THE CUBAN MISSILE CRISIS

The Cuban Missile Crisis

Mark J. White
Lecturer in American History
University of St Andrews

First published 1996 by
MACMILLAN PRESS LTD
Houndmills, Basingstoke, Hampshire RG21 6XS
and London
Companies and representatives
throughout the world

ISBN 0–333–63052–1

A catalogue record for this book is available
from the British Library.

10   9   8   7   6   5   4   3   2   1
05 04 03 02 01 00 99 98 97 96

Printed and bound in Great Britain by
Antony Rowe Ltd
Chippenham, Wiltshire

For my mother and father

Contents

Acknowledgements

I am indebted to Lloyd Gardner for his careful supervision of my doctoral dissertation from which this book emerged. Warren Kimball provided me with an immensely helpful and characteristically candid critique of that same dissertation. This book is a lot stronger as a result of Warren's efforts. I also wish to thank Jack Levy, David Oshinsky, and Norman Markowitz for reading the manuscript at various stages. David Healy, Glen Jeansonne, Jim Hershberg, Robert Frazier, Hugh Brogan, Chris Jespersen, Jon Nashel, and Phil Shashko either influenced my thinking on the missile crisis or were generally supportive. Annabelle Buckley of Macmillan has provided generous assistance as commissioning editor. A special thanks to Reginald Horsman. His advice, encouragement, and friendship have been of inestimable value to me.

I wish to thank the John F. Kennedy Library Foundation and the Harry S. Truman Library Institute for grants which supported the research for this book. Chapters 5 and 7 were originally published in somewhat different form in the *Journal of Strategic Studies* 15 (March 1992) and the *Illinois Historical Journal* 86 (Summer 1993). My thanks to those journals for permission to reprint.

Finally, but most importantly, I thank family. Brenda and Vincent Miccio have been of considerable practical assistance. Robert Perry has always encouraged my interest in American diplomatic history. My wife, Karen, my parents, Mavis and Michael White, and my brothers, Roger and Nicholas, have sustained me through my graduate career and the completion of this project.

MARK J. WHITE

Introduction

A camera rolled. A president spoke. A nation gasped. Time: 7:00 p.m., 22 October 1962. The moment represented the zenith of the Cold War. "Good evening, my fellow citizens," John Kennedy began:

> This Government, as promised, has maintained the closest surveillance of the Soviet military build-up on the island of Cuba. Within the past week, unmistakable evidence has established the fact that a series of offensive missile sites is now in preparation on that imprisoned island. The purpose of these bases can be none other than to provide a nuclear strike capability against the Western Hemisphere.

As Kennedy explained to a television audience of millions that the United States would respond to the Soviet deployment of nuclear missiles in Cuba by imposing a naval blockade around the island, the implicit aspect of the Cold War – that it might at any moment produce a superpower "Hot War" – became ominously explicit.[1]

While Kennedy addressed the nation from the Oval Office, America's Ambassador to the United Nations Adlai Stevenson, the Democratic Party's presidential candidate in 1952 and 1956, watched him attentively on a television set in his New York City office. Historian and White House aide Arthur Schlesinger was one of several officials who joined the ambassador to listen to the president's address. Schlesinger found Stevenson "unperturbed in the midst of pandemonium." A few hundred miles further north, Republican Senator Kenneth Keating was preparing to deliver a speech in Utica, New York. Keating, a companion recalled, was "very excited" by Kennedy's speech. It confirmed what he had previously told the American public – that the Soviets had installed offensive missiles in Cuba. Across the Atlantic, former Secretary of State Dean Acheson marched down the corridors of power in Paris, briefing and reassuring anxious NATO officials about the Cuban situation. The result of the consultations in which Acheson participated was, according to an American official present, a "satisfactory recognition of [the] importance [of the] need for allied solidarity." Late at night in Moscow, meanwhile, Premier Nikita Khrushchev convened a meeting of the Presidium in the Kremlin after hearing reports that Kennedy was about to deliver a speech of considerable importance. That meeting was still in progress as JFK started his address. The whereabouts of Attorney General Robert Kennedy at the moment the president began his speech is unclear. One former official thinks he may have been working in the Justice Department at that time.[2]

These six men – John and Robert Kennedy, Khrushchev, Stevenson, Acheson, and Keating – are the central figures in this account of the Cuban missile crisis. Using their stories, an attempt will be made to answer two questions: First, why did the missile crisis happen? Second, how was it handled and defused?

The aim is not to provide comprehensive coverage of all the policy-makers who played a significant role in the creation and resolution of the crisis. The likes of Robert McNamara, Dean Rusk, and Edward Lansdale would be important figures in that sort of book. The individuals in this study have been selected because they can be used effectively to explore the general issues surrounding the confrontation over Cuba. This is because they either personify important themes or were of representative significance in that they belonged to discrete blocs of officials who shared common viewpoints during the missile crisis. Adlai Stevenson and Kenneth Keating fall into the former category. Stevenson, as the leading liberal in the Kennedy administration, can be used to examine the important relationship that existed between JFK and the liberal Democrats in his administration, while the role played by Keating in the fall of 1962 sheds light on the general assault launched by Republicans on Kennedy over Cuba.

Robert Kennedy, Dean Acheson, and Stevenson were the leading advocates of the three main policies prescribed by American officials during the crisis: the imposition of a naval blockade around Cuba, the execution of some sort of military attack on the island, and the promotion of a diplomatic solution. Robert Kennedy, because he was closer to JFK than any other official, Dean Acheson, because of the force with which he made his arguments, and Stevenson, as the only senior official to explore the diplomatic approach in depth, were the most influential supporters of the blockade, military, and diplomatic alternatives, respectively. John Kennedy and Nikita Khrushchev, it goes without saying, were the two central figures in the crisis.

One additional caveat: Although Fidel Castro obviously played an important role in these events, the purpose of this study is to examine the missile crisis from the context of the Soviet-American Cold War, to reveal the assumptions and objectives of officials in Washington and Moscow, and to explain how these interacted to produce the crisis in October 1962. There is a steadily increasing literature on the Cuban role and this was certainly an important facet of the missile crisis, but that is not the focus of this account.[3]

The story starts with John Kennedy.

1 Approaching Camelot: John F. Kennedy and the Tools of a New Frontiersman

The differences between the competing historical views of John F. Kennedy could not be more stark. The traditional interpretation, propagated by the president's own advisers, depicts him as a knight in shining armour. In their judgement, he displayed in abundance the attributes of great leadership – courage, sagacity, and vision. Over the last two decades, however, a more sober picture of the man and his presidency has gradually emerged. This view emphasises the discrepancy between the reality of Kennedy's leadership and the mythology that has come to adorn it. That reality, it is argued, included a vast and unnecessary increase in military expenditure, an expansion of American involvement in Vietnam, and a reluctance to pursue forcefully such noble but controversial goals as civil rights. On a personal level, Kennedy has been portrayed as superficial, promiscuous, and profane. In this debate over his presidency, the issue of Cuba looms large. To his supporters, the successful resolution of the missile crisis represented Kennedy's crowning accomplishment. His detractors, on the other hand, have castigated him not only for authorising the disastrous Bay of Pigs invasion, but also, in large measure, for precipitating the October 1962 confrontation.

To evaluate the merits of these contrasting views of Kennedy's leadership in general and his Cuban policies in particular is exceedingly difficult. In contrast to a president like Theodore Roosevelt, he was not a larger than life leader whose personality and ideas come charging toward the historian. He is far more elusive. This is due in part to his skill at telling people exactly what they wanted to hear. Part

1

of both his charm and shrewdness was his ability to determine the agendas of other officials, politicians, and friends,
and then to express agreement with their ideas in order to
win support. During his early days in the Senate, for example, Kennedy told Governor of Michigan G. Mennen Williams,
an ardent New Dealer, "I wish I could be a liberal like you
and Hubert Humphrey, but you can't do that in Massachusetts. You can't do in Massachusetts what you can do in liberal states like Michigan and Minnesota."[1]

Another illustration was his November 1960 meeting with
former Secretary of State Dean G. Acheson. The president-
elect, Acheson recalled, indicated that "one of his troubles
now was that he had spent so much time in the last few
years on knowing people who could help him become President that he found he knew very few people who could
help him be President." Kennedy's comment was subtle and
brilliant. This was precisely what Acheson wanted to hear.
He had always viewed the electoral process as a grubby, dis-
tasteful affair. (Note his disgust at the decision of his old
Groton friend W. Averell Harriman to seek the Democratic
presidential nomination in 1956.) Linked to this was his belief
that for the making of policy a president should rely not
on political hacks but upon Establishment expertise. It was
thus no surprise that Acheson found Kennedy's comments
"true and touching." JFK's tendency to tell others what they
wished to hear obfuscated the real man. To different people,
he seemed to be very different things.[2]

As president, his authentic views were also difficult to discern because he customarily solicited his advisers' opinions
without expressing his own. Reflecting on Kennedy's participation in meetings, Deputy Under Secretary of State for
Political Affairs U. Alexis Johnson noticed that he "did it
more by the questioning technique – the probing, questioning technique – than by direct contribution." Florida Senator George A. Smathers, a close friend to Kennedy, recalled
that "many times he picked the brains of others. And on
those occasions he would very rarely express his own view."
Related to this was JFK's habit of concealing his agency by
taking action, especially if it was of an unsavoury nature,
through the proxy of his brother, Robert F. Kennedy. Consequently, it is not always easy to determine whether steps

taken by the attorney general were done on his own initiative or at the president's behest.[3]

By the way he conducted his political life, John Kennedy
in effect placed a smoke screen between himself and those
who would later evaluate him. What then were the core
foreign policy convictions which lay behind that screen? Any
answer to that question should begin with Kennedy's ex-
periences in Britain during the late 1930s. For this period
furnished the cornerstone of the belief-system that would
permanently shape his approach to international relations.
After President Franklin Delano Roosevelt appointed his
father, Joseph P. Kennedy, ambassador to the Court of St.
James in 1938, John Kennedy developed an intense interest
in British politics, especially the issue of Britain's appeasement of Adolf Hitler. He decided, therefore, to write his
senior thesis at Harvard on that subject, and, through his
father's connections with the journalistic profession, managed in 1940 to convert the thesis into *Why England Slept*,
his first published work.[4]

In formulating his ideas for this project, John borrowed
heavily from Joe Kennedy's thinking on defence issues,
although he would come to disagree with his father's isola-
tionist point of view. As ambassador, Joe Kennedy had urged
the Roosevelt administration to stay out of World War II.
It was his firm belief that Nazi Germany would comprehen-
sively defeat a Britain ill-prepared for war. Hence, it would
be myopic for the United States to support the British struggle
which, although magnanimous, would nevertheless
prove to be a losing cause. Poor military preparation on
the part of the British was the principal theme of the
dispatches Joe Kennedy sent back to Washington. "The British
are going to forget that they did not prepare," he predicted
in June 1940 to Secretary of State Cordell Hull. "The entry
of the United States into the war would be only to hold the
bag." Two days after this he lamented that Britain's capacity to wage war against Hitler "still appears to be appallingly
weak. I am of the opinion that outside of some air defence
the real defence of England will be with courage and not
with arms . . . the preparedness for carrying on a war here
is pitiful."[5]

These ideas percolated through the pages of *Why England*

Slept. Here John Kennedy argued that it was harder for a democracy like Britain to augment armament production than it was for a totalitarian state such as Nazi Germany. A dictatorship could increase its military strength without restraint because it did not have to placate pressure groups or public opinion in general. But the resolve of a democracy to forge ahead with defence spending was divided and reduced by such groups as labour, pacifists, and ardent League of Nations supporters. America's leaders needed to compensate for the inherent weaknesses of democracy by pressing ahead with military spending regardless of domestic political pressures in case the fascists defeated Britain and turned their attention to the United States.[6]

Created during his impressionable, formative years, this conviction remained a permanent feature of his outlook. For Kennedy, military preparedness was always the *sine qua non* of a sound foreign policy. Another ramification of his assessment of 1930s appeasement was the hero-worship he developed for Winston Churchill. His prediction that Nazi aggression would lead to war had proven, in Kennedy's words, "to be so accurate." In future years, JFK would appear to ape Churchill by continuously warning that the international situation was critical and that war was at hand.[7]

After his election to the House of Representatives in 1946, Kennedy supported the initial elements of the containment programme, the Truman Doctrine and the Marshall Plan. Nevertheless, he emerged as a sharp critic of President Harry S. Truman and his administration. Using the lessons of appeasement as maxims for the postwar period, he argued that the United States should devote more resources to expanding its military power – just as Britain should have done in the 1930s. This would serve to constrain Soviet belligerence and to ready America for any future war against the communists. During his three terms in the House, Kennedy constantly called for increases in defence spending. His description of the period of the Eisenhower presidency as the "locust years" (to denote a time when American military power and prestige had declined to a dangerous level) during his campaign for the presidency in 1960 is common knowledge. What is less well known is that he had first used Churchill's phrase in reference to the Truman years. "The most serious deficiency in our military strength is our weakness in the air," declared JFK in April 1952. "We started late, and even with a maximum effort at the present time it will be 1952 before we overtake the lead the Soviets developed during the "locust years" of 1946 to 1950."[8]

As well as chastising the president and his advisers for allowing America's military power to atrophy, Kennedy generally accepted the criticisms of the Truman administration levelled by only the most zealous and usually conservative critics of American (and Soviet) policy. He felt Truman had failed to recognise that Moscow did have a definite plan and timetable to invade Western Europe. He also believed America, in waging the Cold War against communism, should have fewer qualms about dispensing military aid to such reactionary governments as that of fascist Spain.[9]

It was on the issue of China, however, that Kennedy most vigorously assailed the Truman administration. When the communists began to prevail over the forces of Chiang Kai-shek, JFK thought the ineptitude of American officials was the root cause. On 25 January 1949 he presented these conclusions to his fellow congressmen. "The responsibility for the failure of our foreign policy in the Far East," he claimed, "rests squarely with the White House and the Department of State." Their reluctance to lend vigorous support to Chiang out of concern over the alleged corruption in his government had allowed the Chinese communists to succeed. By implementing such misguided policies, Truman and the State Department had in effect forfeited the right to make national security policy. The House of Representatives, therefore, should "now assume the responsibility of preventing the onrushing tide of communism from engulfing all of Asia." These were strong words indeed, the sort that Republicans on the right would have found congenial.[10]

Kennedy used the opportunity of a speech in Salem, Massachusetts, a few days later to sustain his assault on recent American policy towards China. "It is of the utmost importance," he urged in what would soon sound like McCarthyistic tones, "that we search out and spotlight those who must bear the responsibility of our present predicament." This time he added FDR to his list of incompetents: "A sick Roosevelt, with the advice of General [George C.] Marshall and other Chiefs of Staff, gave the Kurile Islands as well as the control of various strategic Chinese ports, such as Port Arthur and Darien [*sic*], to the Soviet Union [at the 1945 Yalta conference]." Kennedy's position on China exemplified well his basic critique of late 1940s United States diplomacy: in dealing with the communists overseas, America had not been tough enough.[11]

Another aspect of JFK's early hardline approach was his tendency to conceptualise international affairs in terms of crisis periods. This stemmed from the way he analogised between the present and the late 1930s, ascribing to the contemporary world the characteristics of the pre-World War II years. Put another way, he was convinced Moscow jeopardised the security of the Western powers in the same way that the Nazis had before, and, consequently, that a major war was close at hand. In August 1951, for example, he argued that unless Truman devoted more divisions to Western Europe's defence, a Soviet attack on that region was likely. One year later he suggested that Washington encourage vigorous rearmament among the NATO powers, otherwise the Soviet Union might "move into Western Europe" by the end of 1952. Neither of those ominous scenarios materialised, yet he continued to use this sort of alarmist rhetoric. He continued to regard crises as almost the natural units by which international relations unfolded.[12]

In the 1948 presidential election Henry A. Wallace, who had been Roosevelt's vice-president and Truman's secretary of commerce, broke from the Democratic Party and ran on the Progressive Party ticket. The gist of his arguments was that Truman had erred by departing from Roosevelt's policy of co-operation with the Soviet Union. If Wallace represented the left in the spectrum of early Cold War opinion in the United States, and Truman occupied a fairly central position, then it is no exaggeration to say that Kennedy was located on the centre-right during his years in the House.

After his election to the Senate in 1952, JFK displayed an increasing gravity and a heightened sense of purpose. Indeed, he liked in later years to view himself as something of a Prince Hal – admittedly rather frivolous in his youth, but that period proving to be only the prologue to a subsequent maturity. The Duke of Exeter's comment on Henry V

in Shakespeare's drama – that there was "a difference...
Between the promise of his greener days, And these he
masters now" – would have resonated with Kennedy. This
increasing maturity produced a greater sophistication in his
approach to foreign policy. His old ideas remained intact.
Throughout the 1950s he remained committed to increased
military spending. He also continued to exhibit a "crisis
mentality." In March 1954, for instance, he claimed that the
situation then developing in Vietnam meant this and the
following month constituted the "most critical period" in
the Far East since World War II. The United States might
"easily take the first step which could result in losing all of
southeast Asia to the Communists."[13]

Yet alongside his 1930s-inspired convictions, Kennedy developed a cluster of quite different ideas. He now argued
that the United States should not bolster Western colonialism by supporting French efforts to thwart independence
movements in Vietnam and Algeria. He asserted that the
1953 riots in Berlin and the 1956 uprisings in Poland and
Hungary demonstrated the inadequacy of a monolithic view
of the communist world. Kennedy capped his evolution to
a more moderate, nuanced approach to international affairs
by embracing disarmament in the late 1950s as a viable goal
for American diplomacy, and by supporting a nuclear test
ban treaty as an intermediate step towards the accomplishment of that objective.[14]

There were two salient factors behind Kennedy's modifi-
cation of his foreign policy philosophy. One was the fall
1951 trip that he made to various countries in the Middle
and Far East, including Indo-China. Because of this first-
hand experience, he began to suspect that nationalism and
not communist agitation emanating from Moscow was the
fundamental cause of upheaval in the Third World, as sub-
jugated peoples attempted to gain independence from colonial rule. The change in his outlook was also politically
motivated. From 1955 onwards he viewed himself as a possible vice-presidential candidate, and after the 1956 Democratic Convention, at which he narrowly failed in his bid to
secure that position, he immediately focused his attention
on winning the 1960 Democratic presidential nomination.
To do that, he knew he had to gain support among the

liberals of his party, whose champion during the 1950s had been Adlai E. Stevenson. The two-time presidential candidate had introduced new ideas such as a nuclear test ban treaty into the national vocabulary, and in order to demonstrate his ideological soundness Kennedy began to borrow this and other concepts from Stevenson's lexicon and that of the liberals in general.[15]

As JFK declared himself a candidate for president on 2 January 1960, his foreign policy philosophy was a mélange of traditional 1930s-inspired ideas and new 1950s-acquired approaches. The dilemma for Kennedy was which persona would he project to the public – the tough, uncompromising Cold Warrior or the more subtle, nuanced foreign policy thinker? His answer to that question came in two parts. First, he emphasised his newer ideas in order to gain the support he needed from liberals to secure the Democratic presidential nomination. Second, he reverted to his more traditional views after capturing the nomination in Los Angeles at the July 1960 Democratic Convention in order to defeat the Republican nominee, Vice-President Richard M. Nixon.[16]

This, Kennedy did in part to avoid the standard Republican attack on a Democratic candidate, most associated with the late Wisconsin Senator Joseph R. McCarthy and Nixon himself, that he or she was "soft" on communism. In his 1946 and 1950 campaigns for the House of Representatives and the Senate, Nixon had shamelessly smeared his Democratic opponents, Jerry Voorhis and Helen Gahagan Douglas, by suggesting they were sympathetic to communism; and JFK clearly wanted to undercut any attempt by the vice-president to repeat those tactics in 1960. To do that, however, was no stretch for Kennedy because he was more deeply attached to those hardline ideas anyway. The more sophisticated notions which he had embraced during the 1950s were undoubtedly sincere convictions. But they constituted an intellectual shell (that could easily be discarded) covering the core ideas which he had acquired during his formative years in the 1930s and to which he was viscerally committed.[17]

Kennedy's main assertion in the campaign against Nixon, one he had originally made in 1958, was that American prestige and power, particularly military power, had declined precipitously during the 1950s. Consequently, a dangerous "missile gap" was sure to emerge in the years from 1960 to 1964 between a strong Soviet Union and a relatively weak United States. The next president's first term would thus constitute a crisis period (again, like the late 1930s) that Moscow would use to expand its influence and further its goal of world domination. The new chief executive would need to increase defence spending and adopt a recalcitrant posture (like British Prime Minister Neville Chamberlain should have done with Hitler in the 1930s) in handling Soviet Premier Nikita S. Khrushchev. As a concrete example of the failure of the Eisenhower-Nixon administration to combat communism with sufficient zeal, Kennedy pointed to Fidel Castro's rise to power in Cuba. Indeed, he made Cuba one of the salient issues of his campaign.[18]

The decision to do that was grounded to a large extent in the simple desire to increase his chances of being elected president. Richard N. Goodwin, who wrote many of Kennedy's foreign policy speeches in 1960, recalled that as they campaigned across the country it became clear Cuba was the international issue uppermost in people's minds and that Castro had done more than Khrushchev to antagonise the American electorate. At the end of each day, while relaxing on the *Caroline*, Kennedy's plane, Goodwin would read the mail. "Everywhere – in the Dakotas as well as Florida," he has written, "there were more questions about Cuba and Castro than about any other matter of foreign policy." The Democratic candidate and his advisers decided, therefore, to make "the "issue of Cuba" a major staple of our campaign."[19]

Kennedy received encouragement from other quarters to employ the same strategy for the same reason. When he arrived in Florida during the campaign he was joined by George Smathers. While riding to Bay Front Park, Miami, to deliver a speech, the Democratic candidate asked Smathers whether he had any suggestions for the address he was about to make. The Florida senator recommended he "talk about the importance of Cuba in our whole national relations problem, to recognize that it was a danger and a threat to the rest of Latin America." Kennedy said he already had a speech on that topic scheduled for Tampa, but on Smathers' advice he also devoted a portion of his Miami address to

Cuba. He talked again about the problem of Castro later that afternoon in Tampa. His comments went down so well he decided to speak once more on the subject in Jacksonville. The address, Smathers recalled, "was enthusiastically and warmly received, not only because of himself, but because of the things he had to say, particularly about Cuba." This experience undoubtedly helped convince Kennedy of the effectiveness of the Cuban issue in bolstering support for his campaign.[20]

As the 1960 presidential race proceeded, JFK attacked Nixon on Cuba with increasing ferocity. In essence, he tried to discredit Nixon by claiming that the incompetence of the Republican administration, in which he was vice-president, had resulted in the "loss" of Cuba to the communists. It was reminiscent of the Republican attack on Truman for "losing" China in which Kennedy had joined. In defence of JFK, it could be argued that by emphasising Cuba he was simply responding to the genuine concerns the American people had about Castro. But the strategic timing as well as the vehemence of Kennedy's speeches on Cuba indicated that his main motivation was to make as much political capital as possible. On 6 October 1960, the evening before the second televised debate, he assailed the Eisenhower-Nixon administration for failing to prevent the communisation of Cuba. This was "the most glaring failure of American foreign policy," one which jeopardised "the security of the whole Western Hemisphere." Not surprisingly, the first question which Nixon had to fend off during the second debate was about Cuba. The correspondent who posed the question, Paul Niven of CBS, referred specifically to Kennedy's speech of the previous day.[21]

Even more biting was the attack made by JFK in a 20 October statement, the evening before the important final debate in New York. Not only did he claim the economic sanctions just imposed on Cuba by the Eisenhower administration would be completely ineffective, he also accused the vice-president, who had visited Cuba in 1955, of gross negligence. With reasoning that was transparently facile, he asserted that "Nixon saw nothing wrong in [his 1955 trip to] Cuba – he made no recommendations for action – he did not warn America that danger was growing – and, as a result the Communists took over Cuba with virtually no opposition from the United States." The Democratic candidate, in addition, said Castro was already attempting to foment communist uprisings in Latin America, and expressed his determination, if elected president, to deal vigorously with such insurrections. He then made a serious of proposals, the most provocative of which was his promise "to strengthen the non-Batista democratic anti-Castro forces in exile, and in Cuba itself, who offer eventual hope of overthrowing Castro."[22]

Once again, the opening question in the final debate held the following evening centred on Cuba. This time Nixon felt compelled to describe Kennedy's proposals for supporting the non-Batista, anti-Castro elements as "probably the most dangerously irresponsible recommendations that he has made during the course of this campaign." His opponent's suggestions implied American involvement in Cuba's internal affairs, and this would not only damage the image of the United States throughout Latin America, but might also lead to a superpower war.[23]

The main reason for Nixon's anger at Kennedy's 20 October proposal was not so much the recommendation itself for action against Cuba, but more his belief that it represented a breach of confidence. On 23 July and 19 September 1960, Director of the Central Intelligence Agency Allen W. Dulles had, at President Dwight D. Eisenhower's behest, briefed the Democratic candidate about various national security issues, including Cuba. When Kennedy called for the use of Cuban émigrés to oust Castro, Nixon suspected that Dulles had tipped him off about the administration's secret plans for precisely that sort of action. The vice-president asked Fred Seaton, secretary of the interior, to call the White House to find out whether JFK had been told about this. As Seaton later explained, "The check was made and a reply was made that he (Mr. Kennedy) had been."[24]

Nixon was furious. He believed that Kennedy was "endangering the security of the whole operation by his public statement." Nixon also recognised the irony of the situation. Behind the scenes he himself had been urging administration officials to implement the same policy now publicly prescribed by his opponent. Nixon, however, could not make either of those observations in his campaign because, as he later put it, this "would disclose a secret operation and completely destroy its effectiveness."[25]

Nixon revealed this side of the presidential campaign in *Six Crises*, his 1962 memoir. In rebuttal, Press Secretary Pierre Salinger issued a statement declaring that JFK knew nothing of the covert plans concerning Cuba until a post-election briefing on 18 November 1960 in Palm Beach, Florida. To validate this account, the administration persuaded then former CIA Director Dulles to release a statement in the form of a memorandum to the current director, John A. McCone. Dulles explained that his briefings had dealt with Cuba, but "did not cover our own Government's plans or programmes of action – overt or covert."[26]

Despite these official denials, Nixon's suspicions were probably well-founded. On 14 March 1962 Special Assistant for National Security Affairs McGeorge Bundy supplied President Kennedy with a memorandum on this subject. Of Nixon's allegation, he acknowledged that "there is uncertainty as to how far his exact assertion is wrong." He added that although Dulles' notes for the July briefing "do indicate that he was prepared to tell you that CIA was training Cuban exiles as guerrilla leaders and recruiting refugees for more such training," Dulles was certain he had not mentioned any plans for an invasion of Cuba. The distinction Bundy made here – between Kennedy being aware of the efforts to organise the émigrés but ignorant of the fact that this was geared towards an invasion of Cuba – was nugatory. If the Democratic candidate knew the CIA was training Cuban exiles, the obvious question was: training them for what? Kennedy presumably asked Dulles that at the July briefing. Even if he did not, or if the CIA director evaded such a query, the answer to the question must have been clear to JFK anyway.[27]

Robert Kennedy, who helped arrange the pre-election meetings between Dulles and his brother, later conceded that JFK had been told before the election about the plan which would later become the Bay of Pigs operation. Eisenhower, moreover, authorised Nixon in late March 1962 to say that he had instructed Dulles to brief Kennedy on international issues to the extent of Nixon's own knowledge. This, then, would have included the clandestine plans for Cuba.[28]

The suggestion has been made, however, that Kennedy neither saw nor approved the 20 October statement. Goodwin has written that JFK had told him to "get ready a real blast for Nixon." He then composed a statement on Cuba, including the proposal to help anti-Castro Cuban refugees oust Castro. By the time he had completed the message, Kennedy was asleep at the Hotel Carlyle in New York, and neither Goodwin nor the candidate's other aides wished to wake him. To make the morning papers, Goodwin has further explained, the statement had to be issued immediately, and they decided to release it without JFK's approbation. "It was the only public statement by the candidate in the entire campaign," Goodwin claimed, "that he had not personally reviewed." The fact is, though, that JFK's provocative 20 October statement on Cuba was not released the next morning, but several hours later during the evening. Hence, Kennedy must have reviewed and approved the statement during the day.[29]

When the Massachusetts senator narrowly defeated Nixon in the November election, he had, as one historian put it, "been elected on an anti-Castro platform." Kennedy adviser Harris Wofford, for one, has argued that he "probably did win votes by seeming to be harder on Castro than Nixon." Nevertheless, his pledges on Cuba came with a price: the need to uphold his promise for action against Castro to maintain his credibility. His politically motivated stance on Cuba had, in this way, circumscribed his future presidential policies. During the election campaign Dean Acheson became disturbed by Kennedy's blatant use of the Cuban issue. He advised the Democratic candidate to "stop talking about Cuba" because he "was likely to get himself hooked into positions which would be difficult afterwards." In retrospect, that advice was prescient.[30]

As president, the "lessons" of the 1930s would continue to suffuse Kennedy's whole approach to international relations. Transplanting his sense of the pre-World War II years into the contemporary era, he believed the early 1960s would be years of crisis in which Soviet pressure and the inadequate extent of American military preparedness would necessitate on the part of his administration a specific commitment to increased defence spending and a general determination to be more resolute in dealing with the Soviets and Cubans.

Many other aspects of Kennedy's thinking and personality would influence his foreign policy, including his handling of Castro. Of particular consequence was the importance he attached to the domestic political ramifications of his diplomacy. Domestic politics has obviously been a matter of concern to all presidents. For Kennedy, though, it was more of an obsession. As Alexis Johnson perceived, he was "always a politician in a very big sense of the term, with a very, very keen sense of political realities in this country." George McGovern, director of Kennedy's Food for Peace programme, recalled that after winning the 1960 election, he "never forgot for one minute that he was going to have to face the voters again."[31]

Linked to this was JFK's fascination with image, specifically the cultivation of his own for political advantage. He had long been aware, for instance, of the media's importance. As early as 1956 he had told Smathers that he was determined to woo journalists. When president, he read the *Washington Post, New York Times, Herald Tribune,* and the *Christian Science Monitor* by 10:00 a.m. Foreign policy adviser Walt W. Rostow came to the conclusion that Kennedy was "too much concerned with what Scotty Reston said, or Joe Alsop or Philip Graham. . . . I think the little world of pundits he had to win over – he took too seriously." Nevertheless, his concern was contagious. Military adviser Maxwell D. Taylor, Smathers, and others began to read as many newspapers as possible before meeting with the president on a morning. They knew he would want their reactions to various articles.[32]

Kennedy's fixation with image was evident in other ways. To convey a sense of vigour and vitality, he studiously avoided being photographed playing golf (to distinguish himself from Eisenhower) or using crutches (which he often had to for his bad back). His impressive televised press conferences, in which, as David Halberstam put it, he was able to project himself "not just as leader, but as star," were the product of meticulous preparation. According to Secretary of State Dean Rusk, Kennedy often spent up to three hours prior to those sessions fielding questions from half a dozen advisers. As a safeguard against the unexpected, Pierre Salinger would speak to the press corps beforehand, find out the issues on their minds, and then convey this information back to the president. That way, Kennedy hardly ever received a question to which he had not prepared an answer in advance.[33]

All this reflected the depth of his concern with the cosmetic side of the presidency. As for foreign policy, it meant he would tend instinctively to view decisions in that realm from the perspective of his domestic political credibility. This did not go unnoticed by contemporaries. In a letter written at a time when President Kennedy was soliciting his advice on Berlin, Acheson told Harry Truman that, "There is . . . a preoccupation here with our "image". This is a terrible weakness. It makes one look at oneself instead of at the problem. How will I look fielding this hot line drive to short stop? This is a good way to miss the ball altogether. I am amazed looking back on how free you were from this?"[34]

Another factor to exert a heavy influence over New Frontier diplomacy was Kennedy's inveterate distrust of liberals. The popular depiction of JFK after his death and martyrdom as another liberal-hero president in the tradition of Franklin Roosevelt has become a potent image. But the historical reality belies that idea. The defining individual and political phenomenon for liberals in the 1930s were Franklin Roosevelt and the New Deal. Kennedy was committed to neither. At Harvard, which had been energised in those years by debate over Roosevelt's reforms, he did not join the Liberal Union or the Young Democrats. Charles Spalding, a Kennedy friend, recalled that, "There just wasn't anything about President Roosevelt that stirred . . . Kennedy emotionally." After World War II the young congressman from Massachusetts often attacked FDR's reputation by questioning his competence in foreign policy.[35]

During the early 1950s, Kennedy did not take a stand against McCarthyism, which for many liberals was the key issue of the day. On the contrary, he, like his father, was friendly with Joe McCarthy. The two men had apparently met in the Solomons during World War II, both entered Congress in 1946, often socialised together thereafter, and, for a time, McCarthy even dated Kennedy's sister, Patricia. When the Wisconsin senator launched his attack in February 1950 on the "infiltration" of Communists into the United States government, Kennedy was hardly outraged. Not only did he refrain from criticism of McCarthy, he actually defended him. In a 10 November 1950 address, he was quoted as saying he "knew Joe pretty well" and that "he may have something." At a February 1952 Harvard dinner, to take another example, he responded angrily to criticism of McCarthy by describing him as "a great American patriot." The episode was hushed up. When the Senate finally voted in December 1954 to censure McCarthy, Kennedy, who was ill in the hospital but still fit enough to have registered his opinion, was the *only* Democrat to neither vote nor "pair" against him.[36]

In fairness, it would have been difficult for JFK to oppose McCarthy openly in a state like Massachusetts where many Catholics (and the influential *Boston Post*) ardently supported the provocative Wisconsinite. However, his lack of concern with the obscene excesses of McCarthyism was due not only to those political realities and his friendship with the Wisconsin senator; it was also because he found McCarthy's ideas palatable. Like McCarthy, he too thought the Truman administration had been suspiciously "soft" on communism.[37]

As a congressman from an industrial, urbanised state in the north, JFK often felt obliged to vote for such staples of the liberal agenda as public housing. But he also voted to reduce funds for the old New Deal Tennessee Valley Authority project. Many Republicans viewed the decision on whether to cut the TVA as a conservative litmus test. Kennedy passed with flying colours. He also spoke disparagingly of Social Security in 1953. And when queried about his liberal credentials, he was candid: "I'm not a liberal at all. I never joined the Americans for Democratic Action or the American Veterans Committee. I'm not comfortable with those people." Strikingly, Kennedy's heroes were ardent conservatives – Winston Churchill and Senator Robert A. Taft of Ohio – not Woodrow Wilson, Franklin Roosevelt, and certainly not Adlai Stevenson.[38]

His distate for liberals was grounded in various factors. Most significant was his perception of them as excessively moralising. This was not congruent with his own more pragmatic, hard-headed approach to politics. The influence of his father, an ambivalent supporter of Roosevelt and the

New Deal, was important. Also relevant was the fact that his generally hawkish foreign policy views made him suspicious of those liberals who were less viscerally anti-communist. Adlai Stevenson's experience in losing twice and by large margins to Eisenhower sustained Kennedy's aversion towards liberals. To Kennedy, the lesson taught by Stevenson's defeats was clear: liberals lose. Rather like Bill Clinton, he thought the Democratic Party had to move to the centre to become electable. As Rostow once explained, JFK believed that "the balance of feeling in the electorate lay with a "moderate, decent, conservative margin," which a Democratic candidate had to reach. It was, therefore, impossible to build a victorious base on the left wing of the Democratic Party."[39]

It was thus no surprise that when president-elect Kennedy came to staffing his administration, he did not appoint liberals to key positions. In fact, not only were his main advisers not especially liberal, they often were not even Democrats. McGeorge Bundy was a Republican, as were Secretary of the Treasury C. Douglas Dillon, Allen Dulles, whom Kennedy kept on as CIA director, and John McCone, who was appointed to replace Dulles later in 1961. Secretary of Defense Robert S. McNamara claimed to have voted for Kennedy in 1960, but during the 1950s was generally regarded as a Republican. Even Attorney General Robert Kennedy had voted for Eisenhower in 1956, not Stevenson. In fact, it is almost certainly true to say that most of JFK's important foreign policy advisers voted for Ike and not Adlai in the 1956 presidential election. The New Frontiersmen, then, formed more a bipartisan than a New Deal-type administration.[40]

Kennedy did appoint some leading liberals, but almost always to peripheral posts. Stevenson, the favourite of many pundits for secretary of state, only made ambassador to the United Nations. Mennen "Soapy" Williams was appointed assistant secretary for African Affairs. Harlan Cleveland, a leading supporter of Kennedy in New York State during the 1960 campaign, became assistant secretary for international organizations. Old New Dealer Chester Bowles, as the new under secretary of state, did the best, but he did not last out the year. In November 1961 he was demoted to a far more obscure position.

For Kennedy, then, the liberals were always an attractive

garnish but never part of his substantive diet. Names like
Stevenson and Bowles added a certain prestige to his administration and their appointments appeased the liberal
section of the Democratic Party. But as far as the actual
ideas of these liberals, his attitude towards them ranged from
ambivalence to distaste. When the new president came to
construct policy towards Cuba, he would either pay little
attention to their advice or else would fail to consult them
at all. These Democrats, who emphasised negotiation and
the sparing rather than sweeping use of military force to a
greater degree than Kennedy himself, would in general be
relegated to a secondary status in the New Frontier.

Another factor shaping JFK's foreign policy was his own
character. Care must be taken, of course, to avoid making
facile connections between personality and public policy. For
instance, Kennedy's personal life was obviously conducted
according to a macho code of conduct, as evinced by his
sexual excesses, his disdain for those he thought effeminate
(like Stevenson), and his respect for those he thought virile
(like German Chancellor Konrad Adenauer). But did a macho
personality mean an aggressive foreign policy? Such a link
is hard to establish. If Kennedy's machismo was the decisive
driving force behind his approach to international affairs,
he would presumably have dispatched American troops to
Cuba either during or just after the Bay of Pigs invasion
(several advisers would have supported him in this). Similarly, he would have agreed with the "hawks" during the
missile crisis and have executed an air strike on Cuba.
Kennedy may still have had "macho" impulses that could
be satisfied in the foreign policy realm, but there were clearly
other drives or considerations more paramount. It could
also be argued that Kennedy's competitiveness influenced
his diplomacy. This may have come into play in the aftermath of the Bay of Pigs, when the president sought through
various means to exact revenge upon Castro for the humiliation he had inflicted in routing the CIA-organised Cuban
exile army. But again it is difficult to establish a clear nexus
between his competitiveness and his foreign policy.[41]

The personality trait which may have had a more significant influence upon Kennedy's policies was his tendency to
differentiate sharply the public and private spheres of his

life. Some, like Smathers and journalist Benjamin C. Bradlee, were familiar with the juicier aspects of Kennedy's lifestyle. They knew him as the man who liked to travel to pre-Castro Havana for the nightclubs, who would go to the French Riviera to enjoy adulterous liaisons while his wife was eight months pregnant, and who liked to watch X-rated movies. Others, such as Rusk, had absolutely no inkling of that side of Kennedy. To some people, JFK displayed his professional deportment; to others he revealed his private disposition.[42]

In his conceptualisation of foreign policy, Kennedy, as with his own life, tended to think in terms of a public–private dichotomy to a greater extent than most policy-makers. Tied to this was his ambivalence towards democracy. On the one hand, he was very comfortable with the American people, supremely confident of his own ability to charm them. Yet he also harboured deep suspicions towards the public domain. This attitude was apparent as far back as *Why England Slept*. Here the young Kennedy argued that because of public opinion, particularly certain pressure groups, it was harder for a democratic leader to ensure an adequate level of defence expenditure than it was for a dictator. Implicit in this was the notion that at times an American president had to take steps outside the public domain to accomplish foreign policy objectives.[43]

This idea developed in the late 1950s and during his White House years into a fascination with the clandestine aspects of foreign policy, especially counterinsurgency. In his spare time, Kennedy liked to read the works of Ernesto Che Guevara and Mao Zedong in order to understand better the tactical approaches and mind-set of revolutionaries, and he also enjoyed the James Bond stories of Ian Fleming. As president, he continued to exhibit a keen interest in the covert component of foreign policy – and those who implemented it. On one occasion he praised the CIA's Major General Edward G. Lansdale for being America's James Bond. When Lansdale said the epithet was inappropriate because another CIA figure was the authentic 007, Kennedy asked to meet the man. As Harris Wofford relates the story, "a pistol-carrying, martini-drinking adventurer was found and sent over to the White House." The official was William K. Harvey, who during the 1950s had made his name in intelligence

by organising the construction of a 600-yard tunnel under
East Berlin.[44]

President Kennedy, as journalist Stewart J.O. Alsop has
written, also "loved to pore over intelligence reports, ab-
sorbing even the smallest details." Every morning he would
devote a half-hour to reading through a daily report entitled "INTELLIGENCE CHECK LIST – FOR THE PRESIDENT
– TOP SECRET." So that he could receive this information
first thing in the morning, the CIA staff had to start work at
Langley at 3:00 a.m. or even earlier. Kennedy, therefore,
clearly brought with him to the presidency the conviction
that an effective foreign policy, in addition to its public
execution, should be pursued surreptitiously as well. This,
of course, was something which Eisenhower had plainly accepted. His use of the CIA to overthrow the governments
of Iran in 1953 and Guatemala in 1954 was testimony to
this. But for JFK the commitment to covert action was even
more pronounced.[45]

Kennedy's presidential policy towards Cuba was also affected
by his own temperament and intellectual qualities. Perhaps
his greatest attribute was his ability to grow. During the 1950s,
for example, he had become increasingly diligent and mature. His grasp of domestic issues had become surer, his
perception of the international scene more subtle. Throughout his presidency, he would exhibit the same capacity to
learn and constantly to improve.

Less impressive, though, was Kennedy's tendency to be
easily bored. The advisers to which he paid the most attention were those who were terse and humorous. Conversely,
he disliked those aides who tended to speak in depth and
were of a more serious, philosophical disposition. Rusk recalled that JFK was "an impatient fellow who didn't waste
time. I learned to speak precisely to the point at hand, then
shut up and go back to my office." In describing the young
president's mind-set, Wofford writes that:

> Man-eating sharks, brutal analysis, and covert action were
> not boring. Lectures about morality, legality, and prin-
> ciples were. The secret use of power (to overthrow Castro
> or Diem) was not boring. The public support of Nehru
> or Nyerere was. Foreign aid and even perhaps the Peace

Corps were boring. The CIA was not. Chester Bowles was often boring. Richard Bissell never was.[46]

There was indeed a certain superficiality to Kennedy. Suggestive of this perhaps was the chasm between the popular view of JFK as an intellectual and the reality. His own penchant was in fact for Ian Fleming and show tunes rather than Jean-Paul Sartre or Chopin. On one occasion Rusk asked to meet with the president in the Oval Office. Kennedy, who had just attended an arts function, expressed his gratitude to Rusk: "Thanks for calling me. I was up to here (drawing his hand across his throat) in art."[47]

Kennedy's superficiality affected his formulation of policy, limiting his ability to plumb the depths of an issue. As Alexis Johnson perceived, the president tended to make decisions "in the light of the immediate circumstances at the time without trying to look too far ahead." "He was not a man to whom you could present a plan," Johnson further noted, "extending six, eight, ten months down the road and expect anything in the way of a reaction from him." Despite the increasing maturity and thoughtfulness that Kennedy had displayed throughout his career, his impatience and myopia made it doubtful whether one of the promises implicit in the New Frontier, that there would be a rigorous reassessment of the premises behind and the goals of American foreign policy, would be made good.[48]

Indeed, during the last weeks of 1960 and the first days of 1961, as the Eisenhower administration drew to a close and the Kennedy presidency approached, one question acquired salience: How would the New Frontier in fact differ from what had preceded it? Two leaders – one in Havana, the other in Moscow – were particularly anxious to see how Kennedy would answer that question.

2 Kennedy's Cuban Policies: Misconceptions and Missed Opportunities

The day before President-elect Kennedy assumed the duties of his new office, he met with the outgoing chief executive for a briefing on foreign policy issues. If Kennedy's determination to take action against Cuba had been fashioned in the midst of the presidential campaign against Nixon, his resolve was doubtless fortified by his conversation with Eisenhower on that morning of 19 January 1961. Eisenhower, who a month before had referred sardonically to JFK as a "young whippersnapper," now advised his successor to support guerrilla activities against Castro "as we cannot let the present government there go on." Secretary of the Treasury Robert B. Anderson, also present at the meeting, agreed, arguing that "in the final analysis the United States may have to run Castro out of Cuba and wait until the foreign ministers of Latin America countries publicly complain about our action."[1]

On the following day, 20 January 1961, Senator Kennedy became President Kennedy. In his inaugural address, delivered on that bitterly cold afternoon, the new chief executive embroidered the theme of change which he had initially developed in his July 1960 "New Frontier" acceptance speech at the Democratic Convention. "The torch," he declared, "has been passed to a new generation of Americans." He spoke of the horrific dangers of nuclear weaponry, and the consequent need for the United States and Soviet Union "to begin anew." Holding out the prospect for improved superpower relations, he stated that although America must "never negotiate out of fear," it should "never fear to negotiate."[2]

Despite these expressions of optimism for a more harmonious future, Kennedy also framed the international scene in terms reminiscent of the 1930s. The coming years, he suggested, would be ones of crisis. "Only a few generations have been granted the role of defending freedom in its hour of maximum danger. I do not shrink from this responsibility – I welcome it." Part of the answer to this upcoming challenge was provided by the new president: "Only when our arms are sufficient beyond doubt can we be certain beyond doubt that they will never be employed." The words might have been culled straight from *Why England Slept.*[3]

The extent to which Kennedy was committed to the pursuit of new avenues of co-operation with both Moscow and Havana was soon put to the test. Khrushchev and Castro were, for reasons of self-interest, hopeful that a Kennedy presidency would facilitate improved relations with the United States. At this point in time Khrushchev was under pressure from his own military to reverse defence cuts he had initiated a year earlier. A less acrimonious relationship with the United States would seem to justify his reductions in defence, whereas a heightening of superpower tensions would appear to necessitate the new increases in defence spending advocated by his military. After the presidential election, Khrushchev wrote to veteran diplomat Averell Harriman to say that he was pleased by the Democratic victory. "There was some indication," recalled Harriman, "that he (Khrushchev) felt this (the election of Kennedy) would mean that we could find methods of resolving some of our differences." In early 1961, a British official wrote privately of "Mr. Khrushchev's attempts to woo President[-elect] Kennedy." So when the Soviet premier (along with Leonid I. Brezhnev) wrote to congratulate Kennedy on his inauguration and to express the hope for "a fundamental improvement in relations between our countries," he was probably not being merely perfunctory.[4]

Castro was also interested in ameliorating relations with the United States. During the last days of the Eisenhower administration, he had lived with the prospect of an imminent, American-organised invasion of his country. With reliable sources in the Cuban exile community in Florida, Castro was well aware of the CIA's plans for what would later become the Bay of Pigs operation. In late November 1960 he partially mobilised his 200 000 strong rural militia in case such an attack took place. On 2 January 1961 he ordered the ejection from Cuba of most of the officials working at the American embassy in Havana on the grounds that they were spies. Eisenhower responded by immediately severing diplomatic ties with Cuba. The mobilisation of the militia, however, created economic strains. Castro adviser Che Guevara felt Cuba would be unable to furnish the Soviet Union with the quantity of sugar that had been arranged without using some of the mobilised militia to help with the harvest. Accordingly, Castro demobilised his militia on the occasion of Kennedy's inauguration. He also frankly stated his hope that the new administration would abandon the plans for invading Cuba that it had inherited. A 25 January speech by Secretary General of the Cuban Communist Party Blas Roca, an interview given six days later by President Dorticós to Patrick O'Donovan of *The Observer*, and an 8 February conversation between Che Guevara and a Canadian journalist further indicated the willingness of officials in Havana to enter into negotiations with Washington. For reasons of security and economic well-being, therefore, Castro and other Cuban leaders were eager at the start of the Kennedy presidency to foster better relations with the United States.[5]

Khrushchev and Castro were not the only ones with these thoughts in mind. Harriman, for example, wanted to explore the depth of Khrushchev's interest in a rapprochement with the United States. In the early days of the new administration, Kennedy held a meeting with the pantheon of America's Soviet experts – Charles E. Bohlen, George F. Kennan, Llewellyn E. Thompson, and Harriman himself. During their discussion, Harriman argued that "some preliminary talks" between the Soviets and Americans would be helpful before Kennedy met with Khrushchev at a summit.[6]

Adlai Stevenson had a similar idea in mind. In a 13 January telephone conversation with the president-elect, he proposed a plan he had previously suggested to Dean Rusk and Chester Bowles. He told Kennedy that "the most important first thing that this administration has to do . . . is to discover what is in K[hrushchev]'s mind." Stevenson thus thought it would be salutary to organise "direct talks in Moscow." He argued that the United States needed to come to an adequate understanding of Khrushchev's difficulties, including the pressure he was under from, "Extremists in the Presidium and China."

Stevenson volunteered to go to Moscow himself, but suggested that Kennedy send Harriman if he was uncomfortable with that arrangement. Without committing himself, Kennedy replied, "Good. We will have a chance to talk before we come to a final judgment on this."[7]

The overtures from Khrushchev and Castro – and the recommendations from his own advisers – were certainly food for thought for a new president rhetorically committed to change. At least they should have been. Under Kennedy's stewardship, these opportunities were left unexplored. Diplomatic manoeuvres designed to harmonise relations with Moscow and Havana were not what Kennedy had in mind at all. Instead, the new chief executive set a quite different tone for his presidency in the 30 January 1961 State of the Union address. In that speech he once again expressed his belief that the early 1960s would constitute a period of acute crisis similar to the late 1930s. He spoke ominously of "the harsh enormity of the trials through which we must pass in the next four years." "In each of the principal areas of crisis," he warned members of Congress, "the tide of events has been running out and time has not been our friend."[8]

"In Latin America," he argued, "Communist agents seeking to exploit that region's peaceful revolution of hope have established a base on Cuba." To meet this and other challenges, the new president proposed *inter alia* a strengthening of America's military power. He talked about the need to increase air-lift capacity so that conventional forces might be deployed swiftly, to expedite the Polaris submarine programme, and, in general, "to accelerate our entire missile programme." Over the course of the next year, Kennedy made good on his promise to bolster defence expenditure. As Khrushchev was trying at this point to forge ahead with defence cuts, JFK was by contrast increasing military spending by large amounts. To some extent, the new president's decision to initiate such increases represented a rebuff of Khrushchev's overtures for improved superpower relations. At least the Soviet leader probably took it that way.[9]

As for the idea of a Cuban-American rapprochement, Kennedy had no interest in it. In fact, he was at that time mulling over plans designed to overthrow Castro. Allen Dulles and the CIA's Deputy Director for Plans Richard M. Bissell had fully briefed the president-elect in Palm Beach, Florida, on 18 November 1960 of the plans to topple the Cuban leader; and Kennedy had indicated his general agreement with the scheme at that meeting.[10]

By the time JFK entered the White House, the plan was for a single amphibious invasion at Trinidad on the southern coast of Cuba, to be carried out by an American-backed Cuban exile army, trained in Guatemala. The proposed operation was first discussed at a National Security Council (NSC) meeting before President Kennedy on 28 January 1961. Dulles opened the discussion by depicting Cuba as "a Communist-controlled state" that was constantly enlarging its military strength in the face of mounting internal opposition to Castro. Without committing himself, Kennedy instructed the Defense Department to "review proposals for the active deployment of anti-Castro Cuban forces on Cuban territory."[11]

During the first weeks of his administration, Kennedy did not categorically endorse the plan to invade Cuba. His 6 February memorandum to McGeorge Bundy indicated that the matter was not then settled in his mind. "Have we determined," he asked, "what we are going to do about Cuba?" The position he came to adopt was that he would authorise a plan to transport Cuban exile forces to their homeland, provided the hand of American involvement could be concealed. At an 8 February meeting Kennedy asked his advisers to consider "alternatives to a full-fledged "invasion," supported by U.S. planes, ships and supplies." "Could not such a force [of Cuban exiles]," he queried, "be landed gradually and quietly and make its first major military efforts from the mountains – then taking shape as a Cuban force within Cuba, not as an invasion force sent by the Yankees?" Again at a White House meeting nine days later he argued for the infiltration of exile forces into Cuba rather than an overt invasion. By early March, though, he had decided to execute at least some version of the CIA plan. On 11 March Bundy reported in National Security Action Memorandum No. 31 that the president "expects to authorize U.S. support for an appropriate number of patriotic Cubans to return to their homeland."[12]

In line with Kennedy's obvious preference for as clandestine

an operation as possible, and at his insistence in an 11 March
NSC meeting, the CIA reluctantly agreed to discard its plan
to land forces at Trinidad. JFK wished for a less conspicuous, less populated location. Accordingly, the CIA modified
its thinking. Within a few days, it had selected the Zapata
Peninsula, adjacent to the Bay of Pigs, about thirty-five miles
from Trinidad. With its few roads and sparse population,
the Bay of Pigs was thought less likely than Trinidad to produce powerful resistance from the local population. On 15
March Bundy was able to assure Kennedy that CIA officials
had "done a remarkable job of reframing the landing plan
so as to make it unspectacular and quiet, and plausibly Cuban
in its essentials." The Joint Chiefs of Staff (JCS) gave their
tepid approval to the operation on the same day. By mid-
March, then, the Bay of Pigs plan had emerged.[13]

In addition, the Kennedy administration was considering
other approaches, some linked to the invasion plan, in their
campaign to topple Castro. One was the possible use of the
Organization of American States (OAS) to ostracise Cuba
from other countries in the Western Hemisphere. The State
Department was concerned about the impact of a United
States-organised invasion of Cuba on Latin American opinion,
and so recommended that the operation be preceded by
consultation with and approval from the OAS. Only eight
days into his presidency, Kennedy instructed the State Department to "prepare a concrete proposal for action with
other Latin American countries to isolate the Castro regime
and to bring against it the judgment of the Organization of
American States." On 11 March he ordered State to consider ways of prompting the OAS to demand free elections
in Cuba. Ultimately, the administration was able to use the
OAS against Cuba. But this would not occur until after the
Bay of Pigs.

Another instrument in the campaign against Castro was
the Alliance for Progress. Regardless of whether the Cuban
Revolution had taken place, Kennedy would have probably
created this programme. But the issue of Castroism injected
a greater urgency into the president's developmental plan
for Latin America, which he unveiled on 13 March 1961.
An American aid programme, it was hoped, would make
Latin American governments more favourably disposed

towards Washington in the long-term, and less attracted to
Havana or Moscow. Reducing poverty throughout Central
and South America, moreover, would mean those societies
were less likely to experience leftist revolutions. In the short-
term, the Alliance for Progress would help cushion the hostile
reaction to the Bay of Pigs. As Richard Goodwin stated, "If
that attack was to go forward . . ., it should take place in
the generally benign and progressive context of a new
American policy, lest it appear merely the latest in a long
line of self-serving military interventions." When Castro
claimed that there would have been no Alliance for Progress
without the Cuban Revolution, he was, as the same presidential adviser acknowledged, "only part right – less than
he liked to think . . . [but] more than we were willing to
admit."[14]

Kennedy also considered in spring 1961 the establishment
of a complete economic embargo against Cuba. Eisenhower
had terminated all American exports there, apart from food
and medicine. But when JFK entered the White House, the
United States was still importing sixty to seventy million dollars
worth of goods (primarily tobacco, molasses, fruits, and veg-
etables). Senator Smathers, always vocal on Cuban issues,
encouraged the president to prohibit the importation of those
products. Kennedy instructed the State Department on 15 February to consider that option in National Security Action
Memorandum No. 19. "Would it make things more difficult
for Castro?" he asked. Rusk's answer came back nine days
later in the affirmative. It would hurt Castro because the
Cuban economy would be deprived of valuable dollar exchange. He advised Kennedy to invoke the Trading With
the Enemy Act in order to end Cuban imports. On 9 March
Rusk told the press that this issue was "under very urgent
study indeed." A year later the Kennedy administration would
establish such an embargo. For the time being it was put
on hold.[15]

Another anti-Castro weapon in the New Frontier arsenal
was the whole range of covert activities falling under the
rubric of counterinsurgency. What in particular prompted
Kennedy's interest in this approach was a speech delivered
by Khrushchev on 6 January 1961, in which the Soviet leader
reviewed the November 1960 Moscow meeting of world com-

munist parties. In this address Khrushchev, in addition to extolling the virtues of peaceful coexistence with the West, provided a typology of wars. There were, the Soviet premier explained, three main sorts: world wars, local wars, and wars of national-liberation. The latter "began as uprisings of colonial peoples against their oppressors, developing into guerrilla wars." As examples, he mentioned the conflicts in Algeria, Vietnam, and Cuba. In the case of Cuba, the revolution "began as an uprising against a tyrannical internal regime, backed by American imperialism. Batista was a henchman of the U.S.A." Khrushchev pledged his active support for these sorts of movements, including, "Solidarity with revolutionary Cuba."[16]

Kennedy was alarmed. Maxwell Taylor noticed that the president "took [the speech] very seriously." Four months later, in May 1961, Kennedy was still expressing his concern about it to the distinguished journalist Walter Lippmann. Special Assistant to the President Arthur M. Schlesinger, Jr, recalled that administration officials generally "overreacted" to Khrushchev's speech. To Kennedy and his team, it suggested that Moscow intended to make most of its inroads in the capitalist sphere by providing surreptitious support for ostensibly indigenous "guerrilla" movements. To counteract Soviet backing for national-liberation wars, the administration believed it had to respond in kind. Beginning on 17 February 1961, a group headed by Bissell began to review this issue. As Walt Rostow recalls, the animating question behind the group's deliberations was, "How could we organize our military and civil assets – including covert assets – to make guerrilla operations unattractive or to deal with them if they start?" Chester Bowles summed up the dominant attitude in the early days of the New Frontier: "It was assumed that by borrowing the guerrilla techniques of Mao Tse-Tung and Che Guevara, with some of our own cowboys-and-Indians tradition thrown in for good measure, we could beat our adversaries at their own game."[17]

The response of Kennedy and his aides to Khrushchev's speech was a simplistic one. As Schlesinger has cogently argued, the speech was aimed at two different audiences. By emphasising peaceful coexistence, Khrushchev sought to reassure the West. By stressing Soviet determination to espouse wars of national-liberation, he attempted to placate the Chinese, who had become severely critical of Moscow's lack of vigour in promoting world revolution.[18]

The general failure of Kennedy and his team to perceive the competing and not-so-subtle agendas behind the speech was due in large measure to their monolithic view of world communism. By the early months of 1961, for example, the extent to which relations between China and the Soviet Union had deteriorated was obvious. A 1 April 1961 CIA report, for example, remarked on how the tension between Moscow and Beijing showed that "the monolithic unity of all Communist parties once enforced by Stalin's overpowering authority is giving way to a looser system in which unity can be maintained only by negotiation and compromise." Yet as Robert Kennedy later acknowledged, the issue of the Sino-Soviet split did not receive much attention from the upper echelons of the new administration. "I don't know whether anybody really assessed it very well during that period of time," he recalled. "I never heard any great discussion about . . . what an effect this was going to have."[19]

Consequently, the Kennedy administration still thought and talked in terms of monolithism. A 3 April 1961 State Department pamphlet on Cuba devoted a large portion of its analysis to, "The Delivery of the [Cuban] Revolution to the Sino-Soviet Bloc." Kennedy himself, despite his call as senator for a nuanced view of world communism, now fell back on more traditional, less politically daring concepts. At a 12 April press conference, for instance, he groused that Castro had "associated himself most intimately with the Sino-Soviet bloc." Nor were these references to Sino-Soviet unity for public consumption only. Internal Kennedy administration memoranda also talked in terms of communist monolithism. Of course, events in Yugoslavia in 1948 and Poland and Hungary in 1956 had already revealed fractures in the communist world. But more than those developments, the tension generated by the Sino-Soviet rift should have made clear to policy-makers in Washington, including Kennedy, the need for a reassessment of the assumptions upon which American foreign policy had for so long been based.[20]

This had implications for the president's approach towards Cuba. Making, as he did, the erroneous assumption that world communism was still essentially a unified movement, he viewed Castro as Khrushchev's puppet and Cuba as a Soviet satellite. In terms of the Soviet-American balance of power, this was disconcerting to the Kennedy administration. But such a view of the Soviet-Cuban relationship never approximated the reality. The furnishing of Soviet economic and military assistance to Cuba no more made Castro a puppet of Khrushchev than the same types of American aid made Western European leaders Kennedy's marionettes. All Soviet initiatives dealing with Cuba (including the later missile deployment in 1962) occurred only with Castro's approval. The Soviet Union and Cuba were allies, therefore, in a way that was comparable to the relationship between the United States and the Western European nations. Kennedy and his aides thus exaggerated the threat posed by Cuba because they erroneously viewed it as the sixteenth Soviet republic. As a result, they tended to underestimate the degree of internal support still enjoyed by Castro during the early 1960s. To a large extent, this lay behind their palpably false conviction in the Bay of Pigs that at the first opportunity the Cuban people would rise to cast him out.

Kennedy should have known better too because he had access to information which did indicate the depth of Castro's popularity. On 31 March 1961, for instance, Schlesinger wrote to the president about a recent conversation with Joseph Newman of the *New York Herald Tribune* in which the journalist had spoken of his recent trip to Cuba. Newman had been struck by the "impressive amount of intense enthusiasm for and faith in Castro," and had added that an invasion by Cuban exiles would not spark an uprising against Castro. The British were telling Washington the same thing. Reports compiled by Her Majesty's Embassy in Havana had been passed on to the Kennedy administration since January 1961, and their gist was that an invasion of Cuban émigrés "was not repeat not likely to be accompanied by an uprising in Cuba on a sufficiently large scale to affect the issue."[21]

Not only did Kennedy and his advisers conceptualise Cuba in terms of a monolithic view of communism, they also placed that country in the context of the domino theory. Time and again, they argued that the continuation of the Castro government would lead to a series of leftist revolutions throughout Latin America. "We are," the president declared on 8 February 1961, "giving the matter of Cuba and its export of its revolution throughout Latin America a matter of high priority." On occasion it was argued that Latin American dominoes would fall because of Cuban meddling in the affairs of its neighbours. On others, the mechanism by which the Cuban Revolution would produce revolutions throughout the Western Hemisphere was not even defined – it would apparently happen through some sort of osmosis.[22]

With this logic, the threat of Castroism assumed outrageous proportions. Failure to extinguish the Cuban Revolution would mean the communisation of huge chunks of Latin America. The shortcomings of this view were twofold. First, it may well have exaggerated the degree to which Cuba was tampering in the affairs of other countries. Rusk has acknowledged that although administration officials did worry about the extent to which Latin America was "under the influence of the Castro pressure," they "learned that Castroism was not as much of a force . . . [in that region] as we had supposed." Second, the domino theory, as in its application to Asia, was flawed because it failed to take into account that, fundamentally, the political fate of Latin American countries would be decided by indigenous processes. In part because they subscribed to monolithism and the domino theory, Kennedy and his aides endowed the Cuban issue with the sort of "life or death" significance that it did not intrinsically possess. In terms of the premises upon which it was based, New Frontier diplomacy seemed much the same as the Truman and Eisenhower foreign policies that preceded it.[23]

These standard Cold War assumptions helped fuel a burning desire in Kennedy to oust Castro. Although he had developed various strategies in spring 1961, the Alliance for Progress, covert harassment, economic pressure, and OAS action, the president relied chiefly upon the Bay of Pigs for the accomplishment of that objective. Looked at today, the most enduring myth about the operation is that it received nearly unanimous support from American officials, with the implication being that Kennedy was not especially culpable for the failure because almost everybody around him had enthusiastically backed the plan. "We had virtual unanimity at the time of the Bay of Pigs," claimed Robert Kennedy. McNamara agreed, explaining that, "Not a single advisor to the president, other than Senator Fulbright, recommended against the operation." In truth, a wide range of officials opposed the plan – and JFK knew it.[24]

Most persuasive and forthright in his demurral was the chairman of the Senate Foreign Relations Committee, J. William Fulbright. In a 29 March memorandum to the president and at the 4 April NSC meeting, he enumerated the shortcomings of the Bay of Pigs plan. The extent to which the United States had organised the operation was already clear to other countries; any Cuban government installed in the aftermath of Castro's overthrow would be perceived throughout Latin America as a United States puppet and so would lack legitimacy; American business would not have, even with Castro out of the picture, the privileged status it had enjoyed up to 1959; an invasion of Cuba would probably meet with "formidable resistance" from the local population; and the operation would violate certain domestic legislation as well as treaties (such as the OAS charter) to which the United States was a party.[25]

Fulbright was far from being the only dissenter. In memoranda and in a personal conversation with the president, Schlesinger indicated his own reservations. That opposition ended abruptly when Robert Kennedy told Schlesinger that he was "performing a disservice to bring it [the issue of whether to proceed with the operation] back to the President," and that "he should remain quiet." Bowles assailed the plan in a 31 March memorandum to Rusk, who passed those criticisms on to the president. Rusk himself told Kennedy privately of his dissatisfaction with the operation, although he appeared at least tacitly to endorse it in meetings. Vice-President Lyndon Baines Johnson, according to Rusk's recollection, regarded the invasion as "a harebrained scheme that could not succeed." Edward Lansdale told Defense Department official Paul H. Nitze and others that the plan was sure to fail as it was ineptly organised and based on the false assumption that the Cuban people would aid the invading émigrés. Adlai Stevenson, to the degree that he was briefed about the Bay of Pigs, felt the plan to be misguided. Even Dean Acheson thought the idea was ludicrous. When Kennedy privately broached the matter with the former secretary of state in March, Acheson responded contemptuously. "It was [not] necessary to call Price, Waterhouse," he told the president, "to discover that 1500 Cubans weren't as good as 25 000 Cubans. It seemed to me that this was a disastrous idea." Others also opposed the plan, including the head of the US Information Agency Edward R. Murrow, Director of the State Department's Bureau of Intelligence and Research Roger Hilsman, legal aide Leonard C. Meeker, Charles Bohlen, and Richard Goodwin.[26]

One probable factor behind Kennedy's reluctance to heed these warnings was his disdain for liberals. For many of those who disapproved of the Bay of Pigs were those sorts of Democrats who were indispensable to his administration's progressive image but whom he viewed as weak and ineffectual. Hence, Bowles, Goodwin, and Murrow were ignored; Schlesinger silenced; Stevenson only partially briefed about the operation; and the liberal Theodore C. Sorensen (a close adviser and speechwriter whom Kennedy liked) was not informed about the plan presumably because his opposition was anticipated.[27]

The idea then that there was inexorable administrative pressure compelling Kennedy to authorise the Bay of Pigs is a fallacy. These dissenters did not constitute a united whole. In most cases they were unaware of each others' opposition. They also approached the issue from different angles. Some, like Bowles, grounded their dissent in ethical considerations, arguing that the notion of invasion was repugnant. Others like Acheson opposed the scheme simply because they did not think it would succeed, thereby implying they would have supported it if the operation had been logistically feasible. None the less, there was still a potentially large constituency which would have backed Kennedy against the CIA had he wished to scrap the plan. It would seem, therefore, that despite his anxiety over the ease with which American involvement could be masked, Kennedy positively wished to carry out the operation.

The reasoning behind Kennedy's decision to authorise the Bay of Pigs – or "Operation Castration" as one official called it – was undoubtedly multi-faceted. His twin assumptions that Cuba was a Soviet satellite and the likely source of future

Latin American revolutions certainly contributed to his sense that Castro had to be ousted. Eisenhower's status as a war hero, and, hence, the presumed wisdom of any military scheme with which he was associated, was also an important consideration – especially for a young president who had been in office only a few weeks. The legendary reputation of the Dulles-Bissell partnership was significant for the same reason. Kennedy seemed to assume that the team which had displaced unsatisfactory governments in Iran in 1953 and Guatemala a year later would once again deliver the goods in Cuba. The president was also convinced of the operation's viability by CIA assurances that even if the invading Cuban exiles were unable to overcome Castro's forces, they could still hide in the Zapata swamps, then re-emerge in the Escambray mountain range as an anti-Castro guerrilla unit. Another factor was the problem of what to do with the Cuban exile force being trained in Guatemala should the mission to overthrow Castro be abandoned. They were attracting inordinate publicity, and, furthermore, President Miguel Ydigoras Fuentes was demanding their removal from his country. In early March he told Kennedy that they had to leave by the end of April.[28]

Another important consideration was the fact that in JFK's quest for the White House, he had promised to take action against Castro if elected. That pledge delimited his policies as president. To have refrained from the attempt to dislodge Castro, especially when the CIA had a plan ready to go, would have been to renege on an electoral commitment. Kennedy wished to avoid that because a supine policy towards Cuba would have exposed him to Republican accusations of "softness" on communism. As one scholar has written, JFK, on learning of the Bay of Pigs operation in detail, "faced a plan that fit his campaign rhetoric ... after his own attacks on Republican passivity towards Castro, canceling the operation could hardly fail to create an uproar that the president's rhetoric was mere sham, and that in truth, Kennedy had made his peace with Castro when Eisenhower would have swept him away."[29]

When the operation was finally executed in mid-April, it proved to be an unmitigated disaster. On 15 April, two days before the invasion, six B-26 bombers flew from Nicaragua to attack Cuba's three main airfields under the pretext that the pilots had just defected from Castro's air force. The assault apparently destroyed over fifty per cent of Cuba's air force, but left intact several T-33 jet trainers which would prove to be highly effective later on. Kennedy released the Cuban exile fleet the following day. Worried that America's involvement was becoming clear (the cover story about defecting pilots was revealed almost immediately as a chimera, and Cuban Foreign Minister Raúl Roa had already raised the issue in the United Nations), the president rescinded the second air strike on the main Cuban airfields, scheduled for the morning of the invasion. The invading force itself was soon severely depleted when coral reefs on the approaches to Cuba caused all but one of their small boats to break down. Meanwhile, Castro had mobilised his militia of approximately 200 000 men on 16 April. When the Cuban leader was awakened in the early hours of 17 April with news of the attack, he not only sent forces to the beachhead, he also rounded up 100 000 Cubans believed to harbour anti-Castro sentiments. The CIA hope that the Cuban exile force would spark a popular uprising against Castro, always an unlikely scenario, was now completely quashed.[30]

The portion of Castro's air force that had survived the initial assault attacked the invading force with success on the morning of 17 April. Kennedy wanted to shore up the landing force by authorising an air attack on Castro's interior airfields, but haze on the morning of 18 April prevented the raid from being carried out. When Castro was finally able to bring his field artillery to bear, the already bedraggled landing party disintegrated further. By the afternoon of 19 April, the exile force began to surrender. The Bay of Pigs had failed.[31]

Kennedy was crestfallen. His emotional response to the fiasco ranged from shock and anger to an uncharacteristic despair and self-pity. "Let me tell you something," he confided in veteran Democrat Clark Clifford. "I have had two full days of hell – I haven't slept – this has been the most excruciating period of my life. I doubt my Presidency could survive another catastrophe like this." Perhaps the best explanation for his anguish was offered by one of his advisers:

"This is the first time that Jack Kennedy ever lost anything."
As the operation collapsed, the president was seen to be
constantly shaking his head and rubbing his eyes. When aide
Kenneth P. O'Donnell spoke with him in the early hours of
19 April, the adviser noticed that he was "as close to cry-
ing" as he had ever seen. Shaken and exhausted, JFK took
a lonely, soul-searching, forty-five minute walk by himself in
the White House gardens at 4:00 a.m. on 19 April. Indica-
tive of the depths of his emotional anguish was an episode
involving Arthur Schlesinger. One night during the operation, Schlesinger apparently peeked through either the
keyhole of the president's bedroom or a crack in the door,
and saw Kennedy sobbing in his wife's arms. JFK also turned
to his father for support and advice, calling him every hour
during the Bay of Pigs. But Joe Kennedy was not altogether
sympathetic. "Oh hell," he told his son, "if that's the way
you feel, give the job to Lyndon." To further distress Kennedy,
Jackie became irritated by his reliance on his father during
this time of crisis. The president's sense of anxiety was du-
plicated throughout his entire administration. As McNamara
recalled, the experience was "shattering."[32]

The Bay of Pigs also created the first of what would turn
out to be a great many superpower crises in the Kennedy
years. On 18 April the Soviet government issued a statement roundly chastising the invasion attempt. That attack,
the statement maintained, contravened Cuba's right to self-
determination, was unwarranted because Cuba represented
no threat to United States security, and demonstrated Washington's desire to crush the current Cuban experiment so
that it could not become a model for Latin American countries. It warned that further American military interference
in Cuba might compel the Soviet Union to supply "necessary aid" to Castro. On the same day Khrushchev dispatched
a letter to Kennedy expressing his outrage at recent events.
As with the government statement, he promised that Moscow would provide "every assistance necessary to repulse the
armed attack on Cuba." Perhaps hinting at possible Soviet
retaliation in Berlin, he also wrote that "it is hardly possible
to handle matters in such a way as to settle the situation
and put out the fire in one area while kindling a new con-
flagration in another area."[33]

Kennedy fired back a reply to Khrushchev's message the same day. The Bay of Pigs, he suggested to the Soviet leader, was less an example of American incursion and more a case of Cubans fighting Cubans – of freedom-loving Cubans fighting an oppressive government. As a counter-warning to Khrushchev's caveat on Soviet determination to help Castro, he stated that although the United States had no desire to launch an attack on Cuba, it would, should there be "any military intervention by outside force" in the affairs of that island.[34]

Two days later, in an address before a meeting of the American Society of Newspaper Editors in Washington, Kennedy was even more stern. He once again indicated that his administration would take action if the Soviets intervened militarily in Cuba. "Our restraint is not inexhaustible," declared the president. The lessons of the Bay of Pigs, he went on to say, included the need to avoid underestimating "the forces of communism," and the importance of preventing Cuba from spreading communism throughout Latin America. Even some of Kennedy's own advisers were shocked by the truculence of his speech. Goodwin entered the Oval Office a few hours after the address and expressed his reservations about the president's threats of intervention in Cuba. "I didn't want us to look like a paper tiger," Kennedy explained to Goodwin. "We should scare people a little, and I did it to make us appear still tough and powerful."[35]

The mutual vilification between the superpower leaders in the wake of the Bay of Pigs demonstrated that Kennedy's opportunity to improve superpower relations, afforded by the Soviet leader's own desire for such a state of affairs in order to justify his defence cuts, had been missed. The Bay of Pigs had changed Soviet attitudes towards Kennedy. A senior member of the Presidium told a British official in private that "the Soviet Government had been wrong in expecting a different and more progressive policy from President Kennedy and they had now given up the hopes they had placed in him." Similarly, the 18 April government statement from Moscow declared that, "Recent events show that the present government of the U.S.A., which has proclaimed itself the heir to F. Roosevelt's policy, actually is carrying on the reactionary imperialist Dulles-Eisenhower policy, condemned by the peoples."[36]

As the president considered his response to the Bay of Pigs calamity, he was subject to considerable pressure from his aides to take action, even to the point of launching an invasion of Cuba. One of the most zealous advocates of that approach was his own brother. At a 19 April meeting Robert Kennedy argued that "we would have to act or be judged paper tigers by Moscow. We just could not sit and take it." When at a subsequent meeting Bowles suggested that Castro was firmly entrenched as the leader of Cuba and that the United States would just have to accept this, the attorney general responded with unrestrained anger: "That's the most meaningless, worthless thing I've ever heard. You people are so anxious to protect your own asses that you're afraid to do anything. All you want to do is dump the whole thing on the president." In meetings held on 20, 22, and 24 April, there was much talk of exacting military revenge upon Castro. "The reactions around the table in the Cabinet Room," recalled Bowles, "were emotional, almost savage." On the evening of 20 April the under secretary of state wrote down that, "Military-CIA-paramilitary-type answers" were dominant during the day's discussion, and "I found it alarming."[37]

Advice solicited by Kennedy from outside his administration was often of the same type. Dwight Eisenhower, in a 22 April meeting with Kennedy at Camp David, did contend that "the American people would never approve direct military intervention [against Cuba] . . . except under provocations against us so clear and so serious that everybody would understand the need for the move." But Richard Nixon, in line with Kennedy's more pugnacious advisers, recommended forceful action during a 20 April White House meeting between the two former presidential rivals. At the start of their discussion Nixon listened to an obviously agitated Kennedy. "I was assured," the president told Nixon, "by every son of a bitch I checked with – all the military experts and the CIA – that the plan would succeed." Nixon advised Kennedy "to get Castro and communism out of Cuba [immediately]." He suggested that the president, after finding some legal justification (such as the need to defend American citizens at the Guantánamo base on the eastern tip of the island), authorise military action against Cuba.[38]

Nixon's arguments echoed those already made by Barry

M. Goldwater. Apparently on 15 April, the day the Bay of Pigs operation got off to such a conspicuously bad start, JFK asked to meet with the crusty Arizona senator who would be the Republican presidential candidate in 1964. Kennedy greeted Goldwater profanely: "So you want this fucking job, eh?" "You must be reading some of those conservative right wing newspapers," the senator replied. Kennedy no doubt called for this tête-à-tête to cultivate bipartisan understanding for an operation that was faltering. Goldwater, however, used the meeting to exhort the president to do "whatever is necessary to assure the invasion is a success." Specifically, he recommended the use of American air power to ensure that the Cuban émigrés advanced from the beaches and engaged Castro's army.[39]

Ultimately, Kennedy decided against the belligerent advice he received from both inside and outside his administration. At a NSC meeting on 24 April he told his advisers that they would simply have to accept the humiliation inflicted by the Bay of Pigs. The main reason he refused to invade Cuba was his belief that Khrushchev would probably respond by moving on Berlin. In his 20 April meeting with Nixon, he explained that he could not attack Cuba because, "Both Walter Lippmann and Chip Bohlen have reported that Khrushchev is in a very cocky mood at this time. This means that there is a good chance that, if we move on Cuba, Khrushchev will move on Berlin. I just don't think we can take the risk, in the event their appraisal is correct." Robert Kennedy also confirmed in later years that one of the reasons why the decision was made against the use of American military force to help out the Bay of Pigs operation when it was failing was the fear that "the Russians would move on Berlin."[40]

If he was not going to invade Cuba, then how would Kennedy respond to the Bay of Pigs fiasco? In shaping a response to that question, his liberal advisers urged restraint. Goodwin, in a memorandum written within two weeks of the failed operation, advised the president to expedite the Alliance for Progress. "This program," he stated, "with its emphasis on social and economic advance is the real hope of preventing a communist takeover." He also argued that indigenous groups, not Castro, were responsible for the left's popularity in certain Latin American countries. The influence of those groups, Goodwin warned, would be enhanced by another American attempt to overthrow Castro.[41]

Bowles, who had opposed the Bay of Pigs before its execution, counselled similar temperance in its aftermath. In a 20 April memorandum, he urged Kennedy "to get the Cuban situation in perspective . . . [and] to minimize its implications at home and abroad." If action needed to be taken against Cuba, it could be done through the OAS. But in general the United States should concentrate on building more constructive relations with the underdeveloped world. "Castro is a disaster," acknowledged Bowles, "but a greater disaster would be to ignore the forces which created him and now sustain him."[42]

Kennedy, however, was in no mood to follow Bowles' advice. The under secretary of state's opposition to the Bay of Pigs had been leaked to the press by Rusk, and the president regarded this as a public embarrassment. "We're going to get him!" barked Pierre Salinger to Harris Wofford in reference to Bowles. And they did. In November 1961 Kennedy demoted him to an insignificant post several rungs further down the State Department ladder. For being right on the Bay of Pigs, Bowles had to go.[43]

The adviser who made the most concerted effort to place the Bay of Pigs in an appropriate historical context was Stevenson. In a long 23 April memorandum to Kennedy, entitled "Some lessons from Cuba," America's UN ambassador analysed the Cuban issue from the perspective of colonialism. The Soviet Union, he argued, enjoyed a certain popularity in former colonial countries because Lenin's anticolonial outlook had obvious appeal to these societies and because "Communism, as the most systematic example of the 'soak-the-rich' approach, is inherently popular." It was inevitable, therefore, that some countries would turn to communism, but the West should not respond with "hysterical panic" to this. For instance, the domino theory did not necessarily apply. "Herr Ulbricht and the East German regime," Stevenson stated by way of example, "ensure that there are virtually no Communists in Western Germany."[44]

The ambassador proceeded to argue that intervention was not the most appropriate way of dealing with leftist movements because it reaffirmed the image of Western countries as old colonialists. The more effective way of ensuring the long-term viability of democracy in the underdeveloped countries was through the dispensation of "long term sustained economic assistance." This would not only help to reduce poverty and build-up the middle class, it would gradually replace the image of the West as the source of colonial exploitation with a more progressive, benevolent one.[45]

As for Cuba, it did not merit the sort of obsessive concern that it had hitherto generated in the Kennedy administration. "We are not going to be destroyed in our beds," Stevenson told the president, "even if Castro does continue to mismanage Cuba for another decade." What the United States needed to do was focus on improving living standards throughout Latin America in order to demonstrate the inadequacies of Castroism. "Of one thing we may be sure," Stevenson added in reference to Cuba, "the 19th century system of gunboat diplomacy or landing the Marines is highly unpopular." The general thrust of his arguments was that Kennedy should leave Castro alone and focus upon developing a sound economic aid programme for countries that had not yet gone Communist.[46]

As was par for the course in the New Frontier, Kennedy dismissed the counsel offered by his liberal advisers. Their proposals described long-term objectives requiring steady patience, ones which would only discredit and perhaps weaken Castro indirectly. Stevenson's comment on the feasibility of living with Castro for another decade was just the sort of idea which did not appeal to an action-minded president who felt under siege. Kennedy did indeed view his current situation as critical. One effect of the Bay of Pigs was to convince him of the correctness of his pre-presidential depiction of the early 1960s as a crisis period in the Cold War. In his 20 April address on Cuba, he asserted: "history will record the fact that this bitter struggle [between communism and the West] reached its climax in the late 1950s and the early 1960s." With his burning desire to make immediate repairs to his damaged image and credibility, Kennedy decided to respond to this crisis by weakening Castro's grip on Cuba through a multiplicity of methods – in fact, everything short of the sort of direct military attack on the island which might provoke a Soviet response in Berlin.[47]

His post-Bay of Pigs approach was defined in National Security Action Memorandum No. 2422, which described the decisions made at a NSC meeting on 5 May. "U.S. policy toward Cuba," it made clear, "should aim at the downfall of Castro." Although it was agreed at the meeting that the United States "should not undertake military intervention in Cuba," that approach was to be kept as a definite option. Hence, the administration should "do nothing that would foreclose the possibility of military intervention in the future." American intelligence was thus instructed to determine the amount of military aid being furnished by the "Sino-Soviet Bloc" to Cuba. The information would be used so that "U.S. capabilities for possible intervention may be maintained at an adequate level."[48]

Meanwhile, various other steps would be taken. Kennedy called for the publication in the press of the "terroristic actions" of Castro's government. He further instructed the CIA, in conjunction with other government agencies, to study the "possible weaknesses and vulnerabilities in the elements which exert control in Cuba today." It was also decided to press ahead with the Alliance for Progress, to expand the programmes of the US Information Agency in Latin America, and to initiate discussions on the hemispheric dangers of Castroism between United States military officials and their counterparts in the various Latin American governments. In addition to the policies enumerated in this memorandum, Kennedy also made administrative changes. Now distrustful of the military and intelligence "experts" in the Pentagon and CIA, he encouraged advisers like Bundy, Sorensen, and especially Robert Kennedy to play a greater role in the foreign-policy making process.[49]

NSC Action Memorandum No. 2422 also called for discussions with Latin American governments about the possibility of taking OAS action against Castro. Eisenhower had recommended that approach in his 22 April meeting with Kennedy. During the next nine months, the utilisation of the OAS would emerge as one of the principal themes of Kennedy's policy towards Cuba. This was one tactic which received the blessing of liberals like Stevenson and Bowles.

With their preference for non-military methods of combatting communism, their interest in close co-operation with under-developed nations (including those of Latin America), and their Wilsonian commitment to the use of international organisations like the OAS in order to undertake collective policy (as opposed to unilateral action like the Bay of Pigs invasion), liberals generally endorsed the effort to use the OAS to isolate Castro from the rest of the Western Hemisphere.[50]

The first part of this post-Bay of Pigs attempt to activate the OAS was Stevenson's goodwill trip to Latin America. In a 5 May message to all United States diplomatic posts in Latin America, Rusk defined the goals of Stevenson's upcoming mission. The trip was designed to change the "negative political atmosphere" arising out of the Bay of Pigs and to convey a sense of Washington's commitment to the Alliance for Progress. But Rusk revealed the surreptitious motive when he explained that, "In private conversation, with a minimum of public discussion, [Stevenson was] to solicit reactions and Latin American initiatives in connection with our then current plans for steps in OAS for action on Cuba." In a 24 May conversation between Kennedy, Stevenson, Rusk, and Cleveland, it was finally agreed that the UN ambassador should undertake the mission. Five days later the president issued a public statement announcing the trip.[51]

On 4 June Stevenson commenced his Latin American tour. In the memoranda he sent back to the State Department and the White House, he reported the degree to which Kennedy could rely on support from various governments for OAS action against Castro. The ambassador also made a full report to the president on his return. In it, he encouraged Kennedy to postpone any moves in the OAS against Cuba until after the summer meeting of the Inter-American Economic and Social Council in Uruguay. That conference, Stevenson suggested, should be used to "obliterate the memory of the April invasion effort" and "to show to dissident left-wing elements" in those countries the administration's commitment to improved social and economic conditions in Latin America. After the conference, Kennedy should carry out two suggestions made by President Lleras Camargo of

Colombia. First, a meeting of OAS foreign ministers should be called soon after the economic conference. At this time Cuba would be asked "to rejoin the American community by disassociating itself from the Communist block." Assuming Castro would refuse to make the pledge, a second meeting would convene to arrange, amongst other things, the diplomatic isolation of Cuba. By soliciting these sorts of proposals and by at least partially reducing the ill will generated throughout Latin America by the Bay of Pigs, Stevenson had laid the groundwork for the subsequent actions taken by the OAS against Cuba.[52]

As well as consulting with Latin American governments, Kennedy may also have responded to the Bay of Pigs by seriously considering ways to assassinate Castro. Plans to kill the Cuban leader had been developed by the CIA as early as August 1960 when the agency ordered one of its officials to contaminate a box of Castro's favourite cigars with a fatal poison, botulinum toxin. This was the first of at least eight CIA plots to assassinate Castro hatched between 1960 and 1965. Many of those plans involved the recruitment of major underworld figures to the anti-Castro cause. In late summer 1960 the CIA hired Robert A. Maheu, an ex-FBI agent, who in turn solicited the help of mobster John Rosselli. Rosselli brought into the operation, Momo Salvatore ("Sam") Giancana, the head of the Chicago mafia, and another underworld figure, Santos Trafficante. This CIA-organised crime alliance made at least one and possibly two attempts to kill Castro in the weeks immediately prior to the Bay of Pigs. The plan or plans apparently involved the passage of poison pills from a Cuban émigré to a contact in Cuba. The pills were supposed to be placed in Castro's food at a restaurant frequented by the Cuban leader.[53]

The extent of John Kennedy's knowledge of the assassination plots is not clear. Because of the CIA practice of "plausible deniability," there would be no documentary evidence proving the president's knowledge of them even if he had been briefed. What is certain is that Kennedy did broach the question of assassination with various people. Just before the Bay of Pigs, he asked Smathers about the merits of killing Castro. When the senator expressed his disapproval, Kennedy said he felt the same way, yet still requested a memorandum from Smathers describing a plan for the assassination of the Cuban leader. Later in the year, the president asked Tad Szulc of *The New York Times* his opinion on the same subject. Szulc unequivocally opposed killing Castro, and Kennedy, as in his conversation with Smathers, said he shared that sentiment.[54]

There were only three possibilities. Either the CIA had not informed the president about the assassination plots but JFK was seriously considering them on his own initiative (why else would he even discuss such a sensitive subject with Smathers and Szulc?); or the CIA had informed him, he had told the agency to desist in its planning to kill Castro, but he manifestly had no control over the CIA as it forged ahead with the assassination attempts anyway; or the CIA had apprised him and he had endorsed the effort to eliminate Castro. The last seems the most likely. Even if the CIA had not briefed him, Kennedy would have presumably raised the issue with the agency, as he had been sufficiently interested in assassinating Castro to discuss the idea with those outside his administration. The CIA would have been more than willing to supply a president actively considering assassination with plans that were already underway. Furthermore, JFK's James Bond-type view of covert work as an infinitely exciting and exhilirating world might have actually attracted him to the notion of assassination.

What lends credence to the idea that Kennedy knew of the attempts to kill Castro is the role played by Judith Campbell (later Judith Exner), with whom he had a two year affair after being introduced to her in February 1960 by Frank Sinatra. Campbell later claimed that Kennedy used her as an intermediary to arrange meetings with Sam Giancana (whom she also knew well, and with whom she had an affair either at this time or, as she insists, later) and to convey sealed envelopes between the two men. The first Kennedy–Giancana meeting was apparently held at the presidential candidate's instigation on 12 April 1960 in Miami Beach in order to solicit help from the Mafia in the crucial West Virginia primary. Federal Bureau of Investigation (FBI) records indicate that organised crime did help Kennedy in the primary by pumping money into his campaign and by paying off various state officials.[55]

Campbell has also revealed that JFK asked her to collect an envelope from Rosselli in Las Vegas and to take it to Giancana only a few days after the collapse of the Bay of Pigs operation. She then organised a meeting between the president and Giancana for 28 April 1961 in her room at the Ambassador East in Chicago. As the two men talked in the early evening, Campbell stayed in the bathroom, sitting on the edge of the tub, until they had finished. During the next few days she went to Florida, spent time with Giancana and Rosselli, and collected another sealed envelope which she delivered to Kennedy at the White House on 5 May. She had intended to hand the envelope to the president the following day, but he told her it was an urgent matter and that she should bring it round immediately. If Campbell's account is accurate, and if the assumption is made that the president was discussing (in his meeting and possibly their correspondence as well) matters more substantive than the vagaries of the weather, then Kennedy's frenetic contacts with Giancana and Rosselli in late April and early May may have involved a discussion about how Castro could be punished for the Bay of Pigs through assassination. Even if that was not the case, other officials certainly were thinking in those terms. During a meeting in mid-May, McNamara strongly recommended the assassination of the Cuban leader. "I mean it," he told Goodwin, "it's the only way." Edward Lansdale would reach the same conclusion a year and a half later. In 1977 he recalled that he had "asked [the] CIA about the feasibility of eliminating Fidel Castro in my contingency planning at the time of the Missle [*sic*] Crisis."[56]

Not only did Kennedy respond to the Bay of Pigs by marshalling support from the Latin American nations and perhaps by furthering plans for assassination, he also began to initiate CIA harassment activities against Cuba. Khrushchev's January 1961 speech championing national-liberation wars had prompted the president to think more in terms of developing counterinsurgency and associated covert tactics. The Bay of Pigs now convinced him that those approaches were of vital importance, as his 20 April address to the newspaper editors indicated. The failed invasion of Cuba, the president argued, showed that communist countries were not to be underestimated. "The advantages of a police state – its use of mass terror and arrests to prevent the spread of free dissent" – had to be acknowledged. In advancing their cause, Kennedy continued, communist states seldom used their armies and nuclear weapons. Instead, they relied upon more secretive methods, such as "subversion, infiltration, and a host of other tactics." In meeting this challenge, the United States needed to respond in kind. "We dare not fail to grasp the new concepts, the new tools, the new sense of urgency we will need to combat it [communism] – whether in Cuba or South Vietnam."[57]

Kennedy's speech showed that the Bay of Pigs experience had convinced him of the soundness of the conclusion he had reached two decades earlier in *Why England Slept* that democratic leaders, because of the pluralistic nature of their societies, were never accorded the sort of unanimous support for their diplomacy that their counterparts in totalitarian states enjoyed. Hence, dictators had fewer constraints on their stewardship of foreign policy than democratic statesmen, and so were able to fight the Cold War more effectively. Kennedy may have been thinking of the need he had felt during the Bay of Pigs to limit the sort of direct American military involvement that might have ensured the operation's success. He had tried to conceal Washington's hand in order to prevent waves of criticism throughout the United States (as well as Latin America). Put another way, the self-exonerating logic which Kennedy used to explain the Bay of Pigs was that it failed, not because it was a poor decision on his part, but because of the systemic differences between democracies and dictatorships, and the consequences of this for foreign policy-making. This reaffirmation of his belief in the inherent handicaps of a leader who has to cater to interest groups and public opinion strengthened JFK's determination to overthrow Castro through covert means, which could be employed without having to deal with a potentially censorious public.

In his assignment of the investigation into the Bay of Pigs failure to a team headed by Maxwell Taylor, Kennedy indicated the new emphasis he placed on the whole range of covert tactics. On 22 April he asked Taylor to reassess "our practices and programs in the areas of military and paramilitary guerilla and anti-guerilla activity which fall short of outright war." Kennedy also established a new Task Force on Cuba chaired first by Paul Nitze, then Richard Goodwin, and assisted by covert specialist Edward Lansdale. "Our objective," as Goodwin recalled, "was to contain the spread of Castroism and unseat the communist government in Cuba." The Defense Department and CIA soon supplied the Task Force with a myriad covert projects. By July 1961 the NSC Special Group, which was responsible for the authorisation of the CIA's secret operations, had declared that "the basic objective toward Cuba was to provide support to a U.S. program to develop opposition to Castro and to help bring about a regime acceptable to the U.S." A 1975 Senate report stated that during the summer of 1961, "Occasional harassment operations" were carried out against Cuba.[58]

As a perceptive 27 April 1961 London *Times* article argued, James Bond, Kennedy's favourite fictional character, had "emerged as part of the Administration's answer to communist political warfare." Through clandestine, counter-guerrilla, 007 techniques, the New Frontier would fight the Cold War. *The Times* responded with skepticism to the new emphasis on unconventional warfare. "There would appear to be a national inability," the article asserted, "to comprehend that sincere men can believe in communism, or that a people will not necessarily rise up against a dictator such as Dr. Castro, who has at least introduced basic reforms." Prophetically, the article contended that "the national self-confidence here would seem due for more bruising if the assumption remains that American soldiers or agents can arouse an Asian or Latin American peasantry."[59]

Kennedy's concern over communist guerrilla activities was evident in his talks with Khrushchev in Vienna at their one and only summit meeting. In the afternoon discussions on 3 June 1961, the president frankly stated that he was disturbed by the support expressed by the Soviet premier in his January 1961 speech for national-liberation wars. The broader significance of that summit for American foreign policy was that it heightened both Kennedy's anxiety over the gravity of the communist challenge and his determination to combat it. The two leaders did speak briefly about Castro. Kennedy admitted that he had "made a misjudgment with regard to the Cuban situation." Khrushchev agreed,

arguing that the Bay of Pigs had served only to solidify support for Castro as the failed invasion had evoked fears among
the Cuban people that Kennedy intended to install another
leader like Batista. The whole episode, he suggested, had
probably moved the Cuban leader further to the left: "Castro
is not a Communist but US policy can make him one."
Khrushchev also pointed out that if Kennedy thought the
invasion of Cuba justified, he could not object to Soviet
incursion in a country like Turkey, where the United States
had deployed missiles. In response, Kennedy made clear that
he "held no brief for Batista," and suggested that his principal qualm with Cuba was Castro's desire to stir up trouble
throughout the Western Hemisphere. By way of analogy to
the Cuban situation, he wondered "what the USSR's reaction would be if a government associated with the West were
established in Poland."[60]

If the Bay of Pigs produced the first confrontation between Kennedy and Khrushchev, their discussions at Vienna
generated the second – this one even more personal in nature.
The main bone of contention between the two leaders was
Berlin. Khrushchev told Kennedy during their morning conversation on 4 June that he was determined to conclude a
peace treaty with East Germany. Under this arrangement,
West Berlin would become a free city, and access between
that sector of the city and West Germany would be terminated. Kennedy centred his arguments on the issue of credibility. If the United States willingly ceded its rights in Berlin,
he insisted, "no one would have any confidence in US
commitments and pledges." American undertakings elsewhere
would be viewed as "a mere scrap of paper." In their final
discussion at the summit, the two leaders again clashed over
Berlin. Towards the end of that meeting, Khrushchev talked
of the possibility of war arising from the disagreements over
this issue. Unflinchingly, Kennedy replied that in this case
"it would be a cold winter."[61]

What the declassified Vienna transcripts reveal is that the
traditional view of the summit, that Khrushchev dominated,
intimidated, and even browbeat the less experienced Kennedy,
is false. Khrushchev was assertive, but JFK was equally com-
bative. During the discussion on Berlin, for instance, Kennedy
seemed to sense that Khrushchev was trying to take advan-

tage of him. In response, he stated that although he was a youthful leader, "he had not assumed office to accept arrangements totally inimical to US interests." None the less, as Kennedy's advisers noticed, JFK had been surprised by Khrushchev's obduracy at Vienna. Rusk felt the president had been "sobered and shaken" by the summit. Bohlen noticed that on his return to Washington, Kennedy went over the transcripts of his discussion with Khrushchev on Berlin time after time, and he also read them to people like journalist Joseph Alsop and Philip Graham, publisher of the *Washington Post.* When he met with a group of congressional leaders, Kennedy admitted that Khrushchev had been "very tough" and that he was "a persistent counterpuncher." The overall effect of the Vienna summit, then, was to underscore the essential lesson he had learned from the Bay of Pigs experience – that the communist threat was not to be underestimated and that his administration had to be more tenacious in dealing with communist nations, including Cuba. As Robert Kennedy explained, Vienna taught the President that Khrushchev "was tough, and [that] he had to be as tough."[62]

The events of summer 1961 showed that the Vienna summit had initiated the third Berlin crisis of the Cold War era. Khrushchev's demand that the Western powers evacuate the city caused Kennedy to take such steps as bolstering military spending, and these in turn prompted Khrushchev to put up the Berlin Wall. Shortly after the dénouement of that crisis, Kennedy missed another chance to build better relations with Cuba. At the close of the August Inter-American conference in Punta del Este, Uruquay, Richard Goodwin journeyed to Montevideo. Attending a party there on 17 August, he was told that Che Guevara, who had presented him with a box of Cuban cigars during the conference, was also present and that he wished to meet with the American. Goodwin accepted. During their conversation, Che Guevara spoke of his interest in improving relations with the United States. In exchange for an American commitment to cease both the trade embargo and its attempts to overthrow Castro, Cuba would make a number of concessions. It would try to pay for the American properties expropriated after the revolution through trade, not enter into alliances with the com-

munist bloc, pledge not to attack the American base in Cuba
at Guantánamo, and, in order to assuage Washington's fears
of falling Latin American dominoes, agree to curtail Cuba's
involvement in the affairs of nearby countries. Guevara,
Goodwin recalled, "made clear his awareness that any possibility of a *modus vivendi* would depend on Cuba's willingness to refrain from revolutionary activity in other countries."
The Cuban ended by saying he would only divulge the sub-
stance of their conversation to Fidel Castro, and Goodwin
agreed to be equally discreet.[63]

On his return to Washington, Goodwin told Kennedy of
his conversation with Che Guevara. The president seemed
interested and asked Goodwin for a written account of the
meeting, to be distributed to Rusk, Bundy, and other top
officials. Goodwin handed Kennedy the box of cigars from
Guevara. The President asked if they were good. "They're
the best," Goodwin answered. Kennedy then lit one and began
to smoke. He suddenly turned to his aide and declared:
"You should have smoked the first one." "It's too late now,"
Goodwin replied. Kennedy looked troubled but continued
to smoke. If the president had been briefed about the CIA
plan to assassinate Castro by transmitting a box of poison-
ous cigars to him, this would help explain his anguish. If
Castro was trying to do to him what the CIA had attempted
to do to the Cuban leader, he was in trouble![64]

As requested, Goodwin produced an account of his meeting with Che Guevara, and furnished it to the leading foreign policy-makers in the administration. He also sent
Kennedy a memorandum appraising the prospects for future
Cuban–American relations in the wake of the recent Punta
del Este conference and the private meeting with Guevara.
"Do not create the impression we are obsessed with Castro,"
Goodwin warned Kennedy. He encouraged the president to
increase the economic pressure and expand the propaganda
campaign against Cuba. But he also advised Kennedy to find
"some way of continuing the below ground dialogue which
Che has begun."[65]

What should have been clear to the president by this point
was that Che Guevara's proposals were part of a sustained
attempt by Castro to resume more cordial relations with Washington in the aftermath of the Bay of Pigs. On 27 April –

only a week after the failed invasion attempt – President Osvaldo Dorticós of Cuba read a joint statement by Castro and himself to the heads of the diplomatic missions in Havana. Although stressing their determination to fend off any future attack, they also expressed their willingness "to participate in any discussions as may be considered advisable in order to arrive at a satisfactory solution of the tension" between Cuba and the United States. In May Castro offered to return the Cuban émigrés taken prisoner during the Bay of Pigs in exchange for American farm tractors. Then in mid-June the Cuban leader spoke to a group of American journalists of his wish to improve relations with Washington, and as an example of his good faith said he would be prepared to consider compensation for expropriated United States properties in Cuba. Tad Szulc reported the conversation to Schlesinger who in turn apprised President Kennedy.[66]

In this context, then, Guevara's talk with Goodwin represented the culmination of a concerted effort by Castro to normalise relations with the United States during the late spring and summer of 1961. Moreover, the content of their discussion indicated that the Cuban leader had become more accommodating in order to achieve that goal. In his June conversation with the American press he had responded equivocally to a question about whether he would be prepared to desist from attempts to export his revolution overseas. But by August Guevara stated categorically that the Cuban leadership was now willing to make that concession. Despite all this, Kennedy, as in the early months of 1961, failed to take up the opportunities for better relations with Havana. The president and his advisers seem to have simply acknowledged Che Guevara's suggestions and then immediately dropped them. Of course, the Cuban overtures may have been disingenuous, but American officals never made the effort to find out. In downplaying the significance of the Guevara-Goodwin meeting, they even told their British counterparts that Guevara had not made any direct proposals to Goodwin.[67]

To Kennedy and his leading advisers, Cuba remained an issue of vexing concern during the autumn of 1961. "The Cuba thing sits on my desk like a sack of wet potatoes," groused the president to Assistant Secretary of State for Inter-

American Affairs Robert F. Woodward. Frustrated, Kennedy, along with his brother, tore into Richard Bissell during a meeting in the White House Cabinet Room. According to a Bissell confidant, the Kennedys chastised the CIA deputy director for "sitting on his ass and not doing anything about getting rid of Castro and the Castro regime." By the end of the year, Chester Bowles had come to feel that JFK was totally obsessed with the Cuban leader.[68]

Kennedy's enduring determination to oust Castro resulted in his decision to establish Operation Mongoose, a programme of covert actions designed to harass and ultimately topple the Cuban government. The president initiated Mongoose on 30 November with the aim of utilising "our available assets . . .to help Cuba overthrow the Communist regime." To supervise Mongoose, he created the Special Group (Augmented) (SGA for short), which comprised the usual members of the NSC Special Group that oversaw the CIA's covert operations, with the addition of Maxwell Taylor as chairman of the group and Robert Kennedy. The president also selected Edward Lansdale to manage Mongoose directly. Lansdale was to collect and formulate proposals for clandestine action against Cuba, and then submit them to the SGA for approval. Completing these organisational and personnel changes was the appointment of William Harvey as head of Task Force W, the CIA unit designated responsibility for the implementation of Mongoose. Kennedy kept a close eye on this covert programme. During its early days, he met directly with Lansdale to stay abreast of developments. After that, Bundy kept him informed of the operation's progress.[69]

The planning for Operation Mongoose commenced on 18 January 1962 when Lansdale assigned thirty-two tasks to various government agencies. He added one more the next day. By the end of January the SGA had approved the planning for these thirty-three tasks. On 20 February Lansdale formulated a six-stage plan which would culminate in an "open revolt and overthrow of the Communist regime" in October 1962. The SGA, however, did not accept Lansdale's conceptualisation of Mongoose, and instructed him to devote the programme, at least in its initial phase, to intelligence gathering only. It was this task, then, which was to be the nominal focus of Mongoose until August 1962.[70]

The implementation of Mongoose in the spring of 1962 entailed much more, though, than mere intelligence collection. Sabotage and paramilitary activities, including the attempted destruction of an important Cuban copper mine, took place during these months. This was consonant with the Kennedy administration's general tendency towards activism. During the Eisenhower years, the NSC Special Group approved one hundred and four covert operations, an average of thirteen each year. In sharp contrast, it endorsed one hundred and sixty three during Kennedy's presidency, or fifty-seven per annum. Although Lansdale and others framed Mongoose in terms of encouraging anti-Castro forces within Cuba to dispose of the Cuban leader, it was also felt that any anti-Castro uprising would probably require American military intervention to ensure its success. The 14 March guidelines for Mongoose, to which Kennedy apparently gave his tacit endorsement, indicated that planners regarded a United States invasion as key to the success of Mongoose, and that the programme's main purpose was to create a pretext to justify the use of American force in Cuba.[71]

Testimony to the importance attached by Kennedy to Mongoose was its sheer magnitude. Divided between headquarters and Miami, the CIA devoted four hundred agents and officials to the operation. The CIA was given an annual budget of $50 million to run the programme, as well as resources which apparently included a fleet of ships, aircraft, and secret bank accounts. Not surprisingly, the Miami base became the largest CIA station in the world.[72]

As a complement to Mongoose, the Kennedy administration also developed various military contingency plans for Cuba. Kennedy's own attitude in early 1962 was that although the time to use force against Cuba had not yet arrived, it was an alternative which might have to be pursued in the future. "The time has not yet come," he explained at a January 1962 NSC meeting, "when we must force a solution to the Cuban problem." The obvious implication was that a solution might have to be forced at a later date.[73]

Contingency planning for the removal of Castro through military action had commenced as early as November 1959 under the supervision of Admiral Robert L. Dennison, com-

mander in chief of Atlantic forces. The Pentagon developed
two main plans for Cuba. The first was an air strike (Operation Plan 312) to be executed expeditiously on little or no
prior warning. This option was regarded by planners as a
prologue to the second approach, a full-scale invasion (Operation Plans 314 and 316), which would be carried out by
a combination of army, air, and naval forces. The plans were
constantly updated. After a July 1961 meeting between
McNamara and the Joint Chiefs of Staff, for instance, the
secretary of defense instructed Air Force and Army commanders to play a more active role in formulating contingency plans for Cuba.[74]

The establishment of Mongoose injected an even greater
sense of urgency into the military planning for Cuba. When
Lansdale assigned his various planning tasks in January 1962,
he asked the Defense Department to develop within five
weeks "a contingency plan for U.S. military action, in case
the Cuban people request U.S. help when their revolt starts
making headway." The Pentagon obliged, giving the request
top priority. During the intelligence gathering phase of
Mongoose in spring–summer 1962, military contingency planning continued apace. Lansdale made clear that one of the
main objectives during this time was to "continue JCS planning and essential preliminary actions for a decisive U.S.
capability for intervention." By July the planning had been
developed not only for a military attack on Cuba, but also
for a naval and air blockade of the island. These plans to
oust Castro through covert and military action would be further accelerated during the fall of 1962 before the onset of
the missile crisis. The energy invested in this contingency
planning indicates that a direct military attack on Cuba was
always regarded by Kennedy and his advisers, even before
the October 1962 confrontation, as a definite option.[75]

As Mongoose and its concomitant military planning began, Kennedy was at the same time looking to the OAS for
the application of diplomatic pressure on Castro. In August
1961 the Inter-American Economic and Social Council had
promised at a Punta del Este meeting that, as Rostow recalls, "economic and social progress . . .would move to the
center of political life." The criticism of Cuba in this commitment was implicit but obvious. On 9 November 1961

Colombia called a second Punta del Este conference, a request that was approved by the OAS Council six weeks later. With Castro's declaration at the start of December that he had always been a Marxist-Leninist, American officials were hopeful that the time for collective action against Cuba was now ripe. Kennedy himself was determined that the OAS foreign ministers' meeting, scheduled for the last week in January 1962, would serve to ostracise Castro. In notes describing the comments he intended to make at an 18 January NSC session, the president stated that "the elimination of Castro communism remains a clear purpose of this Administration." In the meeting itself, he told his advisers that Castro should be "effectively isolated at the coming meeting." Rostow, an American delegate at the conference, recalled that he and his colleagues left for Punta del Este "under quite unambiguous instruction from Kennedy to effect the removal of Cuba from the OAS."[76]

The Punta del Este meeting succeeded in passing nine resolutions, the majority of which dealt with Cuba. The most important provided for the ejection of the Cuban government from the Inter-American system. Communism, moreover, was declared to be "incompatible with the principles of the Inter-American system." A Special Consultative Committee on Security was also established to counter "the subversive action of international communism" in the Western Hemisphere; Cuba was removed from the Inter-American Defense Board; trade with Cuba in military equipment was to be suspended; and the possible extension of that embargo into other areas of commerce was to be explored. In a statement at the close of the conference, Rusk indicated his pleasure at the "remarkable unanimity" with which the "democratic nations of the Hemisphere" had demonstrated their opposition to Castro. On the same day Kennedy expressed his "satisfaction" at the results of the meeting.[77]

Those results were achieved, however, through the application of intense and at times coercive pressure from the American delegation. The resolution providing for the expulsion of Cuba from the Inter-American system was just approved by the necessary two-thirds of the twenty-one delegations, with the big countries like Mexico, Brazil, and Argentina abstaining. The crucial fourteenth vote, that of

Haiti, was secured only after the United States promised to help increase the size of an airfield in Haiti. The American delegation, which included two senators and two members of the House of Representatives, also made clear that the recalcitrance of allies would be punished by diminishing amounts of aid. Journalist John Crosby, present at the conference, wrote that the essence of what the congressmen told the Latin American delegates was: "If you're not with us, you're against us. If you're against us, Congress is going to take a very cold view of any foreign aid toward your country." Small wonder Crosby concluded that the expulsion of Cuba from the Inter-American system had only occurred after "the most savage infighting behind closed doors." In addition to all this, the CIA may have sought to influence the other OAS delegations by organising demonstrations throughout the Western Hemisphere in support of the OAS conference. "The OAS meeting is to be supported by public demonstrations in Latin America," wrote Lansdale in an 18 January memorandum.[78]

As an immediate supplement to the work of the OAS conference, Kennedy established an embargo against Cuba. The State Department had decided before the Punta del Este meeting to advise the president to take that step, providing the OAS conference, at the very least, condemned Cuba as a tool of "the Sino-Soviet bloc" and declared the island to be a threat to the security of the Western Hemisphere. With the successful outcome at Punta del Este, the State Department now pressed the president to step up the economic pressure on Castro. Kennedy consented and on 3 February he announced the initiation of an embargo, to become effective four days hence on all trade with Cuba. The president's proclamation meant that all imports from Cuba into the United States were prohibited, as were all American exports to Cuba, with the exception of essential foodstuffs and medical supplies.[79]

By spring 1962 Kennedy had made a concerted effort to weaken Castro's position through economic and diplomatic isolation and covert pressure. Capping that campaign was the decision to stage military manoeuvres on a gargantuan scale in the Caribbean. The first, Lantphibex-1-62, began on 9 April, involved forty thousand military personnel, and ended with the landing of an eleven thousand strong force on the island of Vieques, near Puerto Rico. It was described by the *New York Times* as "the largest Atlantic-Caribbean maneuver ever conducted." The exercise, which generated much publicity at the time, was observed by Kennedy in person. After watching a simulated "hunter-killer" attack on a submarine, the president addressed the Atlantic Fleet from the deck of the USS Enterprise. Recalling his own naval service during World War II, he expressed his "heartfelt appreciation" to those who had participated in the manoeuvre. "What you have shown us today," he added, "makes us all return to the capital with a good deal more confidence and hope." Similar large-scale practice operations, such as Whip Lash and Jupiter Springs, were scheduled soon after Lantphibex.[80]

For Kennedy, these manoeuvres had benefits aside from their military value. They presumably served as a therapeutic release for his pent-up frustrations over Cuba. To Castro, however, they were undoubtedly seen as a portent of a future American invasion of his island. And to Khrushchev, they may have spurred him or at least strengthened his resolve to make a decision, the potential consequences of which made it the most grave in the history of the Cold War.

3 Nikita Khrushchev and the Decision to Deploy

For many years, historians had been forced to speculate on the motives behind Nikita Khrushchev's decision in spring 1962 to deploy offensive, surface-to-surface missiles in Cuba. Apart from Khrushchev's own memoirs, the evidence was scant. But with the advent of Mikhail Gorbachev and glasnost, all that appeared to change. Former Soviet officials, some who played a role in the events of 1962 and others who were intimate with those who participated, have recently furnished long-starved students of the missile crisis with their version of events. This has undoubtedly been helpful in reconstructing the Soviet side of the story.[1]

These recent riches should not lead, however, to an exaggeration of the wealth of available primary source material. Only a limited quantity of contemporary documentation has surfaced, so what has emerged in effect is a small number of memoirs on the Soviet side. The limits of such sources are obvious. For instance, a detached view of the Truman administration's accomplishments would hardly be obtained by sampling the memoirs of Dean Acheson, James Byrnes, and Truman himself, although they do provide valuable insights and information. That is even more the case with the memoirs of Ted Sorensen, Arthur Schlesinger, and Pierre Salinger, and their adoring view of the Kennedy presidency. The especially tendentious aspect of such works is the underlying assumption that American foreign policy always flowed from magnanimous motives. Occasionally, memoirs do furnish more critical assessments. The reminiscences of Chester Bowles on the Kennedy administration are a case in point. But generally speaking, memoirs do not provide a dispassionate view of events. So although these recent Soviet reminiscences must be exploited for the information they yield on how the decision was made to put missiles in Cuba and how the deployment was carried out, they cannot at the same time be wholly depended upon for a rigorous,

60

nuanced analysis of the motives behind that decision.[2]

In explaining why missiles were put in Cuba, recent Western accounts have highlighted two factors. First, emphasis has been placed on Khrushchev's own claim that the main objective was to defend Cuba from an imminent American invasion. Second, scholars have stressed the Soviet determination to repair the gap in the strategic nuclear balance between the superpowers, which then lay heavily in Washington's favour. The recent contributions of Soviet participants have added weight to those theories. Foreign Minister Andrei A. Gromyko and Sergo Mikoyan, son of Khrushchev's closest confidant Anastas I. Mikoyan, have emphasised the desire to defend Cuba. While Fedor Burlatsky, Khrushchev's speechwriter and adviser on Eastern European issues, has suggested the main goal was to alter the strategic balance.[3]

Those two arguments, however, are either superficial or rather limited. The shortcoming of the to-defend-Cuba theory is that it fails to differentiate between the professed goals (that is the rhetoric) of Soviet policy and the authentic motivations behind it. To say without any qualification that Khrushchev wanted to defend Cuba implies that Soviet policy was inspired by pure altruism, a noble concern for Cuba's safety. In other words, to argue that the Soviet premier wanted to defend Cuba really begs the question: why did he want to defend Cuba? What did he have to gain from doing so?

The strategic factor was certainly important in itself. By spring 1962, the Soviet Union's position of nuclear inferiority was common knowledge in the West. The Kennedy administration used intelligence findings to present this picture of American strategic dominance to the public in October 1961, and five months later the president displayed his confidence in America's superior nuclear strength by declaring in an interview with Stewart Alsop that the United States, in certain circumstances, should be willing to launch the first nuclear strike in an international conflict. The gap between the American and Soviet nuclear arsenals that prompted Kennedy's brazen observation was enormous, and Khrushchev and other Soviet officials were cognisant of that reality. Given the degree to which the Soviet Union lagged behind the United States in the arms race and given the clumsy and provocative way Kennedy (in contrast to Eisenhower) highlighted this in public, it is implausible to suggest that Khrushchev's decision to put nuclear weapons in Cuba was unrelated to his strategic concerns. None the less, the question can be legitimately asked: Did the Soviet leader put missiles in Cuba only to repair the strategic gap, undoubtedly an important motivation in itself, or were there other advantages he hoped to secure.[4]

Khrushchev's decision to install missiles in Cuba was an extremely risky one, and it is a simple but important observation that if he had not made this decision there would have been no missile crisis. Up to that point, the Soviet Union had not deployed nuclear missiles outside of Soviet territory. So to not only do that, but also to emplace those weapons a few miles off the coast of the United States in an area regarded by American policy-makers as their own backyard, was indeed a gamble. As Burlatsky has argued, it was a step the more draconian but more prudent Josef Stalin would almost certainly not have taken. Stalin thought instinctively in terms of spheres of influence: Eastern Europe was his, but other countries and regions were not. There were occasions when he resisted intervention in countries such as Greece and Egypt because he viewed them as part of the traditional British sphere of influence. Khrushchev himself recalled that:

> King Farouk had once asked Stalin to give him arms so that he could force Great Britain to evacuate its troops from Egypt, but Stalin refused. Stalin said in my presence that the Near East was part of Britain's sphere of influence and that therefore we couldn't go sticking our nose into Egypt's affairs.

In all likelihood, then, Stalin would not have interfered in the affairs of a country as close to the United States as Cuba. Khrushchev, though, was a different sort of leader and a different sort of man.[5]

Khrushchev's personality was undoubtedly a critical element, for there was much about the deployment of missiles in Cuba that appealed to his temperament. At the core of his personality lay an acute sense of insecurity. Born in 1894 into grinding poverty in the village of Kalinovka, the recipient of no more than two or three years formal education, Khrushchev grew up with a gargantuan chip on his shoulder. It remained with him during his ascendancy through the ranks of the Communist Party. Burlatsky, for example, became very aware of this "inferiority complex." Americans who spoke with him often noticed the same thing. When Under Secretary of State for Political Affairs Robert D. Murphy met with the Soviet leader in October 1959, he came to the conclusion that "Khrushchev's anger showed a lack of sense of security." After meeting with Khrushchev in September 1959, John Kennedy also discerned the Soviet leader's "inferiority complex" from his responses to "harmless questions."[6]

Khrushchev's lack of self-assurance accounted for many aspects of his personality. In order to mask his insecurity, for instance, he liked to boast and to denigrate others. "I had no diplomatic training," he once allegedly told a group of Western diplomats. "And yet here we are, and I can make rings round you all." Insecurity also generated in Khrushchev a craving for recognition, for the acknowledgement of his own strength and importance. When he became leader, that sentiment translated into a desire for recognition of Soviet power on the part of the international community, especially the United States. George Weaver of the International Union of Electrical Workers commented on his October 1959 meeting with the Soviet leader that he "showed the need he felt for Russia to be recognized as an equal of the United States." "Above all," British Prime Minister Harold Macmillan wrote Dwight Eisenhower on one occasion, "[Khrushchev] would like to feel himself recognized as an equal by you and by the United States."[7]

Another feature of Khrushchev's temperament was his incorrigible restlessness. He hated to feel restricted. Reflecting back upon a mundane, bureaucratic job he had been given in Kharkov in the late 1920s, he recalled that it was "most disagreeable. It was nothing but paper work. I'm a man of the earth, a man of action. . . . My job in Kharkov was a dead end; I felt stifled and trapped." His dislike for being confined, for having his manoeuvrability circumscribed, was amplified by the very nature of politics in Stalin's Soviet Union. Life for those in the upper echelons of the Communist Party was highly precarious. A single mistake could be politically, even personally, fatal.[8]

For Khrushchev, Stalin's death in 1953 and his own sub-sequent rise to the summit of political power probably pro-moted a profound sense of liberation. Having been forced to toe the line for so long, he could now give vent to his long-suppressed instincts for bold action. As a May 1961 State Department paper put it, Khrushchev liked "on occasion [to] be a gambler and a dissembler." The most dramatic example of his audacity was when at the pivotal Twentieth Party Congress in February 1956 he roundly denounced Stalin in his secret speech before the delegates, thereby legitimis-ing his own leadership by delegitimising Stalin's. Apparently, Khrushchev had no intention of making such an address at the beginning of the Congress. It had been a spur-of-the-moment decision. His boldness was further evident in 1958 when he threatened to make a peace treaty with the East German government, and called for the conversion of West Berlin into a free city. When in spring 1962 the Soviet leader decided to deploy missiles in Cuba, he once again displayed his penchant for the gamble. Without Khrushchev's insecu-rity, restlessness, and risk-taking tendencies, then, there would have been no missile crisis.[9]

To say that is not to suggest that the installation of miss-iles in Cuba was not also consistent with the Soviet leader's long-term foreign, defense, and domestic policy objectives. The decision to deploy missiles in Cuba was a risk. But Khrushchev was no fool, and so presumably it was a calcu-lated risk, designed to achieve certain goals. In attempting to discern those motives, it is important to recognise that everything which happened from spring 1962 onwards is irrelevant. It makes far more sense to place his decision to put missiles in Cuba in the context of his overall policy objectives during the latter part of the 1950s and the early 1960s.

For Khrushchev, one of the great advantages of having missiles in Cuba was that it would vastly improve the Soviet strategic position *vis-à-vis* the United States, and this in turn would allow him to forge ahead with his long-term programme of pruning conventional military forces in order to reduce overall defence spending. He would then be able to divert financial resources into the civilian economy. This goal stemmed in part from Khrushchev's belief, akin to that held by many Republicans in the 1950s, that nuclear weaponry had vastly reduced the significance of conventional forces. On one occasion, in a conversation between Khrushchev and Mao Zedong in Peking, Mao remarked: "If we compare the military might of the capitalist world with that of the Socialist world, you'll see that we obviously have the advantage over our enemies. Think of how many divisions China, the USSR, and the other Socialist countries could raise." Khrushchev disagreed:

> nowadays that sort of thinking is out of date. You can no longer calculate the alignment of forces on the basis of who has the most men. Back in the days when a dispute was settled with fists or bayonets, it made a difference who had the most men and the most bayonets on each side. . . . now with the atomic bomb, the number of troops on each side makes practically no difference to the alignment of real power and the outcome of a war. The more troops on a side, the more bomb fodder."[10]

In line with this thinking, Khrushchev sought to develop Soviet nuclear capabilities rapidly. Most notably, the Soviets fired the world's first intercontinental ballistic missile (ICBM) in 1957. Khrushchev also tried throughout the late 1950s to make nuclear-powered, missile-armed submarines and not the surface fleet the most important part of the Soviet navy. He fired Admiral N.G. Kuznetsov as commander in chief of Soviet naval forces in 1956 because of what Khrushchev perceived to be his anachronistic interest in building up the surface fleet. One of the reasons he was replaced by Admiral S.G. Gorshkov was the latter's previous experience as a submarine captain.[11]

As the complement to his emphasis on nuclear weaponry, Khrushchev sought to reduce conventional forces by cutting troop numbers. The Soviet Union spent far more of its resources on conventional than nuclear forces, and hence the Soviet leader could modernise his strategic weaponry while cutting conventional forces, and still significantly decrease overall defence spending.[12]

Khrushchev's predilection for reducing military expenditure derived not only from his belief in the primacy of nuclear weapons, but also, more fundamentally, from his conviction that if the Soviet system was to work it needed to win the confidence of the people by raising their standard of living. To that end, Khrushchev tried, as Gorbachev would three decades later, to reduce defence spending and to transfer those resources from the miltary sector to the civilian economy. As he himself put it: "It wasn't as though we could afford to concentrate all our attention on military matters. We had a plateful of other problems. We had to increase our economic potential. Above all, we had to find some way of providing more bread, more butter, and other agricultural products for our people." Khrushchev thus resolved to curtail military spending. After the establishment of the Warsaw Pact in 1955, he felt sufficiently confident to do so. In 1955 the Soviet Union had 5 763 000 troops. By January 1960 Khrushchev had reduced the number to 3 623 000. As a proportion of the gross national product, Soviet military expenditure decreased from 11.5 per cent in 1955 to 8.5 per cent in 1959.[13]

Khrushchev's innovations in defence policy culminated in his January 1960 address to the Supreme Soviet. He emphasised in the speech the superiority of nuclear weapons over conventional forces, arguing that missiles were reducing surface navies and huge standing armies to a status of virtual obsolescence. He spoke enthusiastically of the progress of the Soviet missile programme, and added that unless a "mad-man" came to power in the West, a significant Soviet strategic arsenal would deter an adversary from launching a nuclear strike because of the prospect of Soviet reprisals. Having procured the prior support of the Central Committee in December 1959, the Soviet leader also dramatically announced his intention to reduce military manpower by a third.[14]

In the following months, however, Khrushchev began to equivocate over whether his proposed cut was viable, and on 8 July 1961 he issued a retraction. The reductions, Khrushchev declared, would have to be halted for the time being. Various factors had contributed to his change of mind, including opposition from certain segments of the Soviet military to the proposed cuts, a desire shared by Khrushchev and the military to maintain the Soviet Union's military strength at a time when relations with China were rapidly deteriorating, and reduced confidence in the feasibility of centring defence strategy on the nuclear arsenal in light of the slow progress made by the Soviet ICBM programme. Also of importance was the Francis Gary Powers U-2 incident of May 1960, which raised the issue of whether American officials had ascertained the rather limited extent of Soviet nuclear strength, something they had been grossly overestimating during the late 1950s. The subsequent breakdown of the Paris summit between Eisenhower and Khrushchev and the concomitant deterioration in Soviet-American relations was another significant factor.[15]

Probably the chief reason, though, for Khrushchev's suspension of the military cuts was his disappointment over the tough, uncompromising line pursued by the new administration during the early months of 1961. In his view, the necessary complement to the cuts proposed in January 1960 was a more stable international climate, meaning a more accommodating American foreign policy. Khrushchev was sanguine that such a change would take place because 1960 was a presidential election year; and he was confident the American people would choose a Democrat who held a more tolerant attitude towards the Soviet Union than that displayed by the Eisenhower administration, with its inimical concepts of "rollback" and "brinksmanship."

Khrushchev hoped, in particular, that Adlai Stevenson would be the next president. He had spent time with Stevenson on two occasions and felt that he had "a clear understanding of the need for strengthening friendly relations between our two countries." In August 1958 Khrushchev spoke with him for over two hours in the Kremlin during the latter's summer tour of the Soviet Union. On this occasion the two men agreed to disagree on various issues. But towards the end of their discussion the Soviet leader told Stevenson that in the 1956 presidential election, "I cast my vote for you," by which he meant he had offered Stevenson moral support. He explained that while he had "no objection to Mr. Eisenhower," he despised Secretary of State John Foster Dulles, who "if brought together with a saint, would make the saint look like a sinner." Khrushchev proceeded to ask, "Shall I vote for you again in the next election or not?" Stevenson replied that he would not be able to because, "I will not be a candidate again." Responding anxiously, Khrushchev asked, "But how does Mr. Stevenson *know* that he will not be a candidate?" Avoiding the question, the Illinoisan replied that although he was not certain, he thought the Democratic Party would win the 1960 election. The meeting ended cordially, with Stevenson introducing Khrushchev to his sons, Borden and John Fell.[16]

The Soviet leader enjoyed another amicable meeting with Stevenson during his fall 1959 trip to the United States. When Khrushchev visited Roswell Garst, an expert in hybrid corn growing, in Coon Rapids, Iowa, Stevenson joined them. He was in good spirits, and together with Garst he suggested they all have their picture taken together. "We put our arms around each other's shoulders," Khrushchev recalled, "and struck a relaxed pose for the photographer. I took Stevenson's willingness to be in a picture with me as a sign of tolerance toward the Soviet Union."[17]

By the time of his speech to the Supreme Soviet in January 1960, Khrushchev had decided that Stevenson was the man for the White House. He was so anxious for this to happen, he even availed his services as leader of the Soviet state to the Illinoisan to help bring about his election. Stevenson learned of this during a 16 January 1960 meeting with Mikhail A. Menshikov, the Soviet ambassador to the United States, in a parlour on the third floor of the Soviet Embassy in Washington. Menshikov not only furnished Stevenson with various birthday presents from Khrushchev, including caviar and wine, he also conveyed an astonishing message from the Soviet leader. "When you met in Moscow in August 1958," Menshikov informed Stevenson, "he [Khrushchev] said to you that he had voted for you in his heart in 1956. He says now that he will vote for you in his heart again in 1960. . . . We are concerned with the future, and that America has the right President." Menshikov's recital of the message went on to say that both Khrushchev and the Presidium believed that Stevenson was the presidential contender who best understood the need for improved Soviet-American relations.[18]

Khrushchev then offered to help Stevenson win the 1960 election. The message ordered Menshikov to ascertain from Stevenson how:

we could be of assistance to those forces in the United
States which favor friendly relations. . . . Could the Soviet
press assist Mr. Stevenson's personal success? How? Should
the press praise him, and, if so, for what? Should it criticize
him, and, if so, for what? . . . . Mr. Stevenson will know
best what would help him.

Through this message, the Soviet premier also expressed
his annoyance at the way his debate with Nixon in the model
kitchen at the Moscow Trade Fair in summer 1959 had
enhanced the vice-president's credibility in the United States.
Stevenson, presumably in a state of shock at this remarkable offer of Soviet support, responded with propriety. He
expressed his thanks for the confidence Khrushchev had
shown in him, but made clear that he would not be a candidate for the Democratic presidential nomination, and,
moreover, that he could not condone this sort of interference in the American electoral process. Stevenson reiterated those arguments a week later in a letter to Menshikov.[19]
    Despite the rebuff, Khrushchev still sought to help the
Democrats, whoever their presidential candidate might be.
His interest in doing so may well have been the main reason
(rather than the ostensible one of his annoyance at the Gary
Powers incident) why he decided to wreck the May 1960
Paris summit with Eisenhower. This, he seems to have reasoned, would ensure that the Republican presidential candidate did not enjoy an indirect boost from the praise which
the Eisenhower administration would undoubtedly receive
in the aftermath of a successful summit. In his January meeting
with Menshikov, Stevenson had gathered that the Soviets
"were quite aware of the effect on the Presidential election
of the Summit Conference and Eisenhower's [proposed] visit
to Russia; that a "success" would redound to the benefit of
the Republican candidate which seems to leave them in some
dilemma." It appears that Khrushchev resolved the dilemma
by aborting the Paris summit.[20]
    Once Kennedy had successfully garnered the Democratic
presidential nomination at the Los Angeles convention in
July by defeating a group of rivals that included Stevenson,
Khrushchev focused his attention upon helping the Massachusetts senator. Stevenson was better than Kennedy, but

Kennedy was infinitely better than Nixon. Khrushchev had first encountered JFK at a September 1959 Senate Foreign Relations Committee function. Although Kennedy arrived late for the meeting, the Soviet leader had been "impressed" with the young senator. "I've heard a lot about you," he told Kennedy. "People say you have a great future ahead of you." Nixon, meanwhile, had offended Khrushchev during this trip to the United States with his caustic anti-Soviet comments. In a meeting with Eisenhower and Nixon on 15 September 1959, Khrushchev complained about the vice-president's last speech, saying "it was certainly not calculated to reduce tensions and calm feelings on the eve of his [Khrushchev's] visit."[21]

Khrushchev, having resolved to aid Kennedy in summer 1960, decided to delay the release of the captured U-2 pilot, Gary Powers, until after the presidential election, a move clearly designed to help JFK and hurt Nixon. As the Soviet premier explained to a group of his advisers:

> the two candidates are at a stalemate. If we give the slightest boost to Nixon it will be interpreted as an expression of our willingness to see him in the White House. This would be a mistake. If Nixon becomes President, I don't believe he will contribute to an improvement in relations between our countries. Therefore, let's hold off on taking the final step of releasing Powers. As soon as the elections are over we'll hand him over.

Accordingly, Powers was not released until February 1962, and then only in return for the convicted Soviet spy Rudolf I. Abel. At the Vienna summit Khrushchev told Kennedy that he had voted for him in the 1960 election by not releasing Powers. Kennedy, according to Khrushchev, laughed and replied, "You're right. I admit you played a role in the election and cast your vote for me."[22]

With Kennedy's defeat of Nixon in the presidential election, Khrushchev was optimistic that the administration in Washington would facilitate improved Soviet-American relations. At a New Year's Party in the Kremlin, attended by Soviet officials and foreign diplomats, Khrushchev stressed the importance of developing better relations with Washington. Elaborating on the theme, the Soviet leader told those present of his hope that:

with the advent of a new President a fresh wind will blow
and . . . the unhealthy atmosphere in relations between
the Soviet Union and the United States will begin to improve. We would like our bad relations with the United
States of America to become a thing of the past with the
departure of the old year and of the old President.[23]

Corresponding with Averell Harriman through Ambassador Menshikov in the aftermath of Kennedy's victory,
Khrushchev sounded the same theme. Khrushchev's messages, Harriman recalled, "indicated his gratification at the
election of President Kennedy." They further revealed his
feeling that Kennedy's election would ameliorate Soviet-
American relations. Khrushchev must have hoped, in particular, for a more accommodating foreign policy on the
part of Kennedy in order to validate the sizeable military
cuts he had ordered at the start of 1960. If the tension
between Moscow and Washington subsided, then those reductions would appear to make sense, and so he would have
a stronger case against those sections of the Soviet military
opposing the cuts.[24]

Khrushchev, however, became rapidly disillusioned with
the New Frontier. Two developments convinced him that
Kennedy was no more conciliatory than his predecessor. The
first was the Bay of Pigs invasion, which Khrushchev sharply
denounced in messages to JFK on 18 and 22 April. Of even
greater importance were the large increases in military spending initiated by Kennedy at the start of his administration
and during the Berlin crisis in summer 1961. Khrushchev
interpreted Kennedy's actions in the Bay of Pigs and in the
area of defence expenditure as meaning that his hopes for
a new accommodating American foreign policy were naive.
If Kennedy was to be tough, Khrushchev now reasoned, this
was not the most appropriate time for him to reduce Soviet
military strength. "Given Kennedy's policies," two pundits
on Soviet defence policy have concluded, "it is difficult to
see how Khrushchev could have preserved his programme
[of military cuts] intact."[25]

On 8 July 1961, therefore, Khrushchev announced at a
reception for those graduating from Soviet military aca-
demies that he was suspending the military cuts proposed in

January 1960. He added that defence expenditures would be augmented by one-third. In explaining the need for that, Khrushchev emphasised the recent bolstering of American military spending and its deleterious impact on Soviet security. Increases in defence expenditure, he argued, "have been forced on us, comrades. We are taking them because of the circumstances that have arisen, since we cannot neglect the security interests of the Soviet people." Kennedy's policies during the first half of 1961 were indeed the critical factor in Khrushchev's decision to suspend his programme of defence cuts. Reductions amounting to one-half of the 1.2 million men cut proposed in January 1960 were actually carried out up until the spring of 1961, despite much resistance from the Soviet military. Kennedy's policies, especially his large increases in defence spending, not only fortified the argument of the Soviet military that a reduction in manpower would endanger Soviet security, but also convinced Khrushchev that the objection had value.[26]

Khrushchev indicated in his July 1961 address that the reversal would only be temporary. Given the considerable cuts he had made in Soviet troop numbers since the mid-1950s, he was almost certainly being candid. That being the case, the installation of missiles in Cuba would be exceedingly helpful to Khrushchev because it would significantly improve the Soviet strategic position *vis-à-vis* the United States. This in turn would strengthen Khrushchev's voice in the ongoing dialogue with his military for he would then be able to make the case that the missiles in Cuba had so improved Moscow's strategic position that it would now be safe to resume cutting Soviet manpower. The funneling of extra resources to the civilian economy could then take place.

Even if the deployment of missiles in Cuba did not help Khrushchev in the debate with his military, it would still advance his goal of moving resources from defence to the civilian economy. As one authority has argued, Khrushchev must have viewed the emplacement of missiles in Cuba as "a move to offset US strategic superiority cheaply, so as to allocate to civilian needs resources that would otherwise have to be invested (and were later invested) in a costly programme of intercontinental ballistic missiles." One probable element, then, in Khrushchev's decision to deploy missiles in Cuba was the desire to further his long-term goal of transferring resources from the military to the civilian economy.[27]

Another factor was his determination to restore credibility to the strategy of brinksmanship that he had employed so frequently in the past. Although brinksmanship, the threatening of others with nuclear devastation in order to extract concessions, was synonymous with John Foster Dulles, Khrushchev actually practised it far more than Eisenhower's secretary of state ever did. Brinksmanship, for the Soviet leader, was a way of furthering his foreign policy objectives by inducing a more compliant line on the part of the United States and its Western allies, while expending neither military nor financial resources. As one expert has written in reference to the Khrushchev years:

> The Soviet leadership has been more inclined to use verbal and written ultimatums and warnings than to take a high level of risk in actual policy commitment. Skillful use of words has been a weapon to enlarge the sense of risk in other parties, thereby increasing their caution in situations where the U.S.S.R. itself has been reluctant to take more than token action.[28]

On one occasion during his spring 1956 visit to England, for instance, Khrushchev responded to a question from Mrs Anthony Eden about Soviet missiles by saying that "they have a very long range. They could easily reach your island and quite a bit farther." Khrushchev later recalled that Mrs Eden "bit her tongue" and that his aim had been to convey the sense that "we were powerful and deserved respect." The development during the late 1950s of the missile gap theory, the widespread but mistaken belief in the United States that the Soviets were forging ahead in the arms race, further encouraged Khrushchev to engage in brinksmanship. In June 1959, for example, he told Harriman that as far as the Berlin question was concerned, "one bomb is sufficient to destroy Bonn and the Ruhr and that is all of Germany." During the confrontation over Berlin in summer 1961, Khrushchev assured Italian Prime Minister Amintore Fanfani that if the crisis resulted in war, "Not only the orange groves of Italy but also the people who created them and who have exalted Italy's culture and arts...may perish." Apparently,

Khrushchev even authorised the building of phony missile launching sites in order to lend credence to his boasts about Soviet nuclear superiority.[29]

The actual reality of the strategic balance during the late 1950s and early 1960s was that it lay heavily in favour of the United States. But to American officials conditioned to think in terms of a menacing Soviet challenge, Khrushchev's brinksmanship appeared genuinely threatening. By frequently stressing a supposed missile gap in Russia's favour, Khrushchev actually helped increase America's nuclear superiority. Worried about the apparent gap, and having that concern constantly heightened by Khrushchev's boasts, United States policy-makers focused so much energy on repairing the alleged gap that by 1962 the actual strategic position was even more favourable to the United States than it had been in the late 1950s. Khrushchev's repeated threats were also convincing enough to produce increased criticism from China. The Soviet premier, Beijing suggested, should use his presumed military advantage over the West more forcefully to further communist positions throughout the world. In this way, Khrushchev's brinksmanship compounded the emerging Sino-Soviet split.[30]

Khrushchev's predilection for brinksmanship was undercut in autumn 1961. Deputy Secretary of Defense Roswell L. Gilpatric, in a speech delivered on 21 October 1961, disclosed what the Kennedy administration had known for some time, namely that the missile gap theory was a fallacy, that the discrepancy lay in fact in the opposite direction to the detriment of the Soviet Union, and that this chasm was widening. The notion of a missile gap in favour of Moscow had been revealed as a complete sham, and in the process Khrushchev's brinksmanship was immediately deprived of its credibility. That this troubled Khrushchev seems certain. As one authority has put it, brinksmanship had been the Soviet leader's "favoured instrument" in foreign policy. It was what he had depended upon since the mid-1950s, and especially from 1957. The sudden removal of that "instrument" was something he could not have viewed with equanimity. In this context, Khrushchev's decision to put missiles in Cuba made sense. If that deployment was successful, the Soviet strategic position would be and, more importantly, would be perceived as being considerably improved. This would allow Khrushchev to resume his brinksmanship with credibility.[31]

Another probable factor behind Khrushchev's decision to put missiles in Cuba was Berlin. The Soviet leader had long resolved to change the status of West Berlin. For so many reasons, that city was a vexing problem for him. Between 1949 and 1961, 2 800 000 East Germans had fled to the West via West Berlin, an exodus that was particularly damaging because most of those who left were young, and many were highly skilled and educated. Among the absconders were 15 000 schoolteachers, 30 000 students, and 16 000 trained engineers. The West, furthermore, had established an immense espionage network in the city, deep within East German territory. The sharp contrast between the booming economy of West Berlin, into which the United States had invested billions of dollars, and the relatively stagnant economy of East Berlin was an additional source of embarrassment for both the East German government and the Soviet leader.[32]

Linked to those concerns was Khrushchev's dread of a revitalised, rearmed West Germany. American foreign policy since World War II had itself been heavily shaped by the experience with Hitler and the fear that the Soviet Union would disrupt the international order as Germany had in the 1930s and early 1940s. Given the far greater loss of Soviet life in World War II and the fact that large portions of the Soviet Union had actually been occupied and devastated by the Nazis, this anxiety was even greater in Moscow than Washington. But the Soviets analogised not only between pre-1945 Germany and post-1945 America, but also between Hitler's Germany and the present West German government. In a 1959 *Foreign Affairs* article, Khrushchev argued that the "renewed activities of the West German militarists and revanchists" meant that "Western Germany, taking advantage of her position in the North Atlantic Alliance, might provoke hostilities in order to draw her allies into it and plunge the whole world into the chasm of a devastating war." He explicitly raised the possibility of a new Hitler with Harold Macmillan in December 1961. "Can you guarantee," he asked the British prime minister, "that a new madman will not appear in West Germany?"[33]

Bryant Wedge, a social psychiatrist who did work for the CIA, sent an appraisal of Khrushchev to Kennedy for the Vienna summit. In it, he confirmed that the Soviet leader's concerns about Germany were genuine. "Khrushchev's fear of Germany," noted Wedge, "is deadly and dangerous. After all the Soviet Union lost 20 million people to Hitler. . . . Khrushchev himself acted as political commissar at Stalingrad during the German siege. Thus a prime concern of Khrushchev is to keep Germany weak – and this desire should not be underrated." From a conversation with the Soviet premier in spring 1961, Walter Lippmann also discerned that "in Mr. Khrushchev's mind the future of Germany is the key question."[34]

Khrushchev's fear of a dangerous, rearmed West Germany was heightened by Chancellor Konrad Adenauer's acceleration of West German rearmament. As a result, the Soviet leader came to despise Adenauer. In June 1959 he told Harriman that "we will never accept Adenauer as a representative of Germany. He is a zero." On another occasion he referred to the West German as "that evil man." Khrushchev's suspicion of the chancellor increased when the United States furnished West Germany with planes that could carry nuclear weapons and artillery with the capacity to fire nuclear shells. The fear that West Germany might actually obtain nuclear weapons in the near future almost certainly played a role in the Soviet decision to take action over Berlin.[35]

Khrushchev, accordingly, twice made demands over the status of West Berlin, and on both occasions created a crisis in the process. In November 1958, he announced his intention of transferring control of the access routes to Berlin to East Germany. The Western powers had remained in West Berlin after World War II on the basis of occupation rights which would end on the signing of a German peace treaty. The Soviet Union and the Western powers, however, had failed after 1945 to agree upon the terms for a treaty. Unless the Western powers agreed to commence negotiations for a German peace treaty, Khrushchev now declared, he would sign a treaty with East Germany, forcing those countries to request permission from the East German government to maintain their access rights from West Germany to West Berlin. Khrushchev set a limit of six months for a settlement of the Berlin question. He subsequently argued that West Berlin should become a free city, and that the Western powers must withdraw troops from their sector. In short, Khrushchev wanted the Western powers out of Berlin. Eisenhower, however, refused to accede to either Khrushchev's demands on Berlin or those of critics in the United States who urged him to retaliate by increasing military spending. Unwilling to go to war, Khrushchev was compelled to back down as his six month time limit passed.[36]

Influenced by pressure from East German leader Walter Ulbricht, Khrushchev again demanded a settlement of the Berlin question in 1961. This time Kennedy's response was very different to Eisenhower's. After a bold 25 July television address to the nation, JFK bolstered military spending by over $3 billion, dispatched reinforcements to Europe, tripled draft calls, and mobilised reserves and national guardsmen. Khrushchev, after consulting with Warsaw Pact leaders in Moscow, responded by building the Berlin Wall on 13 August 1961. Although he had failed again to force the Western powers out of Berlin, he had at least ensured that East Germans could no longer use West Berlin as an exit to the West.[37]

Given that it had been a perennial objective of Khrushchev to eject the Western powers from Berlin, it is likely that his decision to deploy missiles in Cuba was linked to that goal. As one observer put it in December 1962, missiles in Cuba would furnish the Soviet leader with "the new trump card in the Berlin game." Khrushchev probably did not hope for a trade in which Kennedy would yield to Soviet demands on Berlin in exchange for the withdrawal of missiles from Cuba. If Khrushchev removed nuclear weapons from Cuba as part of a *quid pro quo*, he would be vulnerable to undesirable Chinese and Cuban complaints that he had placed Soviet interests in Berlin ahead of the need to protect the Cuban Revolution. The more plausible connection between the two issues was that the implicit threat of the missiles in Cuba would make Washington more pliable on Berlin. One of Khrushchev's own advisers, Burlatsky, has made the case that the Soviet leader hoped the weapons in Cuba would create "new conditions for negotiations with the United States" leading to American "recognition of East Germany, [as well as] consolidation of the new status of West Berlin and the post-war borders."[38]

Khrushchev's decision to install missiles in Cuba was also rooted in his desire to respond to the increasingly severe criticisms levelled by China at his leadership of the communist world. The deterioration of relations with China certainly shaped his foreign policy in general. Adam B. Ulam has argued that much of Soviet diplomacy can be understood only in the context of "Communist bloc politics." Burlatsky has written that "at every stage in relations with the United States and Western Europe he [the Soviet leader] constantly glanced over his shoulder to check the expression on the face of the Chinese sphinx."[39]

Various factors produced the Sino-Soviet split, including ideological differences (such as Mao's initiation of the Great Leap Forward and Khrushchev's disdain for it), the historical background of conflict between the two countries, and a personality clash between Mao Zedong and Khrushchev. At the heart of the rivalry, though, was an intense battle for power within world communism. Whereas China wished to increase its influence within the communist bloc, the Soviet Union was determined to remain its undisputed leader. Beijing wanted Khrushchev to use his nuclear arsenal to advance the interests of communist nations, including those of China. Khrushchev, on the other hand, was at times more interested in what he termed "peaceful coexistence" with the West. China also wished to develop a nuclear capacity with Soviet assistance. Khrushchev, however, was reluctant to supply the second most powerful country in the communist world with nuclear weapons. Mao assumed that Moscow would support China in its rivalry with India. Khrushchev, though, was interested in courting India, and so preferred to remain neutral in the Sino-Indian dispute. For those reasons, the communist bloc, already loosened by the independent actions of Yugoslavia in 1948 and Hungary and Poland in 1956, began in the late 1950s and early 1960s to fracture along a fault dividing Moscow from Beijing.[40]

Although Sino-Soviet tension simmered during the years from 1956 to 1959, it did so behind the closed doors of the communist world. Then in 1960 the antagonism exploded, and in the process became common knowledge in the West. In April 1960 the Chinese, on the ninetieth anniversary of Lenin's birth, published an essay entitled "Long

Live Leninism" in which they argued that it was China, and not the Soviet Union, that had upheld the revolutionary tradition bequeathed by Lenin. The animosity generated by the episode was evident in June 1960 when Khrushchev and Chinese delegate P'eng Chen attacked each other at the Romanian Party Congress. During the 1950s, the Soviets had granted increasing quantities of aid to their Asian ally, but in July 1960 Khrushchev suddenly changed policy by withdrawing nearly 1400 specialists from China and by terminating various projects involving Sino-Soviet technical cooperation. Four months later, at a meeting of eighty-one communist parties in Moscow, the acrimony had not subsided, as Chinese officials used the occasion to assail Soviet leadership. Although most delegates at the conference indicated their support for the Soviet Union, a dozen parties endorsed Chinese criticisms. By this point, the Sino-Soviet split could not be concealed. The chasm between the two nations was wide and ever widening.[41]

Of all the criticisms levelled at the Soviet Union by China, the most salient was the charge that Moscow had been too timid in supporting world revolution. Khrushchev, the Chinese contended, was more interested in peaceful coexistence with the West than in using his nuclear arsenal to protect the interests of world communism and to promote revolution. The clear implication of Chinese criticism was that Moscow, because of its inept performance, was forfeiting the right to direct the international communist movement. That, for Khrushchev, was a disturbing accusation because it struck at the very legitimacy of the Soviet Union's leadership of the communist bloc. If a significant number of communist parties throughout the world came to accept the cogency of Chinese arguments, then Moscow's position as the leader of world communism would be jeopardised. For Khrushchev, this was a challenge to which he had to respond.

In the context of Chinese criticism, Cuba acquired a special significance for the Soviet leader. Initially, he had not rushed to embrace the Cuban Revolution of January 1959. The Soviet Union arranged to purchase less sugar from Cuba in 1959 than it had during the final year of Batista's rule, and throughout that year the Soviet press did not emphasise the need to support Cuba. It may have been the case that this cautious response was a strategic move on Khrushchev's part. He was probably delighted about the Cuban Revolution, but calculated that the best way to prevent an American invasion of the island was by adopting a detached disposition towards the Caribbean island in order to assure Washington that Cuba was not about to become a Soviet ally or satellite.[42]

The first important milestone on the path to more intimate Soviet-Cuban relations was the visit of Anastas Mikoyan to Cuba in February 1960, the first meeting between high-level Soviet and Cuban officials. As a result of Mikoyan's trip, the Soviet Union agreed to purchase more Cuban sugar, and also granted Havana a $100 million credit to acquire industrial equipment. Three months later formal diplomatic relations were finally established between the two countries. But it was not until the summer of 1960 that Moscow's support for Cuba became unequivocal. After Castro's government assumed control of the oil refineries of Texaco, Shell, and Esso, the Eisenhower administration reacted on 6 July by reducing the amount of sugar it had pledged to purchase from Cuba by 700 000 tons. Khrushchev decided to act. On 9 July he informed the Cuban government that the Soviet Union would purchase all the sugar previously assigned to the United States, and declared that an American attack on Cuba would be followed by a reciprocal Soviet strike. With his confidence thus enhanced, Castro proceeded to nationalise all American companies in Cuba.[43]

By summer 1960, therefore, Soviet support for Castro's government had become overt. The reason Khrushchev had decided to render Cuba greater assistance was probably the same as the motivation behind his earlier reluctance to do so, namely a desire to prevent an American invasion of Cuba. But by summer 1960 Khrushchev had judged it necessary, in light of the more hostile attitude displayed by the Eisenhower administration, to make an open commitment to Cuba so as to deter any American plans to topple Castro.[44]

In supporting Cuba, Khrushchev, in one sense, was simply adhering to what for both superpowers was an established rule of the Cold War, and that was to shore up any allies or potential allies. By 1960, though, he had additional reasons for helping Castro. In the "Long Live Leninism" article, the Chinese argued that the desire to achieve peaceful coexistence with the West conflicted with the need to protect Cuba from American aggression. Hence, Cuba became tied up in the ongoing dispute between Moscow and Beijing, and this continued to be the case when at both the November 1960 Moscow conference and in a 6 January 1961 address Khrushchev expressed his determination to support national liberation movements (which were said to produce national democratic states that were not socialist, but were close to being so, and which held the potential for moving further to the left). His pledge was designed at least in part to undercut the Chinese argument that Moscow had been weak in supporting revolutionary forces. At the November 1960 conference the Soviet Union procured acceptance of this new concept, "the national democratic state," by citing the example of the Cuban Revolution. In his January 1961 speech, Khrushchev further stressed the centrality of Havana to the national liberation movement. "The Cuban revolution," he asserted, "is not only repelling the onslaught of the imperialists; it is deepening and broadening and marks a new and higher stage of the national-liberation struggle, in which the people take power and become the masters of their wealth." As one pundit has put it, by the early 1960s Khrushchev was "in great need of a new socialist state to testify to the dynamism of the Soviet Union and of its leadership." By the start of 1961, he had placed Soviet eggs in the Cuban basket. For the Soviet premier, the defence of the Cuban Revolution had become intimately associated with the credibility of his leadership within the communist world, particularly in terms of the Chinese challenge.[45]

Kennedy's policies, especially the Bay of Pigs invasion, convinced Khrushchev that Cuban defence would require further Soviet assistance, partly because of anticipated Chinese reactions. Suggestive of this was the conversation on 19 April 1961 between Karl L. Rankin, the American ambassador to Yugoslavia, and Edvard Kardelj, the vice-president of Yugoslavia. Rankin recorded in a memorandum that Kardelj felt the Bay of Pigs episode was "most unfortunate. The situation, he said, was a particularly difficult one for KHRUSHCHEV. If he intervened in Cuba and came into conflict with the United States, it would be very bad. But if he failed to support the Cuban Government, he would be in a bad position *vis-à-vis* China." Subsequent American policies, such as the ejection of Cuba from the OAS, must have increased Khrushchev's fear that the Chinese would continue to criticise him for failing to support Cuba with sufficient zeal.[46]

In this context, the Soviet decision to deploy missiles in Cuba made sense. Having been assailed by the Chinese for his weakness in protecting revolution in the developing world, Khrushchev had developed the concept of the national liberation movement, referred to Castro's government as a classic example of it, and pledged to support Cuba along with other states in similar positions. As American pressure against Cuba intensified in 1961 and 1962, the Soviet leader felt increasingly compelled to assist Castro. If Kennedy toppled Castro, Chinese criticisms designed to discredit Soviet leadership of the communist world would escalate. Deploying nuclear missiles in Cuba to forestall an American invasion would prevent that from happening.[47]

For Khrushchev, the years 1960 to 1962 had produced a number of disconcerting developments. He had been forced in July 1961, largely as a result of Kennedy's foreign and defence policies, to jettison his long-term goal of reducing Soviet military spending. The Kennedy administration's October 1961 revelation that the missile gap was a fallacy meant that he was no longer able to engage in brinksmanship with credibility. He had failed by fall 1961 to accomplish his objective of ejecting the Western powers from Berlin. Finally, China had mounted an increasingly stiff challenge to Khrushchev's leadership of the communist world. By spring 1962, the conjuncture of these developments, along with the overall advantage enjoyed by the United States in nuclear weaponry, had produced a multi-faceted crisis for the Soviet leader. It was probably in response to this crisis that he decided to deploy nuclear weapons in Cuba.[48]

The actual process by which that decision was made began at the end of April 1962. According to Fedor Burlatsky, who edited a post-missile crisis letter from the Soviet leader to Castro in which the former explained the origins of his decision to put missiles in Cuba, Khrushchev hatched the plan during a conversation with Marshal Rodion Ya. Malinovsky, the defence minister. Walking along the Black Sea coast, Malinovsky pointed out to Khrushchev that stationed in Turkey just across the water were American missiles which, if fired, would take only six or seven minutes to hit cities in the Ukraine and southern Russia. Khrushchev observed that the Soviet Union could pose the same threat to the United States by putting nuclear weapons in Cuba.[49]

After this Khrushchev discussed the plan with Anastas Mikoyan. Their conversation took place in the garden of Mikoyan's house, next to Khrushchev's own residence at the Lenin Hills just outside Moscow. When the Soviet leader raised the idea of dispatching missiles to Cuba, he remarked that the deployment would not be publicly revealed until after the congressional elections in November. Mikoyan was skeptical, arguing that Castro would oppose such a move on the grounds that it might provoke an American invasion.[50]

Khrushchev then described his plan to a small group of officials. As well as Mikoyan and Malinovsky, he consulted with Presidium member Frol R. Kozlov, Andrei Gromyko, and the commander of the Strategic Rocket Forces, Marshal Sergei S. Biryuzov. When this group met, Mikoyan raised two objections. He doubted whether missiles could be installed in Cuba without being detected by American intelligence, and he also thought that Castro would probably refuse to permit nuclear weapons on his territory. Undeterred, Khrushchev insisted that those two hurdles could easily be overcome, the first by sending a letter to Castro asking for his approval, the second by dispatching a secret mission to Cuba under the supervision of Biryuzov in order to determine the feasibility of deploying missiles on the island without American detection. Mikoyan, and the other advisers as well, accepted these proposals.[51]

Khrushchev consulted with a few more aides in early May, including Sharaf R. Rashidov, an alternate member of the Presidium, and Aleksandr I. Alekseyev, an intelligence agent in Havana. Alekseyev enjoyed a far more intimate relationship with both Fidel and his brother Raúl Castro than the Soviet ambassador to Cuba. For that reason, Khrushchev decided in early May to appoint Alekseyev the new ambassador to Cuba. A few days after informing Alekseyev of his promotion, Khrushchev told him about the idea of putting missiles in Cuba, and asked how Castro might respond. Alekseyev thought the Cuban leader would probably oppose the plan. Malinovsky, also present, argued that Castro would be more accommodating, noting that republican Spain had accepted Soviet military aid during the 1930s. Khrushchev concluded that Castro would be notified of the plan to deploy missiles in Cuba.[52]

To see if Castro would allow missiles in Cuba, and to assess the feasibility of carrying out such a deployment without alerting American intelligence, Khrushchev surreptitiously sent Biryuzov and a few other military experts to Cuba as part of a Soviet agricultural delegation headed by Rashidov. Just prior to the departure of the group, Khrushchev briefed the full Presidium of the plan at his dacha. "For the salvation of the Cuban revolution," he told Presidium members, "there was no other path, other than one which could equalise, so to say, the security of Cuba with the security of the United States." The agricultural team's visit to Cuba began at the end of May, and the Soviet delegation quickly arranged a meeting with Fidel through Raúl Castro. When told of the plan to deploy nuclear missiles in Cuba, Fidel provisionally approved it. He gave his unequivocal endorsement after consulting his advisers in the Secretariat – Raúl Castro, Che Guevara, Osvaldo Dorticós, Blas Roca, and Emilio Aragonés – all of whom shared Castro's inclination to accept Khrushchev's proposal. Despite Castro's claim that the main reason he accepted Soviet missiles was the desire to strengthen the defensive capabilities of the socialist bloc in general, probably the most important consideration for him was that the nuclear weapons would deter an American invasion, which he had been anticipating since the failure of the Bay of Pigs operation. Meanwhile, Biryuzov and his military advisers decided that it would be possible to deploy missiles in Cuba without being detected by American intelligence. After the Soviet delegation's return to Moscow, a meeting of the Presidium was convened on 10 June. The results of the Soviet-Cuban negotiations were reported to the delegates, and the Ministry of Defense plan for a military build-up in Cuba was approved.[53]

Further consultations between Soviet and Cuban officials

took place during the visit to Moscow of a Cuban military delegation headed by Raúl Castro. Raúl's delegation arrived in the Russian capital on 2 July, and held high-level discussions with Soviet officials for more than a week. It was at these talks, which Khrushchev himself attended on 3 and 8 July, that specific arrangements for the missile deployment in Cuba were made.[54]

A formal agreement, renewable after five years, was drafted and initialled by Raúl Castro and Malinovsky during this series of meetings. Its purpose, described at the beginning of the draft agreement, was to establish "military cooperation for the defense of the national territory of Cuba in the event of aggression." After Alekseyev took it back to Havana, Fidel amended it, and Che Guevara and Aragonés returned the modified draft to Moscow in late August. Khrushchev, however, refused at that point to sign the agreement. The Cubans wished to reveal the facts about the missile deployment in public, and he did not. When Che and Aragonés argued that "with the pact unsigned, . . . [and] as the missiles were not yet in full combat position, we could expect a preemptive attack by the U.S. with very grave consequences for ourselves and no ability to respond," Khrushchev declared that if this occurred, he would defend Cuba by dispatching the Baltic fleet to the Caribbean.[55]

In developing the plan to place missiles in Cuba, Khrushchev strove to keep the operation top secret. He placed strict limits on the number of Soviet officials cognisant of the operation. Not even Anatoly F. Dobrynin and Valerian A. Zorin, the Soviet ambassadors to the United States and the United Nations, were informed. Some Central Committee members were not briefed. Correspondence between Moscow and Havana was not conveyed by transmission of cables, as was usual, but by hand.[56]

The actual extent of the Soviet military deployment in Cuba was far greater than perceived by the Kennedy administration at the time. During the missile crisis, American intelligence estimated that Soviet troops in Cuba numbered between 8 000 and 10 000. By early 1963 that figure had been revised retrospectively to 22 000. It is now clear that the authentic figure was 42 000. In addition to combat troops, substantial quantities of conventional military equipment were deployed, including reinforced motorised rifle regiments, surface-to-air missiles, forty-two IL-28 light bombers, Komar PT boats, and MiG-21 interceptors.[57]

The strategic deployment in Cuba involved mainly medium-range missiles, a category which, in the American definition of weapon types, included both medium-range and intermediate-range missiles. Although Khrushchev expressed initial interest in those sorts of missiles, he left it to his military to decide upon the precise nature of the nuclear weaponry to be delivered to Cuba. Khrushchev's military advisers subsequently decided to deploy three SS-4 medium-range missile regiments and two SS-5 intermediate-range regiments. Each regiment comprised eight launchers, and each launcher would have two missiles. In sum, there would be forty launchers with eighty missiles. As each launcher was to be provided with one nuclear warhead, this would mean a total of forty warheads and eighty missiles. The second missile for each launcher was a replacement, to be used only in case of technical problems with the designated missile. After the completion of the Soviet deployment, forty operational medium and intermediate-range missiles with forty warheads would be in Cuba. Recent evidence suggests that the deployment may also have included eighty tactical cruise missiles and six IL-28s specially fitted for atomic bombs.[58]

Three short-range, tactical "Luna" rocket units with twelve nuclear warheads were also sent to Cuba, possibly for use in the event of an American invasion. Before the missile crisis, Khrushchev delegated the authority to decide whether these tactical missiles should be fired in an emergency situation to his senior military officer in Cuba. In late September or early October 1962, for example, General Issa A. Pliyev, commander of Soviet forces in Cuba, apparently received instructions from Malinovsky, stating:

> Only in the event of a landing of the opponent's forces on the island of Cuba and if there is a concentration of enemy ships with landing forces near the coast of Cuba, in its territorial waters...and there is no possibility to receive directives from the U.S.S.R. Ministry of Defense, you are personally allowed as an exception to take the

decision to apply the tactical nuclear Luna missiles as a means of local war for the destruction of the opponent on land and on the coast with the aim of a full crushing defeat of troops on the territory of Cuba and the defense of the Cuban Revolution.

There has recently been speculation over whether the Soviet leadership rescinded this arrangement during the missile crisis to ensure that Soviet military leaders did not fire the short-range missiles without Moscow's prior approval, even if the contingencies listed in the September/October order occurred. It now appears that Malinovsky, presumably at Khrushchev's behest, sent a telegram to Pliyev to that effect on 22 October; and that three and five days later he dispatched additional messages to Pliyev, again forbidding the use of any nuclear weapons without permission from Moscow.[59]

The most improbable aspect of the military build-up was Malinovsky's selection of Pliyev as the head of Soviet forces in Cuba. Remarkably, Pliyev had no experience with ballistic missiles, having been a cavalryman for most of his career. His greatest accomplishment was to have led the last major cavalry charge in Manchuria at the end of World War II. Apart from two years in Mongolia in the late 1930s, he had no experience as a military adviser outside the Soviet Union. It was astonishing in light of all this that Khrushchev approved Malinovsky's selection of Pliyev.[60]

The Soviet military was initially successful in keeping the operation to deploy missiles in Cuba secret. As Sergo Mikoyan describes it, the military personnel who:

> were sent over by ship to protect the missiles were not told where they were going. They were only told that they would be away from home for a long time. And since it was September [1962], they assembled their necessary winter outfits and took them with them – even skis. Only in the middle of the Atlantic Ocean were they told that skis would not be needed – they were going to Cuba. So there were no problems during this stage.

But the attempt to hide the construction of the missile sites was an abysmal failure. They were built in the same con-

figurations as sites in the Soviet Union, making it a relatively simple matter for American intelligence to deduce that
they were for nuclear missiles. If the weather over Cuba had
not been so cloudy during the autumn of 1962, the missiles
may have been detected much earlier than the middle of
October.[61]

As the summer of 1962 passed, the Soviet military build-
up commenced and accelerated. This did not escape the
attention of Americans. CIA analysts noted a sharp escalation in the amount of Soviet cargo being transported to
Cuba, as well as its increasingly military orientation. Journalists
in Florida, with sources in the Cuban exile community, commented on the build-up in their columns. And Kenneth
Keating, the junior senator for New York, began to consider using this information in ways which would ultimately
thrust himself into the national spotlight and, in the process, enlarge the concern of President Kennedy and the rest
of his administration.

4 The Fall Offensive of Senator Keating

He cried that night. As he gazed across his hotel suite in the early hours of 4 November 1964, he noticed his friends and advisers in a similar state of despair. Kenneth B. Keating, elected to the Senate in 1958 to represent the State of New York, had just failed in his bid for re-election. Compared to the national Republican ticket, he had performed with distinction. President Lyndon Johnson had carried the state from Barry Goldwater by 2.7 million votes, while Keating had lost to his Democratic opponent, Robert Kennedy, by only a little over 700 000 in what had been a long, bruising, and at times bitter campaign. The battle with the former attorney general, however, had not been his first confrontation with the Kennedys. Two years earlier he had clashed with them over the most explosive international issue of the day: Cuba.[1]

Born in Lima, New York, at the turn of the century, Keating graduated from the University of Rochester and then Harvard Law School. He subsequently practiced law in Rochester, served as a colonel and taught in the Far East during World War II, and was elected as a Republican to the House of Representatives in 1946. Having been re-elected five times, he embarked upon a successful campaign for the Senate in 1958. A fairly conservative Republican in the House, Keating developed a moderately liberal reputation on domestic issues in the Senate. As the representative of a state that included New York City, the junior senator often felt compelled to vote for the domestic programmes of the New Frontier, such as Medicare and federal aid for urban mass transit. He also emerged as an advocate of civil rights reform, pledging in his 1958 campaign to examine conditions in the still-segregated South personally if elected to the Senate. Good to his word, he visited Jacksonville, Atlanta, and Birmingham, accompanied by the other Republican senator from New York, Jacob Javits. After consulting community and religious leaders, Keating and Javits reached the conclusion that federal legislation was required to curb racial injustice. On their return to New York, they complained about the "open resistance by officials [in the South] to compliance with the Supreme Court's decision ordering desegregation in the public schools." Keating would later support the 1964 Civil Rights Act, and in the same year oppose his party's ardent right-wing candidate for president, Barry Goldwater.[2]

Keating's political attachments reflected his ideological preferences. He associated most closely with those senators from the moderate wing of his party – Hugh Scott of Pennsylvania, John Sherman Cooper of Kentucky, Margaret Chase Smith of Maine, and Prescott Bush of Connecticut. His greatest ally was New York Governor Nelson A. Rockefeller, the most prominent liberal Republican in the country, who persuaded him to run for the Senate in 1958. Although identified with the moderates in his party on domestic issues, Keating, in sharp contrast, exhibited a fervent anti-communism on foreign policy matters.[3]

The silver-haired senator had an affable and gregarious personality. He was very funny too. Quips were his oratorical trademark and in private he liked to entertain friends with impersonations. He seems to have connected better with women than men. In appointing women to senior positions in his Senate office, he was certainly ahead of his time, and whereas the women on his staff recall his warmth and generosity, the men say he was a figure of great integrity but rather detached from the people around him.[4]

Keating's greatest passion in life was the cut and thrust of politics. When his daughter told him in 1958 that she intended to marry James Howe, he persuaded her to delay the announcement until after his Senate campaign. Howe had worked for J.P. Morgan and Keating feared that this might make him appear elitist, thereby wrecking, as he put it, his "poor boy from the country" image. The nature of Keating's personal life, especially his poor marriage, helped fuel his unquenchable thirst for politics. His wife, an invalid, never came down to Washington, and he rarely returned home to Rochester. He preferred to stay active on the Washington social scene, dating various eligible, usually older, women, and if there was free time, he would visit New York, Florida, or Europe. "He had no real home," reflected Mary Pitcairn Keating, his second wife. Political Washington became Keating's home instead. [5]

Although the senator for a major state since 1958, Keating did not emerge as a figure of national repute until the fall of 1962 when he launched his provocative campaign on Cuba. His preoccupation with this issue, however, stretched all the way back to April 1959 when he met Fidel Castro at a Senate reception. "Why have no elections been held?, asked Keating along with Senator Hubert H. Humphrey of Minnesota. "What is your timetable for elections now?" "The people are not ready," the Cuban leader replied. "When the time is ripe, we will have our elections." That conversation sparked Keating's concern over Castro's intentions.[6]

A hearing three months later in the Senate Internal Security subcommittee further stimulated his interest. He listened then to testimony from Major Pedro Luis Diaz Lanz, Castro's first air force commander in chief, who had recently defected because of what he perceived to be the increasing influence granted by Castro to Cuban communists. "That testimony," Keating recalled, "cast the first real doubts in my mind as to what Castro was up to." Following this, he delivered several speeches in the Senate in which he emphasised the troubling developments in Cuba and urged the Eisenhower administration "to recognize the danger and plan to meet or counteract it."[7]

Keating's concern over Cuba was heightened by his constituents. Their correspondence furnished him with an early sense of the potential value of Cuba as a foreign policy issue which resonated with the public. In August 1959, for instance, he received inquiries into the recent hearings on the Cuban Revolution in the Senate Committee on the Judiciary. "I am sure you will agree," Keating reassured one of his correspondents, "that it is necessary always to be on the alert against the possibility that Communism has gained a foothold on the American continent."[8]

After Kennedy became president, Keating's views on Cuba mirrored those of the new administration. His overriding objective was to oust Castro, and like JFK, he thought Cuban émigrés should play the central role in bringing that about. He argued that Kennedy should support their efforts, but not by ordering a direct American attack on Cuba. "The overthrow of Castro," he explained, "cannot and should not be accomplished by intervention of the United States; however, I am sure that the effort of this group [of anti-Castro Cuban exiles] will have the support of the American public."[9]

The Bay of Pigs invasion, which was backed by Washington but did not involve direct American military intervention, was precisely the sort of action to which Keating had given his implicit endorsement. So it was not surprising he supported the operation once it became public knowledge. The Cuban "freedom fighters," he admitted on 18 April 1961, were "meeting some opposition, armed with Communist-supplied weapons and tanks; but they know that they are fighting for the cause of freedom and progress for Cuba and their cause is a just one." If Khrushchev intervened in the present conflict in Cuba, he continued, the United States would have "to blockade the island and prevent the entry of any forces from outside of the hemisphere."[10]

After the failure of the Bay of Pigs, Keating commenced what can be regarded as his first Cuban campaign. In addresses before the Senate, speeches to his constituents, and letters to the State Department, he exhorted the Kennedy administration to strive more vigorously to effect Castro's removal. He also developed a three-point plan to accomplish that objective, and presented it with particular vividness in a speech in Buffalo on 29 April 1961. With rhetoric rather more appropriate for 1776 or 1861 than 1961, Keating declared that the challenge posed by Cuba meant that "we find oursleves [sic] at one of the great moments of truth in our national history." "Do we stand on the ramparts of freedom," he asked, "with our eyes closed in sleep, or do we summon our spirit, our alertness, our valor, and act in defense of what we hold dear?" Explaining the specifics of his plan, he suggested the United States work with the OAS to take concerted action against the Castro government; consider the establishment of a naval blockade around the island to prevent the entry of military supplies from the communist bloc; and impose a complete embargo on all American trade with Cuba. He concluded by reiterating the gravity of the situation: "we stand in a moment of truth, at the crossroads of history."[11]

Despite his relentless efforts, Keating was unable to keep Cuba in the forefront of public attention. As the Berlin crisis unfolded in the summer of 1961, the Cuban issue moved temporarily from centre to side stage. Still, Keating's statements during 1961 were, in retrospect, noteworthy for their prescience. In recommending OAS action, the imposition of a full economic embargo, and the establishment of a blockade around the island, Keating did anticipate many of the directions that American policy towards Cuba would take over the course of the next year and a half. Most strikingly, he foresaw the possibility of a Soviet missile deployment in Cuba. "How long will it be," he asked his fellow senators in July 1961, "before the Soviet Union establishes military bases and missile launching sites in Cuba?"[12]

When Keating began to speak on the last day of August 1962 about the Soviet military build-up in Cuba, he was, therefore, opening his second, not first, campaign on Cuba. In an address before the Senate, he claimed that five different sources had informed him of a Soviet deployment of 1200 troops, not merely technicians, in Cuba during the first half of the month. Elaborating, he provided the precise dates on which the Soviets had installed both troops and conventional military equipment such as torpedo boats and amphibious vehicles. He also talked about "ominous reports" indicating the construction of "missile bases" in Cuba. Keating did not say whether this information referred to bases for surface-to-air missiles only, or to sites for the more dangerous surface-to-surface variety, but at this point in time it was presumably the former. He added that the probable motivations behind the Soviet build-up included the desire to deter any attack on Cuba, and to help Castro quell internal opposition to his leadership.[13]

The senator not only pointed to the increasing Soviet military presence in Cuba but also admonished the Kennedy administration for its handling of the situation. He suggested the White House had been less than frank in presenting the facts about the Soviet build-up, and he charged the administration with shameful neglect in its response to the escalating threat represented by Cuba. He proposed that Kennedy prod the OAS nations into organising "prompt and vigorous action in a concerted way to meet this threat to their future security as well as to the security of the United States." As for the course to be followed by the OAS, he was vague. But his tone was decidely urgent: "Time is short. The situation is growing worse. I urge upon my Government that prompt action be taken."[14]

The identity of the sources from whom Keating obtained the information used in his 31 August and subsequent speeches is a question that has remained shrouded in mystery over the past three decades. The senator died in 1975 without divulging his sources; hardly any documentation on this subject can be found in his papers, now deposited at the University of Rochester. Keating told his second wife that a staff member had stolen the large file he kept on Cuba. He believed it to be a woman, formerly of the press, who worked for him for only a short time. Despite this paucity of documents, some tentative conclusions can be made about Keating's sources.[15]

He certainly depended upon the Cuban émigré community for information. In the months preceding his fall campaign on Cuba, various anti-Castro exile groups, such as the Cuban Freedom Committee and the Cuban Student Directorate, had furnished him with newsletters, information sheets, and manifestos, that explained the shortcomings of Castro's revolution as well as the goals of their respective organisations. These sorts of groups maintained their contacts with Keating in the fall of 1962, supplying him with information about the Soviet build-up in Cuba, which they did in part through correspondence. In mid-October, for example, a letter clearly written by a Cuban émigré was sent to Keating's office, stating that the Soviets were establishing a submarine base at Cayu Frances in Cuba. In his letter the Cuban went on to thank Keating for his letters of 24 and 29 September, thereby confirming the existence of a previous correspondence. The senator conveyed the claim about the Soviet submarine base to Rusk, who denied the allegation. Keating later told the secretary of state that, "Although previous comments from this informant have occasionally been somewhat exaggerated, they have on the whole stood up. The same reports made to me have been made available directly to government sources in Miami." This informant, then, was apparently a member of the Cuban exile community in Miami, whom the senator had used as a source on previous occasions.[16]

As well as writing to Keating, émigrés also updated him on the situation in Cuba by coming to speak in person to either him or his staff. Abbott A. Leban, counsel to Keating, recalled the flow of Cuban exiles into the office. Many of them had only recently left Cuba, and some had maintained contacts with people on the island. Another Keating aide, Robert R. McMillan, also remembered interviewing Cuban émigrés for the senator.[17]

Keating realised that the material he received from these Cubans had to be treated circumspectly. Their agenda – to oust Castro by soliciting American assistance – was obvious, and they might be expected to exaggerate the magnitude of the Soviet build-up and the threat it posed to the United States. That being the case, the senator needed other sources to validate the allegations. He found them within the ranks of the United States government itself – in Kennedy's own Defense Department and in the CIA as well.[18]

Pentagon officials first came to Keating's assistance after he had received important information from Rear Admiral Edward J. O'Donnell, head of the American naval base at Guantánamo. In late November 1961, Robert McMillan had embarked upon a trip to various nations in the Western Hemisphere as part of the Capitol Hill United States Army Reserve Group. While in Guantánamo, he and Harry S. Dent, aide to South Carolina Senator Strom Thurmond and later an adviser to President Nixon, struck up a conversation with O'Donnell at a cocktail party. When they asked how the security of Guantánamo was maintained, the admiral volunteered to have his driver take them along the perimeter of the base. This they did, using infra-red binoculars to look over on to the Cuban side.[19]

As the three men talked, O'Donnell spoke generally about what he regarded as the indefensibility of the base against any Cuban attack. He emphasised not only the strength of the Cuban militia but also the extent of Soviet bloc support for Castro. Moscow, he estimated, had furnished the Cubans with fifty MiG aircraft, and runways had been elongated to permit the use of jet bombers. He also declared, as McMillan recorded it, that "there is . . . conclusive evidence from Intelligence sources that missilesbases [*sic*] are being constructed in Cuba." O'Donnell's allegations, Dent recalled, "startled and concerned Bob and me."[20]

On their return to Washington, Dent and McMillan briefed their respective senators about the meeting with the admiral. Dent subsequently wrote a speech on Cuba that Thurmond delivered in the Senate on 15 January 1962. In it, the senator made a provocative charge, based on O'Donnell's assertions: "There is substantial evidence now . . . indicating that Mr. Castro is constructing missile launching sites in Cuba." Meanwhile, Keating was prompted by McMillan's report on the Guantánamo episode to dispatch a letter to the Navy Department, soliciting comment on the accuracy of O'Donnell's claims. In response to this and other enquiries from Keating in early 1962, couriers brought over letters from the Navy Department directly to his Senate office, assuring him that there was "no hard evidence" of a Soviet surface-to-surface missile deployment in Cuba.[21]

The question arises as to whether O'Donnell continued to be Keating's source during the summer and autumn of 1962. McMillan insists that this was not the case but that the admiral's claims did lead the senator to the sources on whom he later relied for information about the Soviet build-up in Cuba. According to McMillan, sympathetic Defense Department officials, annoyed by what they perceived to be evasive Navy Department responses to Keating's inquiries, came forward with information on Cuba for the senator. McMillan was forced to cede the handling of the Cuban issue in Keating's office to Phyllis Piotrow, the senator's foreign policy expert. He recalls learning about the role played by the Defense Department "from discussion about the subject while I was in his [Keating's] office."[22]

What lends credence to the idea that Pentagon officials helped Keating is the clandestine assistance they also gave Senator Thurmond. Harry Dent has revealed that several people from the intelligence services of the Defense Department funnelled information to Thurmond during 1962. For example, Lieutenant Colonel Phil Corso, who worked under army intelligence chief Arthur Trudeau, passed on information to Thurmond using Dent as an intermediary. The thrust of these leaks was that McNamara and other upper echelon officials in the Kennedy administration were misinterpreting intelligence information, constantly under-estimating the communist threat, including that posed by Cuba. The hyperbole of Oliver Stone's *JFK* film notwith-standing, there clearly was a section of the American mili-tary that thought Kennedy and his senior advisers were "soft" on communism.[23]

Old friends in the Defense Department may have been particularly helpful to Keating, who had worked in the Pen-tagon for a year during World War II, by coming to his assistance in 1962. Although the evidence is entirely circum-stantial, he may have also relied on Defense Department official Colonel John Wright. By 27 September, he had con-cluded from intelligence photographs that the configura-tion of the sites in Cuba showed they were for missiles of the surface-to-surface as well as the surface-to-air variety. Keating, it should be noted, did not claim the Soviets were establishing surface-to-surface missile sites in Cuba until 10 October. Hence, he only made this allegation in public af-ter Wright had done the same in private. There would be chronological plausibility, therefore, to the idea that Wright was Keating's source in the Pentagon.[24]

In addition to the Defense Department, Keating was also aided and abetted by the CIA. Although there has been no evidence that the senator received help from Langley, a number of Keating's former advisers have recently disclosed that this was in fact the case. Most notably, Eleanor Merrill, Keating's assistant press secretary, has for the first time re-vealed that his "original information" came from the direc-tor of the CIA himself, John McCone. She adds that this is not a nebulous impression but rather a specific recollection that someone within the Keating camp told her this at the time. Patricia Shakow, another former aide to the senator, says her information indicates that it was not McCone but another CIA official who conveyed information to Keating through a journalist. Shakow says she came to believe this because "years later someone who did know [the identity of Keating's source] dropped a hint." The senator's press sec-retary, Vera Glaser, though not wishing to reveal anything specific, says the source was someone from within the intel-ligence community."[25]

That McCone may have been Keating's source is plausible.

At four meetings in August 1962, two of which President Kennedy attended, the CIA director urged other administration officials to pay more heed to the military build-up in Cuba. Highlighting not only the dangers of the build-up, McCone also contended that the Soviets intended to deploy surface-to-surface missiles in Cuba. On 23 August McCone left Washington for a month's honeymoon in France. Between 7 and 20 September, he cabled Acting Director of Central Intelligence Marshall S. Carter on five occasions to reiterate his belief that Khrushchev would put offensive missiles in Cuba. Despite his best efforts, McCone's exhortations and predictions fell on deaf ears. It is conceivable, then, that in frustration he turned to a sympathetic senator.[26]

What makes this scenario more probable was the fact that McCone was a deeply conservative Republican. From his philosophical perspective, the CIA director may have viewed the failure of Kennedy and his advisers to listen to his warnings as symptomatic of their naive liberalism, and he may have felt the need to confide in a fellow Republican who had taken an active interest in Cuba in the past and who had easy access to the public domain. Furthermore, it was perhaps more than coincidence that Keating's allegations in public sometimes mirrored McCone's in private. In his 31 August Senate speech, for instance, Keating suggested that one of the objectives behind the Soviet build-up in Cuba was to use electronic equipment to hamper the American space programme at Cape Canaveral. McCone had made exactly the same speculation in a 10 August meeting with Rusk, McNamara, and other senior officials.[27]

An interesting footnote to this was the fact that during the missile crisis the president himself began to question the loyalty of the CIA. On the evening of 25 October Ray S. Cline, deputy director for intelligence, was attending a party hosted by Mrs. Anna Chennault when an angry Kennedy called. According to Cline, the president said:

> he had heard stories that CIA officers were alleging that intelligence on offensive missile bases in Cuba had been available for several days before it was called to the attention of the President. He asked me to confirm that I was responsible for the analysis of this kind of intelligence

and appropriate dissemination of it to higher authorities, and to tell him the facts in the case.

Cline proceeded to assure Kennedy that these rumours were unfounded, an explanation that apparently satisfied the president.[28]

After the resolution of the missile crisis, the senator indicated that in addition to government informants and Cuban refugees, additional sources supplied him with information. One name to have emerged in this context is Karl von Spreti, the West German ambassador to Cuba. He allegedly came from Havana in September 1962 with evidence of missiles in Cuba. A 1970 ABC news report claimed that von Spreti first approached administration officials with the information; having been shunned by them, he turned to Keating.[29]

The recollections of Mary Pitcairn Keating, who married Kenneth Keating about a year before his death in 1975, seem to add weight to this theory. She recalls a conversation with her husband in which they talked about his sources on Cuba: "The one thing I remember... is... the person that Ken got the information from, he met him by a swimming-pool. And I thought he inferred that this was a foreign diplomat or diplomat type who gave him this information." She added that he did not divulge the actual name of the source. "He was still guarding that secret. He really was at that time." The swimming-pool might suggest a vacation spot, and it is interesting to note that in the 1960s Keating liked to go to the Caribbean island of Nassau for holidays. Could Keating have arranged a rendezvous with the West German ambassador to Cuba in Nassau? Although an intriguing possibility, no evidence has been adduced to support that speculation.[30]

Yet further possibilities remain. It has been suggested that the senator's sources were journalists in Florida; or, along the same lines, that he simply culled information about the Soviet build-up from newspaper reports. Keating denied the latter but acknowledged the possibility that he and the journalists who wrote those articles may have used some of the same sources. Roger Hilsman, on the other hand, suspected that Keating's source was a disenchanted member of Castro's government. Even more obscure possibilities remain. For example, one of the women in Ted Sorensen's office had a roommate who worked for Keating. During the missile crisis, Sorensen made sure this staff member had minimal access to sensitive material. Again, none of these allegations or possibilities is easy to validate.[31]

The identity of Keating's sources on the build-up in Cuba is still a murky subject. What does seem clear is that in addition to Cuban émigrés, he relied chiefly upon CIA officials, including perhaps McCone himself, and the Pentagon. It is difficult to gauge the relative importance of these informants, but the aides to the senator who have been willing to speak to this issue have tended to emphasise the role played by American intelligence. It may well be that Keating's most crucial sources came from Kennedy's own CIA.

As for the motives behind Keating's fall 1962 campaign on Cuba, he probably was genuinely concerned about American national security. But it would be naive to discount the senator's desire to augment his own stature and political credibility. Overshadowed in New York by Javits, the better-known senator, he certainly felt the need to bolster his own reputation. As Hilsman discerned, Keating "had been a member of the House for many years representing an upstate district. As senator, he needed to become known in New York City and to build a "statesman" image." In seeking to do that, Keating must have been aware of the prospective value of the Cuban issue. Throughout 1961 and 1962, constituent correspondence on Cuba had poured into his office, and the letters usually demanded more aggressive action against Castro. When he began his series of speeches in fall 1962, his office was flooded by an even greater influx of mail, the vast majority of which commended him for his stance on Cuba.[32]

For Keating, then, Cuba constituted a simple, even classic anti-communist issue that could be utilised (just as Kennedy had done in the 1960 presidential campaign) to elevate his political profile and to garner more attention from both the public and the press. Publicity was certainly an objective for Keating and his staff. On 7 September Vera Glaser assured him that, "You are in all [the] Cuba stories [in the major magazines], and they are including coverage of yesterday's speech." She also wished:

to relay [the] fact that Chas. McWhorter said your Cuba activity is really getting through in NYC. He has been punching doorbells in the primary and said quite a few people brought up this point. (People are seriously disturbed about Cuba everywhere, and I am getting the reaction that you are a great patriot to keep hammering away [at] this.)

Glaser would later describe Keating as "a very publicity-conscious gentleman" who "enjoyed all the exposure" he received in the wake of his speeches on Cuba. She added that "he would probably be turning over in his grave in fury" if he knew his role in the missile crisis had been overlooked by historians.[33]

Keating could not have been oblivious to the political ramifications of the publicity generated by his allegations. He may have been concerned specifically about the 1962 congressional elections. Hurting Kennedy would strengthen his position in his own party by helping the Republicans who were running in November. To damage the president would also aid his friend and possible Republican presidential candidate in 1964, Nelson Rockefeller. Journalist Drew Pearson even suggested in February 1963 that Keating had planned his campaign on Cuba in concert with Rockefeller in order to make Cuba the salient issue in the 1964 presidential campaign, an allegation the senator denied. In all likelihood, Keating was probably more mindful of his own 1964 Senate race than either the 1962 congressional elections or Rockefeller's plans to run for president. "He was very concerned about reelection," recalled one of his advisers.[34]

Although motivated by political ambition, Keating was not driven by any personal animus against the president or his family to launch an attack on Cuba. Both he and Kennedy had been elected to the House of Representatives in 1946, and during the late 1940s they came to know each other well. "They saw each other all the time," recalled Mary Pitcairn Keating. After entering the Senate in 1958, Keating resumed a cordial relationship with Kennedy. Their Senate offices were just down the hall from each other, so there were frequent contacts between the two. Richard P. Nathan, a Keating aide, thinks they even socialised together.[35]

After the 1960 election, Keating stayed on friendly terms with the Kennedys. As a moderate Republican, he espoused many of JFK's domestic policies, working to secure the passage of his legislation in Congress. JFK no doubt appreciated the senator's support. Keating also maintained a constructive relationship with Robert Kennedy. As a member of the Senate Judiciary Committee, he was involved in reviewing court reform, eavesdropping legislation, judicial appointments, and in other issues of common concern to the attorney general and the Justice Department. Jackie Kennedy, too, was acquainted with Keating; she would sometimes send him notes that would be passed around his office. Disagreements over Cuba before the missile crisis and during the 1964 New York Senate race with Bobby Kennedy would ultimately sour the feelings between Keating and the Kennedys. But in the summer of 1962, all that lay in the future.[36]

Although Keating was not moved by any personal animosity towards the president to attack his Cuban policies, he was influenced by Kennedy's 1960 electoral commitments, which fostered first his expectation that JFK would try to topple Castro and then a sense of disenchantment – if not quite betrayal – at his failure to uphold that pledge. Keating spoke in early September 1962 of Kennedy's campaign promise to oust Castro. That commitment, he observed, was made "nearly 2 years ago, before Mr. Khrushchev expanded his foothold by sending missiles . . . and other military equipment to Cuba. Yet we have done nothing." He also mentioned, as he did again two weeks later, the similar pledge made by Kennedy after the Bay of Pigs to take action against Cuba should it become necessary.[37]

When Keating wrote a retrospective article in *Look* magazine on his role in the 1962 Cuban crisis, he once again emphasised JFK's pre-presidential promises. During the 1960 campaign he "made it clear that he had never been taken in by Castro. In fact, to the chagrin of a good many Republicans, he went further than . . . Nixon during their TV debates and pledged to help freedom-loving Cubans regain their homeland." Keating then spoke of Kennedy's "failure to redeem that pledge" with the Bay of Pigs invasion. Evidently, by the fall of 1962 Kennedy's bold promises and his lack of success in making good on them had generated in the senator a sense that the time for the president to act against Castro was long overdue.[38]

After his initial speech on the Soviet build-up in Cuba, Keating sustained a breathless campaign for the next two months, making twenty-five public statements on Cuba between 31 August and 25 October. Although many of these were delivered on the Senate floor, Keating also utilised the airwaves. He taped both a weekly interview show for radio and television in New York state as well as a bi-weekly show for t.v. in New York City and Buffalo. His active, efficient office staff issued regular releases to the press to alert it to his public discussions of Cuba.[39]

Throughout September and October, Keating presented updated descriptions of the size and nature of the Soviet build-up in Cuba. His most significant early revision came on 4 September when he informed his fellow senators that the number of Soviet troops on the island was five thousand, considerably more than he had indicated in his 31 August address. His most dramatic revelation, though, came on 10 October with his first unequivocal assertion that the Soviets were deploying surface-to-surface missiles. "At least a half dozen launching sites for intermediate range tactical missiles" were being built in Cuba, he claimed. Keating had overestimated the actual number of intermediate-range missile sites. As a January 1963 State Department memorandum conceded, this was "the only technically and provably erroneous statement he made during the entire period of the Cuba build-up."[40]

As well as describing the Soviet military build-up in Cuba, Keating also sought to influence Kennedy's response to it. He argued that the president could gain a tactical advantage over Khrushchev and Castro by consulting with his OAS and North Atlantic Treaty Organization (NATO) allies. Military policy towards Cuba should be co-ordinated with the other nations of the Western Hemisphere, and a NATO meeting should be convened to protest the fact that Western European ships were still being used to transport various materials to Cuba for the Soviets. In a 17 September hearing before the Senate Committees on Foreign Relations and Armed Services, Keating suggested the administration consider witholding aid to those countries that continued to allow the Soviets to utilise their shipping.[41]

Despite his emphasis on the importance of consulting

NATO and the OAS, Keating never explained how this would in itself halt the Soviet military escalation in Cuba. Nevertheless, he considered a dialogue with these organisations to be the appropriate initial step for the Kennedy administration. If this failed to retard the Soviet build-up, the United States, he contended, might need to consider the establishment of a blockade around Cuba. Without positively endorsing such a policy, he did discuss on 16 and 17 September the possibility of imposing a quarantine. On the latter occasion he argued that if collaboration with NATO and the OAS proved ineffective, the United States would have to take action "within the realm of force." He made clear that a blockade was certainly an alternative that would merit consideration in this regard. In private, he instructed one of his staff members to prepare a legal memorandum on the question of whether a blockade constituted an act of war. Unlike his fellow Republican Senator Homer E. Capehart of Indiana, Keating did not advocate an American invasion of Cuba. But as his 23 September statement shows, it was not an option he was willing to discount: "I do not advocate, nor favor any invasion of Cuba *at this time.*" As a last resort, therefore, Keating may have been willing to countenance an invasion, but certainly in September and October 1962 it was not a policy he prescribed.[42]

Keating was by no means the only assailant of Kennedy's Cuban policies. Indeed his real significance was that he personified the widespread domestic political pressure exerted upon the administration during this period. Many other prominent Republican senators echoed Keating's criticisms. Karl Mundt of South Dakota, Bourke B. Hickenlooper of Iowa, and Barry Goldwater all urged the president to establish a blockade around Cuba. On 10 September Texas Senator John Tower proposed the creation, recognition, and arming of a Cuban government-in-exile, with a view to helping that government gain control of its homeland. Eight days later Richard Nixon added his voice to those pressing for a blockade.[43]

More than just extravagant rhetoric, this wave of Republican criticism produced tangible political action. In mid-September, the Senate decided to hold hearings on Cuba in a joint session of the Foreign Relations and Armed Services committees. Pat Holt, aide to Senator Fulbright, recalled that "Keating kept making these charges and everybody got excited as hell about it. The main object of the Joint Hearings . . . was to try to find a formula which would satisfy Keating and the hard liners without doing too much damage to the principle of nonintervention." On 20 September the Senate passed the Cuba Resolution by an overwhelming vote of eighty-six to one. It sanctioned the use of military force, if required, to counter Cuban belligerence and subversion in the Western Hemisphere. It also articulated the determination of Congress "to prevent the creation or use of an externally supported offensive military capability endangering the security of the U.S." and to "support the aspirations of the Cuban people for a return to self-determination." The House of Representatives passed an appropriations bill the same day to terminate aid to any nation allowing its merchant ships to be used to carry arms or any other goods to Cuba. On 26 September the House also voted to endorse the Senate's Cuba Resolution.[44]

Amplifying these Congressional and particularly Republican criticisms and expressions of concern was the press. Though the editorials of the *Washington Post* and *New York Times* lent their customary support to Kennedy, the majority sentiment of the print media in September was in favour of the more hardline approach on Cuba championed by Republicans. Such popular columnists as David Lawrence, William S. White, and Arthur Krock were critical of the president. Even a paper like the *San Francisco Examiner*, which had generally supported JFK's policies on Berlin and Laos, now chided the administration for its handling of Castro.[45]

Ever since the Bay of Pigs, Cuba had represented Kennedy's most conspicuous area of political vulnerability, and any exploitation of that issue was taken seriously by the administration. Naturally, then, the president and his advisers were deeply concerned in the fall of 1962 by the torrent of criticism, particularly that levelled by Keating. Surveys conducted during this period by the Public Opinion Studies Staff of the State Department's Bureau of Public Affairs made frequent reference to the role he played. Officials generally viewed Keating's campaign as a blatant attempt to use the Cuban issue to discredit the administration before the

November congressional elections. Two of the president's closest advisers recalled that Kennedy thought Keating was simply trying "to make political campaign propaganda."[46]

JFK was enraged by Keating's charges, particularly his 10 October allegation that the Soviets were constructing surface-to-surface missile sites in Cuba. Deputy Attorney General Nicholas deB. Katzenbach recalls that Keating's charges drove John and Bobby Kennedy "absolutely wild." What may have heightened the president's suspicions was that Keating was generally regarded as a Nelson Rockefeller man, having been elected to the Senate in 1958 on, as one observer put it, "The coattails" of Rockefeller's successful bid for the New York governorship. "Nobody ever had any doubt he [Rockefeller] could beat me in 1960," President Kennedy once observed. "I knew that." More than any other Republican, he feared Rockefeller as the potential GOP candidate in the 1964 presidential election. He demonstrated the depth of that concern in April 1962 when he suggested to Ben Bradlee that he investigate Rockefeller's war record. "Where was old Nels when you and I were dodging bullets in the Solomon Islands?" Kennedy asked the journalist. "How old was he? He must have been thirty-one or thirty-two. Why don't you look into that?" Kennedy was obviously hoping to uncover dirt that could be used to tarnish Rockefeller's reputation. Conceivably, then, JFK may have regarded Keating's criticisms on Cuba as a ploy organised collaboratively by Rockefeller and the senator.[47]

Kennedy must have been concerned not only by Keating's motives but also by his potentially deleterious impact on the upcoming elections. On 11 October he explained to ABC interviewer William Lawrence that from 1930 to 1958 the party in power had lost on average thirty-nine seats in the House of Representatives. If this happened in November, he noted, it would make it virtually impossible for him to get his legislation through Congress.[48]

Behind the scenes, an industrious effort was made to assess the accuracy of Keating's claims. Rear Admiral Samuel B. Frankel stated that in response to Keating's allegations, "Every possible source was exploited and even the agencies which were not military agencies responded to the levy for any information that came into this area." The findings of these efforts were discussed at weekly meetings of officials from the CIA, FBI, the Defense Intelligence Agency, and the Atomic Energy Commission. Intelligence checks often substantiated Keating's claims. After Keating's 31 August address, for instance, CIA experts were instructed to evaluate his allegations by examining the aerial photography available. His description of the Soviet build-up in Cuba was found to be highly accurate.[49]

The administration's attempts to keep tabs on Keating may even have led to the wiretapping of his office, if the senator's own suspicions were well-founded. Keating indicated at the time that "he had good reason to believe that the Kennedys were learning everything he was saying in the privacy of his office." He later claimed that Bobby Kennedy had placed him under surveillance without procuring a court order. Abbott Leban recalled that on one occasion during the fall of 1962, the senator insisted that his conversation with a Cuban exile:

> be carried out in the corridor of the Senate Office Building where ... the passersby and ... general noise would cancel out this conversation ... in the hall, and I believe the reason for that is that he and others on the staff were concerned about the possible CIA wiretaps on the Hill because the Kennedy administration was ... concerned about leaks ... [and] where Keating may have been getting his information from.[50]

JFK's advisers also conducted an ongoing dialogue with Keating in order to dampen his ardour and elicit the names of his sources. Dean Rusk, for example, telephoned on 11 September to berate him for charging that Kennedy and Khrushchev had made an arrangement whereby the Soviets would limit their involvement in Cuba in return for American restraint over Berlin. CIA and State Department officers were sent to speak to Keating in person. Milton Eisenberg, the senator's long-serving administrative assistant, recalled that these officials would sometimes say they had been unable to verify one of Keating's allegations. (This indicates intelligence checks usually did validate his claims about the build-up in Cuba.) On one occasion they made the rather unusual request that Keating not publicly disclose certain sensitive information known already to him and American intelligence.[51]

John McCone also met with the senator during this period. Keating aides recall the CIA chief coming to his office at least once, although the content of their conversation is unclear as they apparently met alone. McCone summoned Keating to his own office after hearing his charge that missile sites were actually being built. According to Dino A. Brugioni, a photographic intelligence expert at the time of the missile crisis, the meeting was acrimonious. With voices rising, McCone challenged Keating to reveal the precise location of the missiles, and said that he would then "prove . . . that they are not there." He also volunteered to fly intelligence aircraft over any part of Cuba that Keating named. The senator declined the offer, and when McCone proceeded to accuse him of lacking patriotism, he stormed out of the office. McCone tried on another day to meet with Keating, but the senator's secretary called McCone's to say Keating was too busy to see him. If the CIA chief was in fact the senator's source for the missiles in Cuba, and if Brugioni's account is accurate, then all of this represented an elaborate, theatrical charade. Far more likely, if this clash did take place, it would suggest that McCone was not Keating's main informant, although it would not discount the possibility that other CIA officials helped the senator. It is important to note, however, that the Keating aides who recalled McCone meeting with the senator in the fall of 1962 did not remember any acrimonious confrontation such as the one described by Brugioni.[52]

In their public response to Keating, the president and his aides sought to limit the harm done to their credibility by downplaying the importance of the military build-up in Cuba in general and Keating's allegations in particular. Katzenbach said later that John and Bobby Kennedy wanted "to shut him up because they were being badly damaged by something they did not believe was true." Hanson Baldwin, the *New York Times*' military correspondent, recalled that there was "a very intense attempt in the Pentagon and the White House to control the news and dampen it. That is, they were quite disturbed about Keating's pronouncements and they were quite disturbed over what they felt some-

times were exaggerated reports." Pierre Salinger exemplified well the administration's standard but rather self-con-
tradictory line on the senator at a 3 September White House
news conference. The president's press secretary, on the
one hand, suggested that Keating had only revealed information already released by the government. On the other,
he maintained that Keating's statements were mistaken in
certain respects. For instance, the Soviets who had been
dispatched to Cuba were military personnel and not troops,
as Keating had insisted. That Salinger refused to speak about
him on the record at this press conference – he said his
comments on the senator were "for *BACKGROUND* only" –
indicated in itself the Kennedy administration's determination to conceal from the American public the true extent
of its concern over Keating.[53]

Roger Hilsman later acknowledged that the pressure
exerted by Keating and other critics was "always a factor to
be taken account of in the policy discussions – and policy
was at times either adjusted to accommodate some element
of their view so as to disarm them or presented in such a
way as to forestall them." The most important example of
this was Kennedy's own effort to dim the spotlight which
Republicans were focusing on Cuba before the upcoming
congressional elections. In speeches on behalf of Democratic candidates, he generally avoided the issue – a strategy in diametric opposition to the one he had employed
during the 1960 presidential campaign. Occasionally, as in
his 20 and 21 September speeches in Harrisburg, Pennsylvania, and Columbus, Ohio, he did mention Cuba. But even
then his treatment of the subject was brief and perfunctory. During an 11 October interview, JFK stated frankly that
he had decided to stress domestic and especially economic issues over international ones. When asked on the
same occasion about the Republican effort to make Cuba
the main focus of the campaign, he argued that this was an
"American problem" and should not be an issue between
the two parties.[54]

In using this tack, Kennedy was following the advice he
received from pollster Louis Harris in a 4 October memorandum. "You can say," he counselled JFK, "that matters
such as the Mississippi crisis, Cuban policy, and Berlin are

not partisan political issues." "You would never seek to exploit them for partisan purposes," he continued, conveniently
overlooking Kennedy's blatant use of the Cuban issue in
the 1960 campaign. Harris encouraged JFK to rebuke
Republicans for their "extreme partisanship" on these
matters.[55]

To downplay the importance of the Soviet military build-
up in Cuba, as he did during September and October, the
president had to explain why it did not represent a threat.
This he did by dubbing the build-up "defensive" on the
grounds that it involved the deployment of surface-to-air
missiles and not surface-to-surface missiles, which could be
fired on the United States. In this way he was forced to
clearly define a Soviet installation of surface-to-surface missiles
in Cuba as "offensive" and something that would necessitate a strong American response.

Kennedy did not embrace this view before Keating's fall
offensive. In National Security Action Memorandum No. 181,
issued on 23 August, the president had instructed the Departments of State and Defense to assess "the advantages
and disadvantages of making a statement that the U.S. would
not tolerate the establishment of military forces (missile or
air, or both?) which might launch a nuclear attack from
Cuba against the U.S." Although at this point, then, Kennedy
was considering the worth of a public statement indicating
his unwillingness to tolerate surface-to-surface missiles in
Cuba, it was not something to which he was committed.[56]

The president first presented his offensive-defensive dichotomy in a public statement on 4 September. Having
described the military build-up in Cuba, he stressed there
was no evidence of any Soviet combat forces, military bases,
or "offensive ground-to-ground missiles; or other significant
offensive capability." "Were it to be otherwise," he warned,
"the gravest issues would arise." Robert Kennedy later wrote
that the decision to issue this statement was made in response to a meeting he had held earlier that day with
Dobrynin during which the Soviet ambassador had reassured
the attorney general that Khrushchev had no intention of
embarrassing JFK by putting surface-to-surface missiles in
Cuba. Skeptical of the sincerity of Dobrynin's pledge, Robert
Kennedy conveyed his doubts to the president and advised

him to release a statement making clear America's opposition to the emplacement of offensive missiles in Cuba. According to RFK, he and Katzenbach wrote the draft on which that statement was based.[57]

Robert Kennedy's recollections were incomplete. They failed, in particular, to acknowledge that the statement was in part a reaction to Keating specifically and Republican criticisms in general. On 4 September the New York senator appeared on Martin Agronsky's segment of the NBC programme, "Today." After the interview, but before Keating had left the studio, a livid Pierre Salinger called Agronsky. "Why," he asked, "did you let Keating go on and make those inaccurate statements?" "We can't stop a Senator from saying whatever he wants to," Agronsky replied. "In what respect was it inaccurate?" "Well, the President will deal with those inaccuracies," replied Salinger. "He'll have a statement later today." The president's 4 September message was to a considerable degree, then, a direct reply to Keating's charges. As one authority on the missile crisis has put it, this statement was made "perhaps largely, though certainly not exclusively, for domestic political purposes."[58]

Kennedy delivered another message on Cuba at a 13 September press conference. As with so many of the important declarations of his presidency, it was written by Sorensen, his most eloquent wordsmith. In both this statement and his answers to subsequent questions, he made it clear that "if Cuba should possess a capacity to carry out offensive actions against the United States, . . . the United States would act." This was an obvious response to a message released two days earlier by Tass, the Soviet news agency, which described the Soviet military build-up in Cuba as "defensive" and characterised recent American policy towards Cuba, including the president's request to Congress for the authority to transfer up to 150 000 reservists into the armed forces, as aggressive. But Kennedy's message was also designed to deal with his domestic critics. In a memorandum written specifically for the president's handling of the Cuban issue at this news conference, McGeorge Bundy warned, "The Congressional head of steam on this is the most serious that we have had." Kennedy obviously had in mind his Republican opponents when he asserted in his statement that "rash talk is cheap, particularly on the part of those who do not have the responsibility."[59]

As well as compelling JFK to define in public the precise point at which the Soviet build-up in Cuba would become unacceptable, Keating also may have influenced the clandestine aspects of Kennedy's policy towards Castro. Operation Mongoose was accelerated during this time. On 4 October Robert Kennedy upbraided his colleagues in the Special Group (Augmented) for failing to implement Mongoose with sufficient zeal. "Nothing was moving forward," he groused, and the president himself was dissatisfied with the operation's progress. Consequently, SGA officials decided that "more dynamic action" was required. They authorised General Lansdale to step-up acts of sabotage, mine Cuban harbours, capture Castro supporters for interrogation, and generally "give consideration to new and more dynamic approaches" to the Cuban problem.[60]

The formulation of contingency plans for military action against Cuba was also expedited during the fall of 1962, especially the first two weeks of October. On the first Admiral Dennison instructed his subordinate commanders to take the steps needed to reach "maximum readiness" for the execution of the air strike option by 20 October. Two days later he initiated preparations for a possible blockade of Cuba, and on 6 October he called for a heightened state of preparedness to carry out the plans for invasion. The intercession of the secretary of defense further crystallised administration thinking on the military planning for Cuba. He enumerated in a memorandum the circumstances which might make an American attack on Cuba necessary. These included not only a deployment of offensive missiles on the island, but also Soviet pressure on West Berlin, a popular anti-Castro insurgency in Cuba, an attack on the Guantánamo base, and Cuban meddling in the affairs of other countries in the Western Hemisphere. The final contingency listed by McNamara represented a carte blanche for JFK: "A decision by the President that the affairs in Cuba have reached a point inconsistent with continuing U.S. national security."[61]

The nebulosity of that final contingency underscored the most striking feature of the frenetic military preparations made in early October, namely that the Kennedy administration was seriously considering military action against Cuba regardless of whether the Soviets installed offensive missiles on the island. McNamara made this abundantly clear when he stated that the aim of any American assault on Cuba would be either, "The removal of the threat to U.S. security of Soviet weapons systems in Cuba," or, "The removal of the Castro regime." Of those two goals, the secretary of defense regarded the second as more important: "Inasmuch as the second objective is the more difficult objective and may be required if the first is to be permanently achieved, attention should be focused upon a capability to assure the second objective." In other words, ousting Castro was more important than removing any weapons from Cuba, and so, by implication, military action against Cuba might well be required even if offensive missiles were not deployed on the island.[62]

President Kennedy kept tabs on the military planning and preparations underway. On 21 September he asked McNamara about the losses that would be incurred in attacking a surface-to-air missile site in Cuba, and also requested, as McNamara recorded it, "assurance as to the currency of contingency planning for Cuba." During the early days of October, he peppered his secretary of defense and Joint Chiefs of Staff with questions and proposals, including the suggestion that "we war-game the effectiveness of a Cuban surface-to-air missile (SAM) site by using models which our aircraft could practice attacking?" On 4 October Kennedy received and read "with interest" a McNamara memorandum on the issues he had raised on 21 September. It is clear, then, that the readying of American military power for a possible attack on Cuba occurred with JFK's approval and encouragement.[63]

As for Keating, some of the officials involved in the military contingency planning for Cuba were actually delighted by his fall offensive. Vice Admiral William P. Mack, who during this period was active in planning aimed in his words at "getting ready to invade Cuba," was hardly outraged by his allegations: "It didn't bother us too much what he was saying because we thought this was probably good. It would condition the people of the country to the fact that we had a severe problem here, and it would make it easier if we had to go to war or mobilize or something else."[64]

In explaining why the military contingency planning and Operation Mongoose were stepped up in the fall of 1962, historian James G. Hershberg emphasises three factors: first, the internal momentum of Mongoose itself; second, concern in the Kennedy administration over the increase in Soviet military aid to Cuba; and, finally, the domestic political pressure generated after August by GOP criticisms of Kennedy's Cuban policies. Although many Republicans participated in the assault upon the administration, it was the senator from New York who played the most active and important role in this attack.[65]

On 14 October, four days after Keating had claimed in the Senate that surface-to-surface missiles were present in Cuba, a U-2 plane took photographs of the Caribbean island which proved the accuracy of the senator's allegation when interpreted later by CIA officials. Arthur C. Lundahl, director of the National Photographic Interpretation Center, called Ray Cline to tell him the news, and Cline, in turn, passed the information on to McGeorge Bundy. Bundy, who was hosting a dinner for Charles Bohlen and his wife when Cline called on the evening of 15 October, decided against relaying the news immediately to the president. JFK, the national security adviser felt, would benefit from "a quiet evening and a night of sleep" before handling the most dangerous crisis of the nuclear era. He would tell Kennedy about the missiles the next day.[66]

5 Belligerent Beginnings: JFK on the Opening Day

Dean Rusk has argued that John Kennedy "showed qualities of genuine greatness" during the Cuban missile crisis. Ted Sorensen has similarly extolled the virtues of his performance. Harold Macmillan, Sorensen wrote retrospectively, was right: the young president had "earned his place in history by this one act alone." And JFK himself, according to Robert Kennedy, regarded his handling of the missile crisis as his finest accomplishment.[1]

That John Kennedy's role in the events of October 1962 can and has been portrayed in such a favourable light is hardly surprising. The cost of failing to resolve the missile crisis would have been staggering, and the stature of any leader who helped effect an escape from such a grave situation would inevitably assume heroic proportions. But in assessing the American reaction to the Soviet missile deployment in Cuba, it must always be recalled that the response was a collaborative endeavour involving many officials in the upper echelons of the administration. Hence, it is important to differentiate, if a distinction can be made, between Kennedy's contribution and that made by his leading advisers. What, then, was the president's own, personal response to the installation of offensive missiles in Cuba, and how did his initial assessment of the situation compare to that made by his advisers? Did the ultimate decision to opt for a blockade over an air strike or invasion of the island take place largely because or in spite of JFK's leadership? An examination of Kennedy's initial reaction on 16 October 1962 to the Soviet deployment in Cuba helps frame answers to those questions.

McGeorge Bundy told Kennedy the Soviets had placed missiles in Cuba at 8:45 a.m. on the morning of 16 October. As he entered the president's White House bedroom, JFK was sitting on the bed, still in his dressing gown, reading the morning newspapers. Bundy promptly told him the

news: "there is now hard photographic evidence, which you
will see a little later, that the Russians have offensive missiles in Cuba." Kennedy's initial concern was that the intelligence information upon which this judgement had been
based was sound. He then decided to convene a special
meeting for 11:45 later that morning, and informed Bundy of
the personnel he wished to attend.[2]

Kennedy entered his White House office at 9:25 a.m. He
devoted most of the morning to matters unrelated to the
impending crisis over Cuba. After greeting astronaut Walter
Schirra, his wife, and their children, he walked out with
them on to the White House lawn. He also met with his Panel
on Mental Retardation, and announced that storm-afflicted
parts of Oregon were entitled to disaster assistance. Kennedy
did take time, though, to call his brother Robert and John
J. McCloy to inform them of the news about Cuba. McCloy,
a Republican with vast experience in government whom
Kennedy used as an *ad hoc* adviser, urged the president to
do whatever was required to remove the missiles in Cuba,
even if that entailed the use of force.[3]

For one half hour before the meeting with his advisers,
Kennedy spoke to Charles Bohlen, his recently appointed
ambassador to France. "There seemed to be no doubt in
his mind," Bohlen later said of the president, "that the United
States would have to get these bases eliminated, the only
question was how it was to be done." Bohlen attended the
first ExComm meeting on Cuba later that morning, and
departed the next day for France.[4]

As midday approached, JFK met with senior officials in
the Cabinet Room in the first of what became known as the
ExComm sessions. A second such meeting convened in the
early evening. Belying his popular reputation for coolness
and rationality, Kennedy's response in those first two ExComm
meetings to the news of Soviet missiles in Cuba was more
rash than restrained, more impulsively hawkish than instinctively prudent. It was left to his advisers to explore safer
means of defusing the crisis.[5]

A few important judgements and decisions were made in
Washington on the opening day of the missile crisis. At first
photoanalysts erroneously identified the missiles in Cuba,
on the basis of their length, as the nuclear-tipped SS-3 type

of medium-range ballistic missiles (MRBMs). By the evening they were correctly adjudged to be the longer range SS-4 type of MRBMs. The president also agreed to increase the number of U-2 flights in order to garner all the necessary information on the missile sites. Most other decisions, though, particularly on what the most appropriate response to the Soviet missile deployment in Cuba might be, would prove less clear-cut.[6]

As for JFK's disposition on 16 October, Rusk has described him as being "as cool as a block of ice" throughout the missile crisis. McNamara recalled that the president was, "Calm and cool – and highly rational and unemotional." It seems rather implausible, however, to think that anyone, including Kennedy, would have responded with this sort of unflappable calm to such dire news. Ros Gilpatric was probably more accurate when he recalled that at the outset of the crisis, Kennedy was "very clipped, very tense. I don't recall a time when I saw him more preoccupied and less given to any light touch at all. The atmosphere was unrelieved by any of the usual asides and change of pace that he was capable of."[7]

As well as being on edge, Kennedy also felt decidedly vexed towards the Soviets. They had promised on various occasions throughout the fall not to deploy offensive missiles in Cuba, and those pledges had now been revealed as acts of mendacity. The president probably felt a sense of betrayal, therefore, a sense of being deceived even duped by the Soviet leadership. Maxwell Taylor, then chairman of the Joint Chiefs of Staff, has suggested this was the case, recalling that on 16 October Kennedy was simultaneously composed and angry. "What seemed to affect him most was the perfidy of the Soviet officials who had gone to such pains to lie to him about the nature of the weapons being sent to Cuba."[8]

Perhaps adding to Kennedy's sense of indignation was a telegram received mid-afternoon in the State Department. Foy D. Kohler, the new American ambassador to the Soviet Union, had met with Khrushchev that very day, and he wasted no time in reporting the contents of their conversation back to Washington. The Soviet premier had opened the meeting by lavishing praise on Kennedy. The president, he said, was a far more adroit politician than Eisenhower, and had succeeded in selecting able men for his administration. Knowing that Khrushchev had just stabbed him in the back over Cuba, Kennedy must have found these ingratiations irritatingly disingenuous. Changing his tack, the chairman proceeded to complain about American missile bases in Turkey and Italy, and to reaffirm the defensive nature of the Soviet build-up in Cuba. Again, given what he now knew about the missiles in Cuba, those statements must have seemed like sheer hypocrisy to JFK.[9]

Another factor *perhaps* contributing to Kennedy's state of mind on 16 October, although it must be clearly labelled as tentative speculation, was his use of certain drugs. He had come into contact with Dr Max Jacobson, a New York physician, during the 1960 presidential campaign. Jacobson's patients included such luminaries as Winston Churchill, Marlene Dietrich, and Tennessee Williams, and starting in spring 1961, Kennedy too made use of his services at least once and sometimes as often as three or four times each week. Jacobson, known as "Dr Feelgood," treated the president by injecting him with potent concentrations of amphetamines and steroids designed to alleviate stress as well as his back pains. During the first few days of the missile crisis, Kennedy had Jacobson inject him several times. Given that amphetamines and steroids can generate supreme confidence and promote belligerence, and assuming that Jacobson actually treated JFK on 16 October, then the president's drug-taking may have left him more inclined than he would have been otherwise to take forceful action in dealing with the Soviet missiles in Cuba.[10]

If Kennedy did in fact feel angry (and perhaps simultaneously confident and assertive because of the drugs), this would help explain the initial policies he advocated. For what was so very striking about his comments during the first two ExComm meetings was his insistence that the United States had to respond militarily to the missile deployment in Cuba. He made his initial analysis of the situation about half way through the first meeting, after Lyndon Johnson had spoken in favour of military action. Enumerating the policy options, he said the first was an air strike limited to the missile sites. The second was a "broader" strike aimed not only at those sites but also airfields, surface-to-air missile sites, and the like. The third involved carrying out either of the first two alternatives in conjunction with a blockade. The fourth issue, he explained, was the extent to which the United States should brief its allies before taking action over Cuba. Robert Kennedy then interjected that invasion was the fifth option.[11]

The president again listed the feasible alternatives a little later in the same meeting. After calling for heightened surveillance over Cuba, he stated: "We're certainly going to do number one; we're going to take out these missiles . . . the questions will be whether, which, what I would describe as number two, which would be a general air strike. That we're not ready to say, but we should be in preparation for it. The third is the general invasion." The president also spoke with a marked sense of urgency. "I don't think we['ve] got much time on these missiles," he warned. "It may be that we just have to, we can't wait two weeks while we're getting ready to roll. Maybe [we] just have to . . . take *them out*."[12]

Kennedy's interest in military action was equally apparent during the second ExComm meeting when he again described the three viable alternatives as being an air strike limited to the missile sites, a more general strike, and invasion. He also argued that it should be assumed the general air strike would be the preferred strategy, but that there should be sufficient flexibility in the military preparation to permit a change to the limited strike if deemed necessary.[13]

Kennedy did consider the broader strike to be less satisfactory than the limited strike in one sense: it carried a greater risk of evolving into a more dangerous, generalised military conflict. "Once you get into beginning to shoot up those airports," he explained, "then you get in, you get a lot of anti-aircraft, and you get a lot of, I mean you're running a much more major operation, therefore the dangers of the world-wide effects . . . to the United States are increased." Despite that acknowledgement, his predilection still seemed to be for the general strike. After explaining why the limited attack would be less likely to produce a broader military confrontation, he said of this approach, "That's the only argument for it."[14]

Apart from delineating these military alternatives, much of the rest of Kennedy's thinking on 16 October centred

on specific military issues. During the middle of the first
ExComm meeting, for example, he asked about the chances
of success for an air strike on the missiles in Cuba. When
an adviser replied that a single strike would never be entirely successful and, hence, there would need to be a series
of continuous air attacks, the president proceeded to explore this possibility. He also asked his advisers to ascertain
the time needed to organise air strikes on the missile sites,
and he continued to examine these sorts of issues during
the second meeting.[15]

Kennedy's initial determination to undertake military action was also apparent from a conversation he had with Adlai
Stevenson outside the ExComm meetings. Both the president and former presidential candidate attended a 1:00 p.m.
White House luncheon in honour of the crown prince of
Libya. After the function, when the two had a moment alone,
Kennedy showed Stevenson the photographic evidence. "We'll
have to do something quickly," he declared. "I suppose the
alternatives are to go in by air and wipe them out, or to
take other steps to render the weapons inoperable." Stevenson
disagreed. "Let's not go to an air strike," he urged Kennedy,
"until we have explored the possibilities of a peaceful solution." Stevenson later acknowledged that he had been "a
little alarmed that Kennedy's first consideration should have
been the air strike. I told him sooner or later we would
have to go to the U.N. and it was vitally important we go
there with a reasonable case." But his advice had no effect
as JFK continued in the evening ExComm session to endorse the military options.[16]

In line with his preference for the use of force, Kennedy
showed no interest in avoiding an immediate military confrontation by establishing a blockade around the island to
intercept further deliveries of missiles from the Soviet Union.
The blockade option emerged gradually during the discussions that day. Taylor was the first person in the opening
ExComm meeting to recommend it, but only as an adjunct
to an air strike on Cuba. The first official to prescribe the
blockade strategy as a policy alternative independent of any
military action was Secretary of Defense McNamara. Towards
the end of the evening session, he began to indicate his
preference for the blockade, and McGeorge Bundy and Under

Secretary of State George W. Ball voiced their agreement. Kennedy, by contrast, never advocated the blockade as an independent course of action on 16 October. He referred to it only once when, during the first meeting, he said it could be a supplement to either the limited or general air strike. When he enumerated the options later on both in that meeting and the following one, he did not mention the blockade again, not even in this context as an appendage to military action.[17]

Kennedy was equally disinterested in engaging in a diplomatic trade, arranging, for instance, the simultaneous removal of Soviet missiles in Cuba and American Jupiter missiles in Turkey. As with all his advisers on 16 October, he did not consider that possibility. The president did raise the issue of the Jupiters in the second meeting but not in the context of a possible diplomatic *quid pro quo*. Speculating on the reason for the Soviet decision to deploy missiles in Cuba, Kennedy asserted, "It's just as if we suddenly began to put a major number of MRBMs in Turkey. Now that'd be goddam dangerous, I would think." "Well," interjected one of his advisers (possibly Bundy), "we *did*, Mr. President." Responding feebly (and erroneously), Kennedy replied "that was five years ago" and "that was during a different period then."[18]

This amusing exchange did have a serious dimension. As JFK himself had unwittingly observed, putting Jupiter missiles in Turkey was analogous to the installation of Soviet missiles in Cuba. Indeed it could be argued that the United States had less justification because Khrushchev had made no systematic effort to undermine the Turkish government such as the attempt made by JFK to overthrow Castro. But the idea of trading the missiles in Turkey for those in Cuba occurred to neither Kennedy nor his aides on 16 October.

The president's initial outlook in the missile crisis, therefore, was quite unambiguous. In his mind, there were only three practical alternatives: an air strike limited to the missile sites, a more general strike, and invasion. Although he was uncertain which course to pursue, his first preference seemed to be for the general strike, his second the limited strike, with invasion representing the third choice. As for non-military responses, such as the blockade or a diplomatic approach, Kennedy regarded them as falling outside the

gamut of feasible policy options. In his judgement, they
did not merit consideration, not even as fourth or fifth
alternatives.

Kennedy's early thinking in the missile crisis was troubling
in other ways. Particularly disturbing was the way in which
his policy suggestions did not appear to be based on his
evaluation of such obviously important factors as Soviet motives
for putting missiles in Cuba, his assessment of the military
threat posed by the missiles to the United States, or any
thorough consideration of the possible consequences of
American military action. A sound American response had
to be predicated to some extent on an understanding of
why Khrushchev had taken this risk. An especially important issue was whether the chairman's decision to furnish
Cuba with missiles was a defensive move, motivated at least
in part by a genuine belief that failure to do so would result in the overthrow of Castro's government, or, alternatively, whether the decision derived from an aggressive desire
to attack the United States or to threaten doing so in order
to extract important concessions. If Khrushchev's motivations
were chiefly defensive rather than offensive, then a more
restrained, less risky response from Kennedy would have
perhaps been in order.

JFK, however, leaped to the conclusion on 16 October
that the United States must respond militarily without making any clear judgement on the question of Khrushchev's
motives. He did make a few comments on the subject, speculating that Soviet leaders were "not satisfied with their ICBMs,"
and that they might use the threat of the missiles in Cuba
to pressure the Western position in Berlin. But Kennedy's
overall attitude was one of bewilderment. As the second
meeting drew to a close, he time and again declared his
inability to understand why the Soviets had put missiles in
Cuba, especially in view of what he perceived to be their
moderate positions on recent issues like Laos and Berlin.
"Well," he confessed, "it's a goddamn mystery to me." That
Khrushchev may have perceived as threatening and thus been
responding, at least in part, to prior American policies, such
as the Bay of Pigs, covert sabotage in Cuba through Operation Mongoose, and the ejection of Cuba from the OAS,
never occurred to him (or his advisers). On the contrary,

Kennedy argued during the second meeting that what the Soviet missile deployment in Cuba showed was that the decision to carry out the Bay of Pigs "was really right." That JFK could have found Khrushchev's motivations so unfathomable, and yet been simultaneously convinced of the need to attack Cuba, was striking.[19]

Nor did Kennedy's support for military action relate to his analysis of the threat posed by the missiles. His advisers took diametrically opposed positions on this question. McNamara argued that they were strategically irrelevant because Khrushchev could already attack the United States with ICBMs from the Soviet Union. Other officials, such as Taylor and the rest of the Joint Chiefs of Staff, disagreed. According to Taylor, the missiles in Cuba were "a rather important adjunct and reinforcement to the strike capability of the Soviet Union." Kennedy's own feeling at this point in the second meeting was that they were significant in that they could be used to soften up the United States on the question of Berlin. But later in the same session he seemed to have come round to McNamara's point of view. The MRBM deployment in Cuba, he stated, "doesn't increase very much their strategic strength."[20]

Kennedy was sure, in addition to this, that Khrushchev would *not* fire the missiles in Cuba on the United States, probably because he knew that the prospect of a retaliatory nuclear strike would deter the Soviet leader from launching such an attack. When in the second meeting Secretary of the Treasury Dillon raised the possibility of the Soviets using Cuba to launch a nuclear strike against the United States, Kennedy replied, "You assume they wouldn't do that." Taylor and Rusk agreed with the president. It is again striking that Kennedy advocated a risky, military course of action on 16 October even though he did not feel certain the missiles altered the strategic balance of power between the superpowers, and he did not believe Khrushchev would use them against the United States.[21]

JFK also supported the use of force against Cuba without exploring the consequences. One obvious problem with an attack on Cuba was that it would compel Khrushchev to consider retaliating in order to maintain his credibility; then there would be pressure on Kennedy to respond again for

the same reason. In this way, there was grave danger that
an American attack on Cuba would spiral into a generalised military conflict. Kennedy did at one point in the second meeting argue that the chances of the missile crisis
escalating into a broader military conflict were greater with
a general than a limited strike on Cuba. Apart from that,
the concern he demonstrated over the possible consequences
of military action was negligible.[22]

All in all, Kennedy's views represented a curious paradox.
On the one hand, he did not believe the missiles in Cuba
significantly changed the strategic balance of power, did not
think Khrushchev would use them to attack the United States,
and was uncertain as to the reasons behind the Soviet missile deployment. On the other, he remained convinced on
16 October of the need for a military response to the Soviet
challenge in Cuba. Why, then, was Kennedy in favour of
military action? Speculation on this issue is unavoidable
because JFK himself did not articulate the reasoning behind
his arguments. Perhaps the most plausible answer is that
his eagerness for a military response flowed primarily from
the need he felt to convey a sense of decisiveness, especially
from the standpoint of domestic politics. Having stated in
September that he would not tolerate the deployment of
offensive missiles in Cuba, Kennedy seems to have considered
his credibility with the American people to have been dependent upon upholding that pledge in a swift and resolute manner – and a military strike was obviously more decisive
than either the blockade or a diplomatic initiative. He did
indeed refer on the opening day of the crisis to his position on Cuba in September. During the second meeting,
for instance, he pointed out that "my press statement was
so *clear* about how we *wouldn't* do anything under these
conditions [a military build-up in Cuba without surface-to-
surface missiles] and under the conditions that we *would* [a
build-up which included these offensive weapons]. He must
know that we're going to find out."[23]

Outside ExComm, JFK did indicate the importance he attached to the domestic political consequences of the missile deployment. In the morning, he spoke to Ken O'Donnell,
who had previously assured him of the Cuban issue's insig-
nificance to the forthcoming Congressional elections. "You

still think that fuss about Cuba is unimportant?" asked Kennedy. "Absolutely," O'Donnell replied. "The voters won't give a damn about Cuba." The president then brought him into his office to examine the photographs of the missile sites. "I don't believe it," exclaimed O'Donnell. "You'd better believe it," Kennedy observed. "We've just elected Capehart in Indiana, and Ken Keating will probably be the next President of the United States." Although Kennedy referred here to the November elections, he was probably more concerned with the general impact of the Cuban situation on his own and his administration's credibility than with the outcome of the congressional elections specifically.[24]

JFK's initial preference for the military options was probably linked secondarily to the extensive pre-missile crisis contingency planning for military action against Cuba that had taken place within his administration. He may well have felt that a military response was logical given the fact that he and his advisers had been seriously considering the need for such action anyway. There is some sense of this in the declassified parts of the transcripts for the first two ExComm sessions, and the still classified portions might well add to that sense as parts of them appear to relate to American military preparations already in progress for Cuba before the missile crisis. During the first meeting, for instance, Kennedy asked, "How long did it take to get in a position where we can invade Cuba? Almost a month? Two months?" McNamara replied, "No, sir." Then an unidentified speaker said, "Right on the beach." The next part of the conversation is classified but in the first statement after the deleted portion, Taylor said, in possible reference to prior military planning on Cuba, that "at least it's enough to start the thing going. . . . It ought to be enough."[25]

In the latter part of the evening ExComm meeting, to take another example, Kennedy asked McNamara about the state of military contingency planning on Cuba. The secretary of defense replied that:

the military planning has been carried on for a considerable period of time, is well under way. And I believe that all the preparations that we could take without the risk of preparations causing discussion and knowledge of this, either among our public or in Cuba, have been taken and are authorised.[26]

As well as referring to the general state of military planning for Cuba, these exchanges may have related directly to an amphibious training exercise called PHIBRIGLEX-62. Scheduled to commence on 15 October, this training operation was to be conducted on a grand scale. Some twenty thousand naval personnel and four thousand marines would launch an amphibious assault on Vieques Island, just off Puerto Rico. Consequently, when the missile crisis began on 16 October, there was, as an April 1963 report by the commander in chief of the US Atlantic Fleet (CINCLANT) put it, "a significant amphibious force . . . already enroute to the Caribbean." Nor was this exercise of negligible concern to upper echelon officials. The same report noted that "as early as about 10 October the National Military Command Center began inquiring informally of CINCLANT as to the nature and scope of PHIBRIGLEX-62. Without ever relating the exercise to the Cuban situation, there were indications of high-level interest in it." To Kennedy, the probable significance of PHIBRIGLEX-62 was that it meant a military response to the Soviet missile deployment in Cuba made sense precisely because his military was well prepared to undertake such action.[27]

In defence of the president's performance at the start of the missile crisis, it can be pointed out that many officials changed their minds several times between 16 and 22 October before rejecting the various military alternatives and supporting the blockade. Hence, it could be argued, Kennedy's endorsement of military action on 16 October was insignificant. Many other officials momentarily supported the idea of a military response before rejecting it in favour of blockade, and Kennedy was no exception.

The flaw with this argument, though, is that there were still marked differences between JFK's thinking and that of many of his advisers. Most of those who came to support the blockade at least showed some signs of moving towards that position during the first two ExComm meetings. This they did by exploring various non-military alternatives for American policy, and also by expressing their fears about the possible consequences of military action. Kennedy evinced little interest in those issues and was far more committed on 16 October to the military options than most of his leading advisers who ultimately supported the blockade. This further suggests that Kennedy's eventual decision not to resort to an air strike or invasion was more a matter of his being persuaded from that line of action by other officials than of he himself quickly and easily changing his own mind.

McNamara was the most vocal of Kennedy's advisers in the first two ExComm meetings. As the hours passed on 16 October, he focused less on the military alternatives open to the United States and more on the feasibility of the blockade. His initial preference was for military action. In his first extended analysis of the situation, he argued that if a decision to launch an air attack on Cuba was made, it should be carried out before the missile sites were operational, thereby avoiding the possibility of a retaliatory strike from those sites. He also stated that any air strike should be made not just on the missile sites but also upon the airfields, aircraft not located in the airfields, and all possible nuclear storage sites, even though this would probably mean the death of two or three thousand Cubans. The United States, McNamara added, should also be prepared to invade Cuba in the aftermath of a strike. To that end, Kennedy should mobilise America's military forces either during or after the air attack.[28]

McNamara again argued later on in the meeting that an invasion might ultimately be necessary. "There's a real possibility you'd *have* to invade," he asserted. "If you carried out an air strike, this might lead to an uprising such that in order to prevent the slaughter of the free Cubans, we would have to invade to reintroduce order into the country. And we would be prepared to do that." Towards the end of the first ExComm session, McNamara still seemed to be assuming that Kennedy would have to respond militarily. He said that when ExComm officials reconvened, they should come prepared to answer three questions. First, should the administration publicly announce it was scheduling reconnaissance flights to verify the presence of offensive missiles in Cuba? Second, should the United States take some "political" steps, such as contacting Khrushchev, before beginning military action? Third, how long would it take to carry out and what would be the likely consequences of air strikes on Cuba? The thrust of those questions showed McNamara's penchant during the first meeting for military action.[29]

By the evening ExComm session, however, McNamara had changed his tune by including a blockade as one of the feasible policy options. In the early stages of that second meeting, he described three alternatives. The first was political action, on the lines proposed by Rusk, such as the initiation of diplomatic approaches to Castro or Khrushchev. McNamara was skeptical about this, arguing that it would "lead to no satisfactory result, and it almost *stops* subsequent military action." The implication was that a diplomatic approach would reveal the administration's knowledge of the missiles in Cuba to Khrushchev and Castro and thus forewarn them of a likely American military response. The next alternative was a blockade in tandem with a public declaration that Washington would use reconnaissance missions to maintain constant surveillance over Cuba. The final option was one of the various types of military action. At this point McNamara appeared undecided between the second and third strategies. Of the third, he warned that "any one of these forms of direct military action will lead to a Soviet military response of some type some place in the world." Yet in the same breath he reflected, "It may well be worth the price. Perhaps we should pay that."[30]

During the course of the second ExComm meeting, McNamara adopted the position that the missiles in Cuba did not alter the strategic balance of power between the superpowers. Having dismissed the military importance of the missiles in this way, he asserted towards the end of the session, "I don't think there *is* a military problem here." Rather, "this is a domestic, political problem" because Kennedy had publicly stated in September that "we'd *act*" if evidence emerged indicating the presence of missiles in Cuba. McNamara clearly implied here that a failure to uphold this promise would seriouly damage the credibility of the Kennedy administration in the eyes of the American public. That was the key issue.[31]

The secretary of defense also became increasingly concerned about the ramifications of military action against Cuba.

After evaluating both the limited and general air strike options, he exhorted his colleagues:

> to consider the consequences. I don't believe we have considered the consequences of any of these actions satisfactorily, and because we haven't considered the consequences, I'm not sure we're taking all the action we ought to take now to minimise those. I don't know quite what kind of a world we live in after we've struck Cuba, and we've started it.

He thus suggested that the Defense and State Departments spend the night pondering the consequences of the various policy proposals.[32]

Having now minimised the military threat posed by the missiles, and having emphasised the potential dangers of an American strike, McNamara accordingly modified his recommendations. When he once again outlined the alternatives as the second ExComm session drew to a close, he cited the same three that he had presented earlier: a political approach, blockade, and one of the various types of military action. By this point, however, his predilection was for the blockade, combined with open surveillance of Cuba and an ultimatum to Khrushchev threatening both the Soviet Union and Cuba with a nuclear strike unless the missiles were removed from the island. Although he said he was not endorsing the blockade, he did indicate his preference for it. "This alternative doesn't seem to be a very acceptable one," he remarked, "but wait until you work on the others."[33]

McNamara's comment on the feasibility of threatening Khrushchev with a nuclear attack was disturbing. His failure to explore the important question of why Khrushchev had put missiles in Cuba was also a major shortcoming in his analysis of the situation. None the less, his views had clearly changed from an initial preference for a general air strike followed possibly by invasion, to tentative support for the blockade. That McNamara would come to endorse the blockade approach unequivocally in the following days was not at all surprising given the development of his ideas during the first two ExComm meetings. Unlike the secretary of defense, Kennedy exhibited no comparable evolution in his

thinking on 16 October. Whereas McNamara quickly recon-
sidered his support for the military options, Kennedy demonstrated nothing but unambiguous support for them.
Whereas McNamara's recommendations were appropriately
shaped by his assessment of both the military significance
of the missiles in Cuba and the possible consequences of
an American air strike or invasion, the president's, disap-
pointingly, were not.

The opening day of the missile crisis was an especially
busy one for Dean Rusk. As well as attending the two ExComm
meetings, he also participated in afternoon sessions at the
State Department with various officials, including Stevenson,
Bohlen, and Llewellyn Thompson. After the second ExComm
meeting, deliberations at the State Department resumed, finally
ending after 11:00 p.m. in Rusk's office.[34]

The secretary of state was decidedly taciturn that day. He
tended to speak at length at the start of meetings but then
keep quiet, and he also had a proclivity to present alternatives for American policy without indicating his own preference. Rusk has subsequently claimed that he did explain
his precise views to the president in private. Even so, his
influence on Kennedy's thinking was probably limited. Comments made by JFK to his aides revealed his general doubts
about Rusk's abilities. Compared to a forceful and imposing adviser like McNamara, Rusk seemed diffident and ineffective. Robert Kennedy later disclosed that before his death
his brother was seriously considering the replacement of
Rusk as secretary of state after the 1964 presidential election with McNamara or possibly Bundy.[35]

In contrast to his more highly rated colleagues, though,
Rusk did examine the issue of Soviet motivation in depth
on 16 October. He believed Khrushchev had put missiles
in Cuba to procure a bargaining-chip *vis-à-vis* Berlin and to
establish a psychological and military counterbalance to
American strategic superiority in general and the missiles
in Turkey in particular. As for the United States response,
he did not categorically support military action, as Kennedy
did. Rather, he viewed it as only one of two alternatives,
the other being the diplomatic option. Specifically, Rusk
suggested the possible initiation of various ploys designed
to induce Moscow and Havana into removing the missiles

without any American military intervention. This would involve encouraging the OAS to demand that an inspection
team be sent to the missile sites in Cuba. Rusk admitted
the request would inevitably be rejected, but implied that
the increased pressure might make Moscow and Havana
reconsider their position.[36]

A message to Castro was another part of Rusk's diplomatic
track. The Kennedy administration, he suggested, could warn
Castro, through either the Canadian ambassador in Havana
or the Cuban ambassador to the UN, that the Soviet Union
had installed missiles in Cuba for its own purposes (like
arranging some sort of superpower trade of Cuba for Berlin)
and was willing to risk the destruction of Cuba to achieve
those ends. Hence, Castro should be informed, it was in his
best interests to break with Moscow and make sure the missiles
on the island did not become operational. Rusk also mentioned the possibility of a message to the Soviet premier.[37]

When ExComm reconvened in the early evening, the secretary of state once again argued that "a direct message to
Castro, as well as Khrushchev, might make some sense."
He then had Edwin M. Martin, assistant secretary of state
for Inter-American Affairs, summarise a letter to the Cuban leader that State Department officials had written during the afternoon. The note presented Castro with an ultimatum: he must provide immediate assurances that steps
were being taken to remove the Soviet missiles or else the
United States would initiate "measures of vital significance
for the future of Cuba." Overall, Rusk's position on 16 October was that a military strike against Cuba might well be
required but consideration should also be given to various
diplomatic approaches that might defuse the crisis before it
escalated into military conflict.[38]

Other ExComm officials also expressed their reservations
about military action. None did so with greater vigour than
George Ball. As the end of the second meeting approached,
he candidly stated his fears. "This come in there on Pearl
Harbor just frightens the hell out of me as to what's going
beyond." "You go in there with a surprise attack," he continued. "You put out all the missiles. This isn't the *end*. This
is the *beginning*." Unsurprisingly, Ball found the blockade
more appealing than the military alternatives. Even McGeorge

Bundy, who during the early ExComm discussions had been attached to the limited air strike option, was at least considering the value of the blockade by the end of the second meeting.[39]

Robert Kennedy was determined after the Bay of Pigs that his brother would never have to endure such an ignominious experience again. To that end, he started to involve himself in the conduct of foreign policy, and even speculated with Nicholas Katzenbach about the possibility of switching from attorney general to under secretary of state, and then using his new position to run the State Department. Rusk, as secretary of state, would remain as only its titular head. Given his burning desire to protect the president's interests in the foreign policy realm, RFK was more than a little concerned when he learned about the Soviet missile deployment in Cuba; he was furious.[40]

After receiving a call from his brother about the missiles in Cuba, Robert Kennedy spoke that morning with CIA Deputy Director for Plans Richard M. Helms about the situation. When Helms confirmed the bad news, he expressed his anger pithily: "Shit!" He was moved to an extended repetition of the same expletive when he examined the photographs of the missiles later on in Bundy's office: "Oh shit! Shit! Shit! Those sons a bitches Russians." According to one official present, he proceeded to pace around the room, hitting his fist into the palm of his hand. His wrath was also evident during the meeting he attended that same morning with the SGA. Reviewing the progress of Operation Mongoose, he groused about its ineffectiveness and cited the failure to carry out acts of sabotage as an example.[41]

Robert Kennedy was far quieter during the first two ExComm sessions. His most famous contribution came when, as officials considered the feasibility of an air strike, he passed a laconic note to the president: "I now know how Tojo felt when he was planning Pearl Harbor." The comments that he made in ExComm revealed his initial support for an American invasion of Cuba. In the first meeting, he pointed out to his brother that invasion was one of the options, and he asked Taylor how long it would take to carry out. Explaining the advantages of an invasion over a general air strike, he warned that with the strike:

You're going to kill an awful lot of people, and we're going to take an awful lot of heat on it . . . [and] you're going to announce the reason that you're doing it is because they're sending in these kind of missiles. Well, I would think it's almost incumbent upon the Russians, then, to say, Well, we're going to send them in again, and if you do it again, we're going to do the same thing to Turkey, or We're going to do the same thing to Iran.

Why he assumed that an invasion of Cuba would not produce the same scenario is not clear.[42]

Robert Kennedy argued along similar lines in the second ExComm meeting. He again seemed to oppose an air strike and to endorse invasion when he pondered "whether it wouldn't be the argument, if you're going to get into it [i.e. Cuba] at all, whether we should just get into it and get it over with and say that [we should] take our losses." Searching for pretexts to justify invasion, he suggested, in reference to the 1898 Spanish-American War over Cuba, that perhaps "there is some *other* way we can get involved in this through Guantánamo Bay, or something, or whether there's some ship that, you know, sink the *Maine* again or something." In this context, the note in which RFK expressed empathy with Tojo for having to prepare an attack on Pearl Harbor appears to have been meant literally. It was almost certainly not, as has usually been assumed, a facetious comment designed to condemn those officials who recommended military action against Cuba.[43]

In apportioning blame for America's entry into the Vietnam War, leading authority George McT. Kahin has argued that most the responsibility should be placed on the shoulders of Lyndon Johnson's advisers rather than on Johnson himself. More than his aides, Johnson was wary of becoming fully involved in a war in Vietnam. The likes of Bundy, Taylor, and McNamara, however, cajoled the president into endorsing a policy of escalation he would not, of his own volition, have pursued. If Kahin is right, then the reverse was the case in the Cuban missile crisis. Kennedy's performance on 16 October made clear that his own instincts coupled with a desire to keep his September public promises to take resolute action if missiles were placed in Cuba led him down the path towards military action. In the missile crisis, it was left to his advisers, especially McNamara and Robert Kennedy (as he modified his views after 16 October), to explore the alternatives to a military approach, and ultimately to convince the president that the blockade was the most appropriate course of action.[44]

It could be maintained, of course, that most officials in the Kennedy administration changed their minds in the period from 16 to 22 October, supporting one option than another before finally espousing the blockade. This, it could be further argued, was the case with John Kennedy. He initially embraced the military approach, and particularly favoured the general air strike option, before supporting the blockade.

That analysis, however, is an over-simplification. The key difference between the initial outlook of JFK and most of the leading officials who subsequently came to endorse the blockade was that the president was far more convinced than they of the need for a military response. It is true that Robert Kennedy, who advocated an invasion of Cuba on 16 October, emerged in the following days as a forceful proponent of the blockade. But generally speaking, most of the leading advisers who came to support that alternative did express reservations towards the military options on the opening day of the crisis. McNamara and Rusk, for example, developed non-military alternatives for American policy. And McNamara and Ball expressed their concern over the consequences of military action against Cuba, suggesting that it might ignite a superpower war.

Given the misgivings expressed by these officials towards military action, it was not at all surprising that they would come to approve the blockade strategy. Given the paucity of objections raised by John Kennedy to a military response, it seems unlikely he would, on his own initiative, have transferred his support from the military options to the blockade. JFK does deserve praise for not clinging dogmatically after 16 October to the military approach he initially favoured, for remaining open to the recommendations of his aides. Nevertheless, in the Cuban missile crisis it was the advisers who were responsible for guiding the president away from a military course of action he would, in all likelihood, have otherwise undertaken.

6 The Battle for Blockade: Bobby Kennedy versus Dean Acheson

After American officials staked out their initial positions on 16 October, two key debates took place in ExComm resulting in the decision to blockade Cuba. The battle between supporters of the air strike and blockade, in which the latter group prevailed, was the first. The second was the discussion on and unequivocal rejection of Stevenson's 20 October proposals, which sought to resolve the crisis through mutual Soviet-American concessions, and in so doing represented the principal alternative to the air strike and blockade options.

The most important advocates in that first debate were Dean Acheson and Robert Kennedy. Acheson was not the only prominent official to favour an air strike on Cuba. Dillon, Taylor, McCone, and (for most of the time) Bundy were similarly disposed. But it was Acheson who was, as Bundy recalled, the "most formidable" of the hawks. This was due in part to his dexterity in debate. As Gilpatric explained, Acheson would:

> make a pronouncement [in ExComm] and knock down any opposing ideas, which he did . . . very masterfully, and then depart the scene. He didn't want to spend a lot of time. So he sort of came and went. . . . But if he was there in full force and wanted to make an issue of it, no frontal attack would overcome him.

John Kennedy himself once told Ben Bradlee that Acheson, along with Clark Clifford, was one of "the two best advocates I have ever heard. Acheson would have made a helluva Supreme Court justice." Acheson's intimidating presence and imperious personality also helped make him the most redoubtable hawk. He was, in addition, probably granted greater respect from ExComm colleagues by virtue of his status as one of the original architects of containment and one of the most conspicuous figures in the American Establishment.[1]

For his part, Robert Kennedy did not introduce the idea of the blockade to the ExComm discussions. That was McNamara's chief contribution. Nor were his arguments original. Rather, they were restatements of comments already made by George Ball. Nevertheless, Robert Kennedy emerged after 16 October as the most vigorous proponent of the blockade and impassioned critic of the air strike. The attorney general's importance as a blockade supporter stemmed not only from the ardour with which he made his case, but also the nature of his relationship with John Kennedy. In what seemed at times to be a symbiotic link, JFK depended heavily upon Robert Kennedy, who in turn served his elder brother with unwavering devotion. As Bowles once observed, the attorney general "may have had as much influence on the President as all the rest [of us] put together."[2]

ExComm members paid close heed to Robert Kennedy's recommendations because they were very much aware of the special nature of his relationship with the president. With campaign commitments dictating John Kennedy's absence from many of the early missile crisis meetings, officials felt that Robert Kennedy was, as Gilpatric put it, "the president's alternate. That was to be the line of communication except for the few meetings we had with the president, particularly later in the week, [until] he returned from Chicago." Gilpatric further noted that RFK's participation in the ExComm sessions had a "disciplinary" effect because, "It was perfectly evident that he was keeping notes as to where everybody stood.... I used to see he had initials of people and put after the initials some comments. He didn't keep detailed notes of everything that was said, but he was keeping some kind of a score sheet, a rating card."[3]

Although it would have been appropriate for Dean Rusk, as secretary of state, to have orchestrated the discussions on Cuba, Robert Kennedy tended to dominate. The attorney general placed little faith in Rusk's competence, and in the secret discussions during the first week of the missile crisis, he plainly felt the need to supply the leadership and direction which, in his view, Rusk could not. A minor incident in the 19 October ExComm session highlighted this. Leonard

Meeker, who took notes during the meeting, wrote that at one point Rusk called for an exploration of the legal aspects of the various military courses of action. He then "turned to me, and seemed about to call on me, when the Attorney General signalled and said "Mr. Katzenbach." Secretary Rusk then called on the latter," and Katzenbach opened the discussion.[4]

Robert Kennedy learned about the missiles in Cuba shortly after 9:00 a.m. on 16 October. After McGeorge Bundy had briefed John Kennedy on the missiles in Cuba, the president called his brother and asked him to come immediately to the White House. When he arrived, JFK explained that the recent U-2 photographs showed that the Soviets were in the process of installing nuclear missiles in Cuba. In the two ExComm meetings later that day, Robert Kennedy was generally taciturn. The little he did say revealed his initial belief that an invasion of Cuba would be the most appropriate American strategy.[5]

Dean Acheson was drawn into the ExComm discussions a day later. When Dean Rusk, a State Department official under Acheson during the Truman years, briefed him about the situation in Cuba, the veteran Democrat responded by emphasising the criticality of time. Assuming the missiles were not yet fully installed (by which he perhaps meant that no warheads had reached Cuba), he argued that:

> we had to consider at the outset whether to deal with the weapons before they became operative, or whether we would take the risk that they would become operative while we were taking other steps to get them out of Cuba. I was very much afraid that if we delayed dealing with them we would get into a situation where we could never deal with them.

This temporal consideration soon led Acheson to propose an air strike on the grounds that it was necessary to destroy the missiles while there was still time to do so in relative safety. Put another way, an attack should be carried out before those missiles became operational and so could be fired in retaliation at the United States.[6]

In preparation for the ExComm meeting he was to attend later on 17 October, Acheson wrote a short memorandum fleshing out the ideas he had first expressed to Rusk. He once again stressed the importance of removing the missiles in Cuba before they became operational, and implied that military force would be needed to achieve that goal. The decision to initiate such action "has to be made now, or not at all. . . . This is [the] time of minimum risk. I would act." He added that the "Other one [i.e. Khrushchev] will not take this quietly," thereby suggesting that the Soviets would most likely retaliate should the president use force against Cuba. Hence, the United States had to be "ready to act instantly . . . in several spots," including Berlin.[7]

Acheson proceeded to discuss the importance of both America's allies and the upcoming November congressional elections to the impending crisis. He felt the Kennedy administration should not consult but must notify its allies about the Cuban situation and the course of action that JFK had chosen. The best candidates for the job of notifying NATO and the OAS were Lyndon Johnson, Dwight Eisenhower, Supreme Allied Commander in Europe General Lauris Norstad, or Acheson himself. Once the judgement had been made to respond militarily to the missile threat, Kennedy, in a spirit of bipartisanship, should immediately cancel all of his planned campaign speeches in order to unite the country. Likewise, the decision as to which day should be selected for the strike on Cuba should not be influenced by considerations relating to the congressional elections.[8]

Acheson refined his ideas in these preliminary notes during the ExComm meeting that he joined later on 17 October. He would soon become disillusioned with his ExComm colleagues, referring to them later as "a leaderless, uninhibited group, many of whom had little knowledge in either the military or diplomatic field." To Acheson, Rusk, along with other foreign policy pundits, should have been the exclusive participants in an administration discussion of an international crisis like the one in Cuba. Cabinet officers such as the attorney general, therefore, should have been excluded.[9]

Reflecting perhaps his irritation at this state of affairs, Acheson clashed angrily with Robert Kennedy during the 17 October ExComm meeting held in George Ball's State Department conference room. The president, keeping to his planned schedule that day, missed the famous confrontation. The recollections of Acheson and Robert Kennedy on how their disagreement emerged differ. Acheson claimed it was he who responded to the attorney general's arguments. Robert Kennedy, on the other hand, said it was a case of the former secretary of state first defining his position and then of his shaping a response to the issues raised by Acheson. George Ball's account of the session substantiates Acheson's version.[10]

In the meeting, Robert Kennedy amplified and injected with passion comments first made by Ball. When the idea of launching an air strike against Cuba was broached, Ball denounced it vehemently. Such a policy, he contended, would contravene America's best traditions and undermine its position of moral authority throughout the world. Robert Kennedy agreed. An attack on Cuba would be inconsonant with American values and history. He later wrote that he had been unwilling to "accept the idea that the United States would rain bombs on Cuba, killing thousands and thousands of civilians in a surprise attack." To his ExComm colleagues, he put the case that an American strike on Cuba would represent an attack by a great power against a small nation, thereby undermining "our moral position at home and around the globe." He capped his argument by using vivid, emotive imagery. An American assault on Cuba would constitute "a Pearl Harbor in reverse," and he had no intention of allowing his brother to become the Tojo of the 1960s.[11]

Acheson, never one to keep his feelings under wraps, expressed his complete disagreement with Robert Kennedy. He "clearly indicated," recalled Ball, "not only by his words but also by the emphatic way he spoke, that Bobby was talking sentimental nonsense." Acheson declared that there was no underlying similarity between the Japanese bombing of Pearl Harbor and a prospective American assault on Cuba. The Japanese had not issued a warning before their attack on Pearl Harbor. The United States, by contrast, had made crystal clear its unwillingness to countenance a Soviet missile deployment in the Caribbean. The Monroe Doctrine itself prohibited foreign military penetration of the Western Hemisphere. The president, moreover, had stated in September that he would take action if the Soviet Union installed offensive missiles in Cuba. On 3 October Congress had authorised JFK to do whatever was necessary to prevent the establishment of a Soviet military base in Cuba, even if this required the use of force. "How much warning was necessary," Acheson later queried with characteristic sarcasm, "to avoid the stigma of "Pearl Harbor in reverse"? Was it necessary to adopt the early nineteenth-century method of having a man with a red flag walk before a steam engine to warn cattle and people to stay out of the way?"[12]

In appraising Soviet motives, Acheson felt Khrushchev was trying to strengthen his position and weaken America's in various ways. Although he did not appear to discuss this issue in ExComm on 17 October, Acheson did present his assessment of Khrushchev's objectives in a letter to a friend at the end of the month. The Soviet premier, he claimed, was attempting to damage American credibility throughout the Western Hemisphere, acquire a bargaining chip which could be used against the United States in Europe and Asia, and augment his nuclear first-strike capability by fifty per cent. Unlike some of his ExComm colleagues, Acheson believed that the missiles in Cuba would substantially affect the nuclear balance between the superpowers. Shorter-range missiles in the Caribbean, because of their proximity to American territory, were as dangerous to the United States as ICBMs located in the Soviet Union. If the Kennedy administration meekly acquiesced in this installation of missiles in Cuba, confidence in American leadership would be eroded both in the Western Hemisphere and Western Europe.[13]

Acheson was convinced, therefore, that the emplacement of missiles in Cuba constituted a very serious challenge which the president had to meet. An air strike limited to the missile sites would be, in his view, the most effective American response. The salient problem with a blockade was that it would not actually remove the missiles from Cuba, and so would merely postpone the military action needed to destroy those weapons. An air strike at a later date would be far more dangerous than one launched immediately because in the intervening period of the blockade work on the missile sites would continue apace. Whereas a subsequent American air strike might carry with it the possibility of retaliation from Soviet missiles in Cuba, an earlier strike, launched before those missiles were operational, would avoid that risk.[14]

Acheson claimed in later years to have felt during the missile crisis that the chances of Soviet reprisals after an American attack on Cuba were negligible. At the time, however, he acknowledged that there was a significant possibility, although not necessarily a likelihood, of a Soviet military response. This he did in both his 17 October memorandum and in a letter written shortly after the crisis. In the latter, Acheson admitted that the consequences of an air strike:

> might have been severe since a good many Russians would have been killed. We should have expected them to be severe . . . . I thought that they [the Soviets] might act in Berlin or Turkey, and that we must be prepared for war. My judgment, on which we could not bank, was that they would not react with spasmodic violence.

The equanimity with which Acheson accepted the prospect that an air strike might lead to a general superpower war was striking.[15]

Much to Acheson's chagrin, the military officials present at that 17 October ExComm meeting expanded upon his proposals to advocate not only a strike against the missile sites, but also against airfields, SAM sites, and fighter aircraft. This was an approach which the former secretary of state regarded as highly dangerous and unsatisfactory because it would produce the scenario that Robert Kennedy feared, namely the deaths of thousands of Cubans. "When you get the soldiers talking about policy," Acheson bitterly observed in later years, "they want to go further and further in a military way so that all possibilities of doubt are removed, until their proposals are apt to be at least as dangerous as the original danger." As for a limited air strike, he viewed this as a relatively moderate strategy. It would endanger no Cubans and only about four and a half thousand Soviet troops and technicians stationed at the missile sites.[16]

Acheson did not discuss the possibility of resolving the crisis by trading the missiles in Cuba for America's Jupiter missiles in Turkey. This was rather curious because in the early days of his administration, Kennedy had asked Acheson

to produce a report on NATO policy. The study recommended *inter alia* the removal of the Jupiters from Turkey, partly because their vulnerability to enemy fire meant
they were unlikely to survive an attack enabling them to be
used in retaliation as second strike weapons. It was also felt
that the missiles' proximity to the Soviet border made them
especially provocative to Khrushchev. Yet although Acheson
thought it was in American interests to withdraw the missiles from Turkey anyway, he did not talk at the 17 October
ExComm meeting in terms of defusing the crisis through
the removal of the Jupiters. He perhaps thought it was inappropriate to make such a concession under pressure because it would suggest a lack of firmness on the part of the
Kennedy administration, and this would serve to undermine
American credibility.[17]

In ExComm's meeting on the morning of 18 October,
Acheson and his colleagues started to ponder the legal ramifications of the various policy options. Despite his background
as one of the outstanding lawyers for the prestigious Washington firm of Covington, Burling and Rublee, Acheson did
not concern himself with the legal nuances of the situation.
On the contrary, he argued that the American response to
the missile deployment in Cuba should not be conditioned
in any way by legal considerations. America's security, prestige, and credibility with the other nations of the Western
Hemisphere were all at stake, and the effort to protect those
interests should not be jeopardised by international law. It
was probably at this meeting that Acheson stated: "The hell
with international law. International law gets made, it's just
a series of precedents and decisions that have been made
in the past. But this is a unique situation and this is one in
which one can, and should, make international law rather
than just follow past precedents." According to Paul Nitze,
Acheson proceeded to propose that the United States use
the term "quarantine," if some officials found the word "blockade" offensive and if the decision was made to implement a
blockade.[18]

For Acheson, his greatest opportunity to shape the American response to the missile deployment in Cuba arose when
John Kennedy asked to meet with him alone on the afternoon of 18 October. The chances of Acheson persuading

the president to implement his preferred policy, the air strike, were diminished, however, by the nature of their previous dealings with each other. Mutual distrust had always simmered beneath the surface of their ostensibly cordial relationship. For his part, Acheson viewed JFK's meteoric political rise as the result of old Joe Kennedy's insidious influence. During the Democratic primaries in the spring of 1960, for example, he sardonically wrote to Harry Truman that, "Maybe we should all give Jack a run for his money – or rather for Joe's."[19]

Senator Kennedy had also irritated Acheson back in 1957 by urging the Eisenhower administration to pressure France into granting Algerian independence. Alienating an important Western European ally out of some nebulous, moralistic concern for a country with which the United States had no cultural or historic affinity seemed completely misguided to Acheson. And in *Power and Diplomacy*, his 1958 work on American foreign policy, he said so, declaring that, "It will not help for us to snap impatient fingers at a people who were great before our nation was dreamt of, and tell them to get on with it." When Jackie Kennedy found herself sitting next to Acheson during a train ride to Washington, she took the opportunity to explain that "the Kennedy family was not pleased" with his criticisms of JFK on the Algerian issue. That displeasure would have been magnified had they known that a year later Acheson would privately describe Lyndon Johnson, in comparison to his Democratic challengers for the 1960 presidential nomination, as "a giant among pygmies." At this time, Acheson thought that Kennedy should only be LBJ's vice-presidential running partner.[20]

Although president-elect Kennedy solicited Dean Acheson's advice on cabinet appointments, and although, as president, he paid Acheson the compliment in spring 1961 of picking his brains on Western European issues, the former secretary of state continued to regard JFK as a callow youth. The air of condescension which characterised his view of Kennedy surfaced most clearly in the aftermath of the Bay of Pigs. Addressing the Foreign Service Association in Washington, he suggested that the young president looked like "a gifted amateur practicing with a boomerang and knocking himself cold." Kennedy was furious. McGeorge Bundy called

Lucius D. Battle, a former special assistant to Acheson, to ask his old boss for a retraction. In mid-August 1961, Acheson obliged, writing to JFK to apologise for his comments. Still, he remained sceptical of Kennedy's abilities. An official who used to lunch with Acheson recalled that "he never really thought much of Jack Kennedy. He came to think more of him, but [his view was that] he was too young, too inexperienced for the job. [He] didn't know what he was doing." A British official who dined with Acheson in early July 1961 noted that "he spoke of the President with scarcely veiled criticism."[21]

Trust and mutual respect were not hallmarks of the Kennedy-Acheson relationship, therefore, and this made it more difficult than it would have been otherwise for Acheson to bring the president over to his point of view on Cuba in their private meeting on 18 October. During their conversation, JFK not only displayed a general awareness of Robert Kennedy's views during their discussion, he also used the Pearl Harbor comparison to explain his concern over the air strike option. Acheson responded by saying he knew from whom the president had heard the analogy, and by once again expressing his disdain for it. He also used the meeting to indicate the value of dispatching a personal emissary to Europe to inform the NATO allies in general and the independently-minded French leader Charles de Gaulle in particular of the situation in Cuba and the response devised by the administration. This was an especially pressing issue because Charles Bohlen, the newly appointed ambassador to France, would be at sea for a number of days before arriving in Paris to assume his diplomatic duties. When Acheson suggested that Kennedy consider sending Lyndon Johnson to brief de Gaulle in person, the president neither concurred nor disagreed with the idea. At the conclusion of their tête-à-tête, JFK rose from his rocking chair in front of the fireplace and walked to the French doors. After gazing out at the Rose Garden for a considerable length of time, he reflected, "I guess I better earn my salary this week." "I'm afraid you have to," agreed Acheson. The meeting ended. Acheson, as developments later in the week would make clear, had failed to influence Kennedy's thinking.[22]

Kennedy had his first contact with a Soviet official since

learning about the missiles in Cuba later that same afternoon. Foreign Minister Gromyko came to the Oval Office at 5:00 p.m. for a meeting that had been arranged before 16 October. The main issues covered were Berlin and Cuba. Gromyko reiterated the demand made consistently by the Soviet government during the past four years, namely that a settlement of the Berlin question involving the withdrawal of the Western powers from the city must be reached. He indicated that the Soviets expected progress on this question after the congressional elections in November.[23]

Turning to Cuba, Gromyko denounced recent American policies in the Caribbean. "I should like to draw your attention," he said:

> to the dangerous development of events in connection with the US government's attitude to Cuba. For some considerable time, the American side has conducted an unrestrained anti-Cuban campaign and made attempts to block Cuban trade with other states. Calls for aggression against that country are being issued in the USA. This course can lead to serious consequences for the whole of mankind.

If Kennedy launched an attack on Cuba, Gromyko warned, the Soviet Union would respond. At the same time, he assured JFK that recent Soviet military aid was only intended to develop Cuban defensive capabilities. Kennedy listened to Gromyko's spiel poker-faced. His advisers had encouraged him before the meeting to resist the temptation to confront the foreign minister with the photographs proving the existence of surface-to-surface missiles in Cuba. This way Kennedy could keep the initiative, ensuring that he, not the Soviets, would be the first to inform the American public of the situation, and that he would be able to do so after having decided on his response to the missile deployment. In his meeting with Gromyko, therefore, the president confined himself to a recitation of his September warnings on the unacceptability of offensive missiles in Cuba.[24]

Although these early days of the missile crisis were almost unbearably tense for Kennedy and Acheson, as well as other American officials, there were lighter moments – sometimes at the expense of the former secretary of state. On one occasion Rusk, Ball, and Acheson took the elevator from the State Department garage to the secretary of state's seventh-floor office, accompanied by Rusk's security agents, Gus Peleusos and Bert Bennington. As the elevator ascended, Rusk told Ball and Acheson that the only sound advice he had received in the past week had been that offered by these two security men. Bennington, a former lineman for the Pittsburgh Steelers professional football team, explained, "The reason for that, Mr. Secretary, is that you have surrounded yourself with nothing but dumb fucks!" Rusk recalled that "George Ball blushed moderately, Dean Acheson turned a scarlet red." The secretary of state had all he could do to prevent himself from keeling over in laughter.[25]

The battle between Acheson and Robert Kennedy, having been joined on 17 October, resumed two days later. On that Friday the ExComm group held an all-day session in Ball's conference room. With the president again absent on the campaign trail in Ohio and Illinois, the discussion was fluid. It began with a debate over the legal implications of the use of American force against Cuba. Leonard Meeker spoke at length, suggesting that the administration obtain prior OAS approval for any action it intended to take. This would justify the use of force against Cuba under the terms of the UN Charter, which permitted regional arrangements in handling threats to international peace and security. Edwin Martin stated confidently that the United States would be able to secure the necessary votes in the OAS. Robert Kennedy expressed his concern over the possibility of embarrassment to his brother should the United States lose such a vote, and he wondered whether it might not be possible to be "perfectly sure of the outcome before seeking OAS concurrence."[26]

The discussion soon reverted to an analysis of the respective merits of the blockade and air strike options. Bundy, who explained that he had just spoken with the president that morning, indicated his support for the latter. Acheson agreed. Khrushchev "had presented the United States with a direct challenge, we were involved in a test of wills, and the sooner we got to a showdown the better. He favored cleaning the missile bases out decisively with an air strike." American action against Cuba was perfectly justified on the grounds of self-defence, and the United States should not, as Meeker had argued, make the execution of a military strike on Cuba dependent upon OAS approbation. Dillon, McCone, and Taylor, all endorsed Acheson's arguments for the air strike.[27]

Other officials remonstrated. McNamara once again affirmed his support for the blockade; and Robert Kennedy made an extended, impassioned case for the same approach. In making clear to Bundy who had the most access to his brother, he said "with a grin" that he too had spoken with the president, "indeed very recently this morning." He went on to enumerate the options. The Kennedy administration could do nothing but that "would be unthinkable." The other alternatives were either to initiate an air strike or to establish a blockade. Of the two, the air strike was the more problematic for the president given "the memory of Pearl Harbor and . . . all the implications this would have for us in whatever world there would be afterward." "For 175 years," he continued, "we had not been that kind of country. A sneak attack was not in our traditions. Thousands of Cubans would be killed without warning, and a lot of Russians too." Although he felt action was required to make Khrushchev aware of the depth of American resolve to remove the missiles from Cuba, "the action should allow the Soviets some room for maneuver to pull back from their over-extended position in Cuba."[28]

The chasm between the air strike advocates and blockade supporters was obviously still vast. To help bridge the gap, Rusk suggested that ExComm divide itself into two groups. One, consisting of designated leader Alexis Johnson, Llewellyn Thompson, Gilpatric, Martin, Nitze, and Meeker, was to flesh out its arguments by writing a precise, detailed draft describing the blockade scenario. The other group, to be headed by Bundy, and also comprising Dillon, Acheson, and Taylor, was to do the same for the air strike. The two groups would reconvene later in the day to critique each other's draft. Before ExComm split into those opposing camps, Sorensen announced that he had "absorbed enough" to begin writing a draft for the president's speech to the nation.[29]

Acheson decided to withdraw not only from the Bundy group's deliberations shortly after they had begun but also those of ExComm as a whole. He later explained his departure by saying that while he thought it appropriate to offer his general opinions, he did not consider it fitting for someone outside of the administration like himself to be privy to detailed secret plans for a military operation that might soon be executed. McGeorge Bundy has since revealed Acheson's authentic motivations. Before leaving the scene, Acheson told Bundy that he had gained the strong impression from his conversation with the president the previous day that he had already decided to follow the advice of Robert Kennedy and McNamara and implement the blockade. He felt there was no point in remaining to argue the case for an air strike when the matter had already been settled. An additional consideration may have been that sentiment within the Bundy group was in favour of a broader air strike rather than the more limited version that he preferred. As a result, Acheson decided to excuse himself from the ExComm sessions on the afternoon of 19 October. Two of Kennedy's close advisers recall that he "departed in a huff" to spend the weekend on his Maryland farm.[30]

Acheson's respite from governmental duties proved to be short-lived. On the evening of Saturday, 20 October, Rusk phoned to pass on the president's request that he travel immediately to France to brief de Gaulle about the situation in Cuba and the decision to initiate a blockade. Acheson readily consented to undertake the mission. He quoted Oliver Wendell Holmes to Rusk on how Americans belonged to the least exclusive club in the world, but the one with the highest dues, namely the United States. "You don't mind that your advice isn't being followed," asked the secretary of state. "Of course not," replied Acheson, "I'm not the President, and I'll do whatever I can do." Intimately involved in the founding of NATO, well-known for his interest in cultivating close relations between the United States and Western Europe, Acheson was certainly an appropriate choice for the mission.[31]

In the early morning of Sunday, 21 October, Acheson went to the State Department and then his Washington abode to garner some money, clothes, and an updated passport. Son-in-law and Defense Department official William P. Bundy drove him to an airfield, where an Air Force plane was preparing to take off for Europe. Once in the air, Acheson discovered that he was not alone. Also on board were the Ambassador to West Germany Walter C. Dowling (who was to brief Adenauer), Sherman Kent of the CIA, two other intelligence officials, and three armed guards. The plane touched down at Greenham Common air base in England around midnight. David K.E. Bruce, the United States ambassador to Britain, was there to meet the passengers. Bruce was provided with one of the CIA officials, a guard, and a set of photographs of the missiles in Cuba to help in the briefing of Harold Macmillan. The ambassador to Britain, for his part, had brought a bottle of Scotch to the air base. Both he and Acheson imbibed while waiting for the plane to depart. A weary Acheson finally landed in France at 2:30 on the morning of Monday, 22 October.[32]

As the former secretary of state prepared for his European sojourn on the morning of 21 October, Robert Kennedy continued to lend his support in Washington to the consensus now in favour of the blockade. When Maxwell Taylor and Tactical Air Command Chief General Walter C. Sweeney, Jr, explored the air strike option at a White House meeting, the attorney general was sharply critical. Such a strike, he contended once again, would represent "a Pearl Harbor type of attack." It might well provoke a Soviet military response that could trigger a general nuclear war between the superpowers. From 17 to 21 October, Robert Kennedy's argument had remained constant: an American air strike on Cuba was reprehensible because it would be equivalent to the Japanese assault on Pearl Harbor.[33]

In formulating their proposals during the first week of the missile crisis, Robert Kennedy and Acheson were motivated by different considerations. For the attorney general, the principal factor behind his opposition to the air attack and his support for the blockade, in addition to the genuine concern he felt about the possibility that a strike would lead to a costly war, was the inveterate desire he always felt to protect the interests of his brother in a personal sense. In fathoming Robert Kennedy's performance during the crisis, it is far more useful to think in terms of his clannish devotion to the president rather than an attachment to any particular foreign policy ideology.

That clannishness had deep roots. Robert Kennedy had been raised in an environment which stressed the importance of familial loyalty. During his formative political years, RFK's role was paternally defined as the protector and promoter of his elder brother's interests. In JFK's 1952 race for the Senate, his 1956 bid for the vice-presidential nomination at the Democratic Convention, and his 1960 campaign for the presidency, Robert Kennedy worked indefatigably on behalf of his brother's political ambitions. His actions at the 1956 Democratic Convention typified the role he played before becoming attorney general. When Mennen Williams, a member of the Michigan delegation that supported Tennessee Senator Estes Kefauver over John Kennedy for the vice-presidential nomination, left the Convention floor, an animated Robert Kennedy grabbed his arm and indignantly asked, "Why are you against my brother?" Williams was "flabbergasted" by such behaviour. This, then, rather than endeavours which involved the thoughtful conceptualisation of foreign policy or any other policy, was the sort of political activity in which Robert Kennedy participated before the "Camelot" years.[34]

After the 1960 election, Robert Kennedy continued to guard his brother's interests zealously. "Bobby's big objective," Nicholas Katzenbach recalled, "was always to serve his brother." This was the "central motivation that he had." In 1964 Walt Rostow described his impressions of the attorney general at the time of the Bay of Pigs: "[He was a] thick-skinned guy: tremendously focused on his brother, Jack. And he could get hurt worse than Jack if things went badly for Jack, as they had just done [in the Bay of Pigs]. But he wasn't acting for himself. His mature personality has still got to emerge."[35]

Robert Kennedy was not afraid to protect his brother by using a mailed fist rather than kid gloves. As Maxwell Taylor observed, "Bobby became to an extent the hatchet man. He did the unpleasant things. I must say he has a rugged nature, and I don't think he ever shied away from it." Many officials, according to Rostow, came to regard RFK as "a kind of tough, conservative thug." Dean Rusk felt that he was "ruthless on personnel matters." John P. Roche, one-time chairman of the Americans for Democratic Action, described him as a "demonic little bastard." Alexis Johnson recalled his behaviour at meetings of the Special Group for Counterinsurgency. During those sessions, he would "bore in with some lower officials of the Government." One particular presentation so dissatisfied him that he "got up and slammed the chair on the floor and stalked out of the room, slamming the door." Johnson came to the conclusion that the attorney general was "the fearless watchdog on behalf of the President. He had enormous possessive pride in the President, and he was looking after the President's interests in a way which, he felt, ... the President could not do."[36]

Robert Kennedy's intense, aggressive devotion to his brother was evident in various ways. One of them was his tendency to judge other officials by the loyalty they exhibited to the president rather than the value of their advice. On one occasion shortly after the Bay of Pigs, when it had become common knowledge that Chester Bowles had opposed the operation, Bobby Kennedy grabbed the under secretary of state by his coat collar and chided him for being disloyal to the president by failing to conceal his dissent. That Bowles had been right about the Bay of Pigs, and hence the idea that his views merited greater attention than they had hitherto received, did not occur to him. He was similarly vexed by John McCone for later revealing that in the months preceding the missile crisis he had told JFK that the Soviets were installing missiles in Cuba. McCone's suspicions proved to be well-founded. Yet instead of praising his prescience, Robert Kennedy would subsequently criticise the CIA director. Motivated no doubt by a sense that McCone had embarrassed his brother, he erroneously claimed that McCone had not explained to the president his belief that Khrushchev would put missiles in Cuba. He also complained that the problem with the CIA director was that although he "liked the president very much, ... he liked one person more and that was John McCone."[37]

In the context of American policy towards Cuba in the pre-missile crisis period, Robert Kennedy's interest in bolstering his brother's credibility translated into a burning desire to overthrow Castro after the humiliation of the Bay of Pigs. Only two weeks before he made his impassioned arguments in ExComm against the air strike, he was browbeating administration officials for the elephantine pace at which they were executing Operation Mongoose. At a 4 October meeting of the SGA he urged his colleagues to organise "massive activity" against Cuba. His exhortations resulted in a decision by the SGA to increase covert actions aimed at weakening Castro's position.[38]

When he learned of the missile deployment in Cuba on 16 October, Robert Kennedy initially favoured an invasion. But the more he considered the situation from the perspective of his brother's reputation, the more perturbed he became by the possibility that the missile crisis would lead to a superpower conflict. Then his brother would be labelled as the president who embroiled the United States in a third and potentially nuclear world war. Military action against Cuba, because of the likelihood that it would provoke a Soviet military response, was the least satisfactory option from this point of view. For the attorney general, it was not just a question of the air strike (or invasion) representing an inappropriate policy for the United States *per se*, but also a case that his brother should not, as he declared in the ExComm group, become the Tojo of the 1960s.

In contrast to Robert Kennedy, Acheson's arguments did flow from a firmly-held cluster of foreign policy convictions, including a commitment to use force if necessary. This, in Acheson's view, entailed a willingness to approach the brink of nuclear war in crisis situations in order to force the Soviet Union to back down and accept American objectives. Acheson came to embrace these ideas as his foreign policy philosophy evolved during the 1950s. Originally, his views had placed him at the centre of the spectrum of Cold War opinion in 1940s Washington that was committed to the avoidance of 1930s-style appeasement and the development of containment. Given his involvement in the enunciation of the Truman Doctrine and Marshall Plan, and the establishment of NATO, Acheson was not only a supporter of containment; he helped define the concept. To the left of that centre were those like Henry Wallace who criticised American foreign policy for having abandoned Roosevelt's policy of co-operation with the Soviet Union. To the right of Acheson were various figures, including a young John Kennedy, who felt that the Truman administration had incompetently 'lost' Eastern Europe and then China to the Communists. Perhaps the clearest indication that Acheson was not one of the most belligerent Cold Warriors in the 1940s is the fact that he was not part of that coterie of officials (which included Under Secretary of State Joseph C. Grew, Admiral William D. Leahy, and Secretary of the Navy James V. Forrestal) who argued in spring 1945 that the opportunity afforded by Roosevelt's death should be used to fashion a more hardline policy towards Stalin. Acheson did not advocate a tougher approach to the Soviet Union until the crisis over Iran in spring 1946.[39]

Whereas Acheson was in the mainstream of Cold War opinion in the late 1940s, he moved to the right during the 1950s. With the election of Dwight Eisenhower as president in 1952, a distinction emerged between those who subscribed to containment, and those, led by the new secretary of state, John Foster Dulles, who suggested it needed to be revamped by the introduction of such concepts as "brinksmanship" and "massive retaliation." On leaving the State Department in 1953, Acheson emerged as a sharp critic of his successor. (He once stunned a dinner party when he declared, after the death of Dulles, "Thank God Foster is underground.") Amongst other things, he assailed Dulles for his advocacy of brinksmanship and massive retaliation. In *Power and Diplomacy*, Acheson argued that these tactics had prevented neither communist aggression in Korea and Indo-China nor the Soviet crushing of the 1956 Hungarian uprising. The United States, he explained, was obviously unwilling to risk nuclear war over these sorts of issues.[40]

Although Acheson ostensibly disavowed the concepts behind Dulles' diplomacy, his foreign policy philosophy developed during the 1950s so that his views began to coincide with those of the new secretary of state. For example, he started to support the idea that it was necessary to approach the brink of nuclear war if international crises were to be resolved without forsaking American interests. In a 1959 presentation to students at the Columbia Journalism School, he indicated his newly-acquired belief in brinksmanship. The United States, he elucidated, must be ready to increase tensions to a point where adversaries "act on the basis of fear. . . . So the Russians will say, 'We may get a strike when we're not expecting it.' This is the only thing to do. This is what you call the delicate balance of terror."[41]

Acheson's commitment to brinksmanship was again evident in the summer of 1961 when he served as an *ad hoc* adviser to the Kennedy administration during the Berlin crisis. On 28 June 1961 he furnished the president with a report recommending the declaration of a national emergency, a full mobilisation of America's military forces, an increase in defence expenditure by $5 billion, and a tax hike. In short, the United States needed to prepare for a possible nuclear engagement. As two authorities on Acheson have suggested, the former secretary of state, "despite his disdain for Dulles, was calling for brinksmanship."[42]

In the missile crisis, Acheson once again displayed his penchant for brinksmanship. The clear premise behind his arguments in ExComm was that the Kennedy administration had to demonstrate its willingness to approach the very brink of nuclear war. He thought it quite likely, moreover, that his proposals would take the United States to the precipice of a nuclear conflict. At one point, possibly during the ExComm session on 17 October, one official asked Acheson how he thought the Soviets would respond to an air strike on the missiles in Cuba. Acheson replied, "I know the Soviet Union well. I know what they are required to do in the light of their history and their posture around the world. I think they will knock out our missiles in Turkey." This was followed by another question: "Well, then what do we do?" "Well," answered Acheson, "I believe under our NATO treaty with which I was associated, we would be required to respond by knocking out a missile base inside the Soviet Union." Asked how the Soviets would react to this, Acheson stated "that's when we hope cooler heads will prevail, and they'll stop and talk." This was, Sorensen recalled, "a rather chilling conversation for all of us."[43]

The transformation of Acheson from a supporter of containment to a proponent of brinksmanship was caused by various factors. No doubt the new examples of communist aggression, as in Korea, and Soviet brutality, such as the crushing of the 1956 Hungarian uprising, had the effect of convincing Acheson that the United States needed to adopt an even tougher approach to the communist challenge than that defined by containment. Also significant was the simple fact that the Democrats lost the presidency in 1952. As a leading member of the party out of power, it was natural for Acheson to develop a critique of the Eisenhower administration's policies, particularly in his area of expertise, foreign policy. It was equally to be expected that this critique would develop the theme that Eisenhower was too timid in dealing with the communist threat – the standard criticism levelled at an incumbent president by the party out of power during the Cold War era. This, then, tended to make Acheson's views increasingly hardline.

The other factor which ossified Acheson's foreign policy outlook during the 1950s was McCarthyism, and specifically the scathing attack launched by Senator McCarthy on Acheson during the latter's tenure as secretary of state. Acheson had originally made himself vulnerable to that assault by the way he handled a January 1950 press conference held only three days after Alger Hiss had been convicted of perjury for lying at a House Un-American Activities Committee hearing about supplying classified documents to a communist agent. Hiss had impeccable Establishment credentials and Acheson had worked quite closely with him in the State Department. Refusing to condemn Hiss, he declared at the press conference: "I do not intend to turn my back on Alger Hiss."[44]

This was fodder for McCarthy. As he began his campaign on 9 February 1950 against what he claimed to be heavy communist infiltration of the Truman administration, Acheson figured prominently among those whom the Wisconsin senator sought to vilify. McCarthy accused the secretary of state of protecting card-carrying communists in the State Department, and used his defence of Hiss as a concrete example. He also resorted to cheap abuse, referring to Acheson as "this pompous diplomat in striped pants with a phony British accent", and dubbing him "the red Dean."[45]

Acheson, of course, responded to McCarthy's charges with stoicism. None the less, the experience was traumatic. The torrent of abuse was so great that he felt compelled to offer his resignation as secretary of state, although Truman refused to accept it. By June 1950 the crank mail generated by McCarthy's assault led to the installation of guards around

Acheson twenty-four hours a day. This was, Acheson later recalled, "a regimen not conducive to relaxation." His wife, Alice, later maintained that McCarthy's attack took ten years off her husband's life.[46]

The fact that Acheson was a notable figure in the American Establishment (educated at Groton, Yale, and Harvard Law School) must have made McCarthy's charges even harder for Acheson to stomach. The very blessing bestowed by membership in the Establishment was, by definition, a sense of legitimacy, endowing members, including the secretary of state, with a feeling of assurance and confidence. By accusing Acheson of nurturing communism in the State Department, McCarthy had in effect questioned Acheson's patriotism and credibility, and, therefore, his legitimacy as well. For someone to whom that was a birthright, this was not only a sobering but also a shattering experience.

McCarthy's attack clearly influenced Acheson's thinking. In *A Democrat Looks at His Party*, published in 1955, he used a sizeable portion of the book to condemn the way in which inordinate fear of communism in the United States during the early 1950s had reduced individual liberties. McCarthy shaped Acheson's foreign policy views, on the other hand, by making them more virulently anti-communist. This did not escape the attention of some of Acheson's contemporaries. Charles Bohlen, for example, stated: "I have always felt that the personal assaults made Acheson more rigid in his anti-Soviet attitude after he left the government. Some of his bitterness welled up later. He became much more caustic in his descriptions of people and downright dogmatic in his view of events." McCarthy's calumnies left Acheson with scars as well as a determination never again to be vulnerable to the accusation that he was "soft" on communism. In the process, it helped generate the array of hawkish beliefs that came to underpin Acheson's foreign policy philosophy.[47]

The factor of McCarthyism probably contributed in another, more obscure sense to Acheson's performance in ExComm. In the early part of his career, Robert Kennedy had worked as an assistant counsel to the McCarthy-chaired Senate Subcommittee on Investigations. As a result of his association with the Wisconsin senator, Acheson had developed a dislike for Robert Kennedy, and that probably made him eager to engage in a debate in which his chief antagonist was the attorney general. For Acheson, it may have been a case, at least to a limited extent, of old scores to settle.[48]

There were perhaps other reasons why Acheson so zealously challenged Robert Kennedy in the ExComm meetings. Acheson was an incorrigible snob and he may have viewed Robert Kennedy, with his Irish, new-money background, as something of a presumptuous, pushy parvenu. Acheson also took great pride in his reputation as a foreign policy pundit, and he tended to feel competitive towards others who also claimed an expertise. He had, for example, clashed in the 1950s with virtually every other prominent authority on international affairs, including Walter Lippmann, George Kennan, Dulles, and Stevenson. It would seem likely, then, that Acheson's competitive instincts were aroused by the attorney general's tendency to dominate the ExComm discussions.[49]

In the contest between Acheson and Robert Kennedy, it was the attorney general who won the day: the president decided to opt for the blockade. Although that decision was not revealed to the American public until JFK's television address on 22 October, he had basically made up his mind several days before. The support he had originally expressed for an air strike in the 16 October ExComm sessions was still evident the next morning. McCone noticed at a 9:30 meeting with JFK that he "seemed inclined to act promptly if at all, without warning, targetting on MRBM's [medium-range ballistic missiles] and possibly airfields. Stated Congressional Resolution gave him all authority he needed and this was confirmed by Bundy, and therefore seemed inclined to act."[50]

By 18 October, however, the president had withdrawn his backing for the air strike. At an 11:00 a.m. meeting with his advisers he was, according to McCone, "non-committal." His main concern with any American policy centred on the "reactions of our allies, NATO, South America, public opinion and others." A few hours later, though, in his afternoon conversation with Acheson, he indicated a preference for the blockade. He did so again at a meeting of senior officials on the evening of 18 October. In the 19 October

ExComm session, one official, reflecting back upon the previous evening's White House talks, commented that the discussion had resulted in "a tentative conclusion to institute
a blockade" and that Kennedy had been "satisfied" with this
consensus. Paul Nitze has written of the same meeting that
the president "listened to our differing recommendations,
and then tentatively decided that in a televised speech he
would reveal to the world the presence of the Soviet missiles in Cuba and our intention of implementing a naval
quarantine." So JFK had provisionally decided to blockade
Cuba as early as 18 October.[51]

According to Robert Kennedy, his brother made the de-
finitive decision in favour of the blockade two days later on
the afternoon of Saturday, 20 October. An Oval Office meeting
held on 21 October and attended by the Kennedys,
McNamara, Taylor, and General Sweeney helped to dissi-
pate any doubt still felt by the president. During the course
of the discussion, Sweeney acknowledged that "even under
optimum conditions, it was not likely that all of the known
missiles [in Cuba] would be destroyed" by an air strike. Taylor
added that, "The best we can offer you is to destroy 90% of
the known missiles." So although a blockade would not in
itself remove the missiles from Cuba, an air strike would
not be wholly successful in that respect, either. In other
words, Soviet reprisals from the missile sites in Cuba was a
real possibility.[52]

An interesting parallel to the transformation in Kennedy's
outlook was the evolution in Dwight Eisenhower's views during
the early days of the missile crisis. At JFK's behest, McCone
informed the former president on 17 October about the
situation in Cuba without indicating how the administration
intended to react. "Throughout the conversation," McCone
noted, "Eisenhower seemed to lean toward (but did not
specifically recommend) military action which would cut off
Havana and therefore take over the heart of the government. He thought this might be done by airborne divisions."
Four days later, though, Eisenhower had switched his support to the blockade. Air strikes, he told McCone after another briefing, were never entirely successful, and American
military action against Cuba "would license other countries
to resort to violent military action without notice." Had Eisen-

hower been at the helm in the missile crisis, then, the American response would probably not have differed.[53]

In the process by which JFK transferred his support from the air strike to the blockade, Robert Kennedy played the crucial role. As president, John Kennedy relied heavily on his brother for advice on the formulation of policy, as well as action to implement it. Bowles once observed that, "Management, in Jack Kennedy's mind consisted largely of calling Bob on the telephone and saying, 'Here are ten things I want to get done.'" After the Bay of Pigs, the president's dependence on his brother increased when he decided to bring the attorney general into the foreign policy-making process. Robert Kennedy recalled that apart from himself, the president trusted no-one in the aftermath of the Bay of Pigs. So disenchanted was JFK with the CIA that he wanted his brother to replace Allen Dulles as director. Robert Kennedy dissuaded him, arguing that a Republican should be appointed to the position.[54]

John Kennedy relied even more than usual on the attorney general's talents during October 1962. In later years, Robert Kennedy acknowledged that along with the Berlin crisis, Bay of Pigs, the steel dispute, and the Oxford, Mississippi incident, the episode in which the president depended upon him most was the missile crisis. As soon as John Kennedy learned on the morning of 16 October of the missiles in Cuba, he called his brother. Even on a day like 19 October when he was away on the campaign trail in Ohio and Illinois, he kept abreast of the situation by speaking to Robert Kennedy on the phone. And the first offiicial that he consulted on his return to the White House from Chicago on 20 October was RFK. As John Kennedy went for a swim, Bobby sat at the side of the pool, and the two men discussed the crisis. They continued to talk as they walked to the Oval Room for an ExComm meeting. As Robert Kennedy later wrote that the president made an unequivocal commitment to the blockade that afternoon, this conversation may have been crucial to the making of that commitment.[55]

For the critical conversations which helped convert JFK from an air strike advocate to a blockade supporter, there is, however, very little contemporaneous documentary evidence. It is clear from Acheson's recollection of his discussion with John Kennedy on 18 October, for instance, that there was at least one crucial meeting (or telephone conversation) in which Robert Kennedy convinced the president of the cogency of the Pearl Harbor analogy. But there is no record of that discussion. That such conversations took place, however, is beyond doubt. The Director of the Office of Emergency Planning Edward A. McDermott recalled that in ExComm the president would on occasion leave the meeting, and walk on to the porch on the second floor of the White House overlooking the South Lawn. Then he:

> would stand out there alone for a few minutes and on another occasion, possibly on both occasions that I'm referring to he would be joined by Bobby, his brother. They would have a discussion – the President would come back and join the group and would indicate a particular decision or judgment that he made.

As a consequence of the anomalous situation of two brothers (and two particularly close ones at that) holding the two most important positions in the administration, many key conversations occurred outside of ExComm and produced no written records. Hence, the influence exerted by RFK on his elder brother was probably even greater than is suggested by the available evidence. Although Dean Rusk was secretary of state, and Robert McNamara secretary of defense, their importance in shaping the president's policies during the first week of the missile crisis paled in comparison to Robert Kennedy's.[56]

If the arguments expounded by the attorney general constituted the primary reason for the President's decision to transfer his support from the air strike to the blockade, the issue of Berlin represented a secondary factor. JFK had resisted the temptation to respond to the Bay of Pigs failure by launching a full-scale attack on Cuba because he feared that Khrushchev would react by moving on Berlin. This appears to have been a consideration during the first week of the missile crisis too. When at one point in discussions with the Joint Chiefs, General Curtis E. LeMay argued that the Soviets would not retaliate to a military assault on Cuba, the president disagreed. The Soviets, he explained, "no more than we, can let these things go by without doing something. They can't, after all their statements, permit us to take out their missiles, kill a lot of Russians, and then do nothing. If they don't take action in Cuba, they certainly will in Berlin." During another meeting, JFK observed that "if we made a move against Cuba," Khrushchev would announce that he was going to "take Berlin."[57]

John Kennedy made the right decision in accepting the fraternal advice he received over that offered by Acheson. The former secretary of state's arguments were unpersuasive for various reasons. Their shortcomings included some convenient double-standards. For example, Acheson maintained that the Soviet Union was obliged to abide by what he regarded as the quasi-legal concept of the Monroe Doctrine. At the same time, he claimed that the Kennedy administration need not worry about whether its response to the missile deployment in Cuba contravened international law.

More importantly, Acheson's arguments were flawed because the general concept of brinksmanship, which his proposals embodied, was itself flawed. Brinksmanship was based on the assumption that in any confrontation Washington could continuously up the ante because any adversary, including the Soviet Union, would inevitably back down before the United States felt compelled to do so. Yet there was no clear reason why that would always be the case. In addition, this approach depended upon being able to determine precisely the point at which the brink would be reached in order to avoid its traversal. But how could anyone, including Acheson, *know* when that point had been reached? How could Acheson assume with such apparent equanimity that an air strike killing thousands of Soviet military personnel and destroying dozens of Soviet missiles would not in itself cross the point at which Khrushchev felt it necessary to respond in kind? Obviously, the location of the brink could not be established with precision, especially because Khrushchev himself had probably not determined what for him constituted the brink, the point at which Soviet retaliation was imperative; and so if he did not know that, there was no way Acheson could either.

Also unwarranted was Acheson's assumption that an air strike limited to the missile sites was a relatively safe option because it avoided the outcome that Robert Kennedy feared, namely the deaths of thousands of innocent Cuban civilians. Only a few thousand Soviets, Acheson observed, would be killed. Yet in terms of the likelihood of a military response from Khrushchev, a strike causing the deaths of thousands of Soviets was presumably far more dangerous than one which killed Cubans. Acheson simply did not broach that issue. There were, moreover, far more than just a few thousand Soviet military personnel in Cuba in October 1962. The actual figure was around 42 000. For all these reasons, his recommmendations were dangerous because they ran the risk of eliciting a Soviet military response, and thereby escalating the missile crisis into a generalised Soviet-American (possibly nuclear) war.[58]

The air strike was a less attractive option than the blockade in other ways. The quarantine had the advantage of supplying a period of time in which a negotiated settlement to the crisis could be reached, and that was what ultimately occurred. The air strike furnished no such temporal benefit. Also the blockade would not damage America's international credibility in the way that an air strike would have done. Acheson argued that the United States was compelled to take action against the missiles in Cuba in part because a supine response would reduce confidence in American leadership throughout Western Europe and the Western Hemisphere. He did not recognise the likelihood that an air strike which ran the risk of a nuclear war, into which America's allies certainly in Western Europe and conceivably in Latin America might be drawn, would have eroded American credibility to a greater extent than if the Soviets had managed to install missiles in Cuba permanently.

Robert Kennedy was a foreign policy novice in comparison to Dean Acheson. The subject had only engaged his attention to any significant degree for the year and a half since the Bay of Pigs. Acheson, on the other hand, had devoted the past quarter-century to the analysis and implementation of American diplomacy. He had held all the important positions in the State Department: Assistant Secretary of State, Under Secretary of State, and Secretary of State. He had been an important promoter of American intervention in World War II, one of the founding fathers of containment, and a leading critic of the Eisenhower-Dulles foreign policy. He had written acclaimed books on diplomacy. In fact, his acknowledged expertise was such that in the early 1960s he was accorded a deference occasionally bordering on sycophancy by many of John Kennedy's own advisers, including Nitze, Rusk, and McGeorge Bundy.

Despite his relative lack of experience, Robert Kennedy supplied his brother with sounder advice during the first week of the missile crisis than that offered by Acheson. It would be fair to say of the attorney general that his was not a great mind. He was neither a sophisticated nor a careful, precise thinker. The analogy between the Japanese attack on Pearl Harbor and an American strike on Cuba was clumsy. Acheson was right: the former was launched without caveat whereas the United States had issued ample warning that it would not tolerate Soviet missiles in Cuba. None the less, Robert Kennedy did possess a sort of native commonsense. Alexis Johnson was exactly right when he said of the attorney general, "his instincts were right. He might not be too well informed, he might fix on the wrong things, but he was generally sound on the big issues." Johnson reflected that this was "particularly true when it came to the missile crisis in Cuba." It was indeed this sense wedded to his desire to protect his brother's reputation which together sparked Robert Kennedy's scepticism towards the air strike and prompted him to support the blockade instead.[59]

The salient shortcoming of the attorney general's proposals, however, was their failure to conceptualise or anticipate how the initiation of the blockade would end the crisis. Robert Kennedy summarised his view of this issue during a 21 October meeting when he argued that after the establishment of the blockade, the United States would have to "play for the breaks." It was, therefore, a matter of Robert Kennedy feeling instinctively that the blockade would somehow defuse the crisis rather than his intellectualising how that might happen. But one adviser did manage to describe a path by which the Kennedy administration might progress from the establishment of the blockade to the resolution of the crisis. He was America's ambassador to the United Nations in New York.[60]

7 Adlai Stevenson: Hamlet in New York

Harry Truman was only one of many observers who likened Adlai Stevenson to Hamlet. "Those who make the comparison," as Richard Goodwin explains, "do so as a metaphor of irresolution. Hamlet is the story of a man who tries to understand and reach for certainty before he strikes." The origins of the analogy lay no doubt in Stevenson's seemingly timid and certainly unsuccessful bids for the presidency in 1952 and 1956. He seemed so much more intelligent, erudite, witty, imaginative, and stylish than his Republican rival, Dwight Eisenhower, altogether the superior candidate, and yet on both occasions the popular war-hero trounced him. It was as if the one-term governor of Illinois liked the smell of success, but was unwilling to do what was required to achieve it. Other episodes contributed to this image, especially his decision in 1956 to forfeit the right of selecting his vice-presidential running partner to the floor of the Democratic Convention. Critics felt such incidents demonstrated his indecisiveness and lack of judgement.[1]

Stevenson's performance in the Cuban missile crisis has been used to buttress this disparaging view of his talents. Whereas other ExComm officials advocated either a blockade or military action, Stevenson, it has been alleged, developed a plan for a diplomatic settlement that was "soft." That harsh assessment was originally made by journalists Stewart Alsop and Charles Bartlett in a December 1962 *Saturday Evening Post* article, "In Time of Crisis." Although Alsop and Bartlett devoted only a few paragraphs to Stevenson, that was all they needed to launch a brutal assault on his credibility; for they condemned him with what they did not say almost as much as with what they did. On one page there was a series of photographs of and information on "the key advisers to whom President Kennedy turned," men to whom he "will turn . . . again with each new challenge in the Cold War." Stevenson was conspicuously absent. The next page had a particularly damning headline: "An opponent charges, 'Adlai wanted a Munich. He wanted to trade U.S. bases for Cuban bases.'" Also included was a full page picture of a pensive, diffident-looking Stevenson. The part of the actual text on the UN ambassador portrayed him as the successor to Neville Chamberlain. Alsop and Bartlett quoted a "nonadmiring official" as saying "Adlai wanted a Munich" in that he wished "to trade the Turkish, Italian and British missile bases for the Cuban bases." The article was obviously an *ad hominem* attack on Stevenson.[2]

Since Bartlett was an intimate friend of Kennedy, there was immediate speculation in the press that the story had been authorised by the president, and, further, that it presaged Stevenson's removal as UN ambassador. The autumn 1961 dismissal of Bowles as under secretary of state had been preceded by a denunciatory Bartlett article that was now viewed as a precedent for Stevenson. Supporters of the ambassador, angered by the treatment of their hero, rallied to his defence. The fervour with which they did so left Kennedy bemused. "Lyndon Johnson doesn't have a cult," he remarked in a telephone conversation with Bartlett, "I don't have a cult, how does Adlai get a cult?"[3]

To allay the suspicions of the press, public, and Stevenson himself, the president issued statements stressing both his continued confidence in the ambassador and his regret over the article. Rumours that he had sanctioned the attack persisted, however, because he did not indicate his disagreement with the article's disparaging description of the Illinoisan's performance. When asked at a 12 December press conference, for example, about the fact that he had not denied the veracity of what Alsop and Bartlett had written about Stevenson, Kennedy dodged the question, saying he was not prepared to discuss "the various positions of the members of the National Security Council."[4]

The Alsop-Bartlett piece left its victim dispirited. "This latest assault," Stevenson wrote a friend, "set a new record for malice and falsehood." In a 5 December 1962 television interview, he explained to the American public that he was "used to assassins. I remember McCarthy, very well indeed." To some friends and colleagues and to Kennedy himself, Stevenson expressed satisfaction at the president's defence

of him during the uproar over the article. But to his closest
confidants, he revealed his true feelings. He told Harlan
Cleveland that he suspected either John or Robert Kennedy
had leaked information to Alsop and Bartlett. Stevenson,
Cleveland recalled, was "extremely distressed" by that
possibility.[5]

Stevenson's suspicions were well-founded. Despite John
Kennedy's disavowal of involvement, he was in fact the central figure in the attack on Stevenson. As early as 29 October 1962, a day after the resolution of the missile crisis,
Bartlett wrote the president, saying he wished to do a piece
with Stewart Alsop on the recent confrontation over Cuba
for the *Saturday Evening Post.* He told JFK that he wanted to
write the article "without involving you directly." The obvious implication was that the president would be involved
indirectly. Kennedy seems to have taken little time in approving the idea, for two days later Bartlett sent him a laconic handwritten note: "Stewart and I are going ahead on
that piece for *The Sateve Post.*"[6]

Sunday, 11 November, was probably the day JFK provided
Bartlett with his account of the missile crisis. The president
and first lady spent that weekend at Glen Ora, their rented
estate in Middleburg, Virginia. After attending mass, they
returned to Glen Ora before leaving for Rattlesnake Mountain Farm in the company of Bartlett and his wife. JFK spent
at least the period from 12:50 to 2:00 p.m. with Bartlett,
easily enough time to furnish the journalist with a cursory
description of the recent crisis. The president's appointment
book does not make it clear, but he may well have spent
the rest of the day with Bartlett as well. Kennedy was certainly of a mind at this time to present Bartlett with an
unflattering view of Stevenson. At a dinner with Ben Bradlee
only four days later, he spoke in terms which, the journalist
noted, "did nothing to dispel the rumors that he was less
than 100 percent behind his UN ambassador."[7]

Over the years, other evidence has surfaced that conclus-
ively demonstrates Kennedy's involvement in the preparation of the *Post* story. Alsop has written that in general JFK
was "a good source as well as a good friend." In specific
reference to the piece on the missile crisis, he has disclosed
that the president not only read the text of the article be-

fore its publication but also made a number of changes in the section on Stevenson. Kennedy, according to Alsop, "cut out two or three sentences which reflected [Stevenson spokesman] Clayton [Fritchey]'s explication and justification for Stevenson's position on the bases. Stevenson's position was thus made to seem less rational than in fact it was." Alsop maintained that this distortion was simply a careless error on the part of the president, caused by fatigue. That argument seems naive. It was far more likely he did this quite deliberately to discredit Stevenson. Bartlett later acknowledged that JFK did feel "the article was accurate. I think he would have stood behind every aspect of the article."[8]

Not only was Kennedy interviewed for the Alsop-Bartlett story, not only did he actually annotate the text, he was himself the "nonadmiring official" who claimed "Adlai wanted a Munich." Stewart Alsop revealed this to Don A. Schanche and Clay Blair, the executive and managing editors of the *Saturday Evening Post*, before the piece went into print. When Blair instructed Alsop and Bartlett to check with Kennedy as to whether he really wished to include such an incendiary quotation, the president was adamant: "I want it in."[9]

Although JFK played the key role in shaping the passages of the article on Stevenson, Alsop and Bartlett did interview many other officials, including Robert Kennedy, McGeorge Bundy, and Fritchey. They may also have used Acheson and McCone as sources. Both had clear motivations for assailing Stevenson. Acheson had disliked him ever since the 1952 presidential campaign when Stevenson sought to distance himself from the Truman administration by refusing to defend Acheson's performance as secretary of state from Republican criticism. During the late 1950s, Acheson and Stevenson again clashed by engaging in a fierce debate within the Democratic Advisory Council over the future direction of their party on foreign policy issues. Although it is true that Acheson and Stevenson were never present in ExComm at the same time, Acheson may well have learned of Stevenson's comments from other officials, possibly McGeorge Bundy. Acheson was close to Bundy, partly because his daughter had married Bundy's brother. Adding to the likelihood of Acheson's involvement in the *Post* article was his relationship with Stewart Alsop. They were friends who often dined together at the Metropolitan Club. They also had much in common, having both grown up in Middletown, Connecticut, and then gone on to Groton and Yale. Stevenson himself, according to a January 1962 newspaper story, suspected Acheson's involvement in the Alsop-Bartlett article.[10]

McCone's distaste for Stevenson stretched back to the 1956 presidential campaign. When scientists from the California Institute of Technology (of which McCone was a trustee) publicly expressed support for Stevenson's idea of a nuclear test ban, an outraged McCone attacked them, claiming they had been duped by Soviet propaganda. He tried, allegedly, to have them dismissed. His antipathy for Stevenson was probably also created by philosophical differences. As an extreme conservative, he must have found the Illinoisan's quintessential liberalism repugnant. Stevenson himself seems to have suspected McCone's involvement in the Alsop-Bartlett affair. In a January 1963 letter to his friend, British economist Barbara Ward, he speculated that Alsop and Bartlett "got most of their untruths from jingoists at [the] CIA."[11]

Why, then, had these officials, led by Kennedy himself, sought to discredit Stevenson? Different officials had different reasons but for John and Robert Kennedy their main goal was probably to prevent any future challenge by Stevenson for the presidency. During the 1950s and into 1960, they had viewed him as their principal antagonist in the contest for the 1960 Democratic presidential nomination. As a rival to JFK, Stevenson possessed superior liberal credentials, but his main point of political vulnerability was the notion that he was "soft" on communism.

The Cuban missile crisis, however, changed that perception. Stevenson's scintillating performance in the United Nations on 25 October won over many who had previously thought him too weak. Mountains of favourable mail poured into his office in the aftermath of the October confrontation. The correspondence indicated that his dramatic showdown with Zorin, the Soviet ambassador to the UN, had added a new constituency to Stevenson's traditional following. Even the Republicans in Lake Forest, an affluent Chicago suburb, who had snubbed Stevenson throughout his career, felt exhilarated by his showing in the Security Council.

As Jane Dick, a close friend of Stevenson, noted, the Lake Forest Republicans "had always thought him too liberal. Then came this speech [on 25 October]. They thought, 'At long last he's got some guts and stature.' Suddenly he was their champion." To the Kennedys, a stylish Stevenson who was the darling of the liberal set was worrying in itself. But a Stevenson with both liberal appeal and anti-communist credentials was even more disconcerting.[12]

The possibility that Stevenson's UN performance had evoked suspicions that he might once again seek the Democratic presidential nomination did not escape the attention of contemporaries. W. LeRoy Garth, a Stevenson supporter in California, speculated in a letter to the ambassador that, "Your enemies began to get jealous and to begin to think of you in terms of 1964 and '68. So they decided to take you down a peg or two?!" Harlan Cleveland stated retrospectively that he could envisage Robert Kennedy:

> having an instinct for the jugular on the political jealousy. It was, "Hey, now. We've got to watch this guy. He's going to become a national hero, coming out against the Communists this way. When the only real chink in his armor has been that he's a liberal and soft and so forth. He might be a real alternative to Kennedy in 1964. And we better cut him down to size, fellas."[13]

It is unlikely the Kennedys wished to force Stevenson's resignation over the Alsop-Bartlett article. His ability to act as a critic of the president's policies was nullified by his presence within the administration. As the United States ambassador to the UN, Stevenson felt obliged to defend Kennedy's policies, especially because of his strong sense of duty and loyalty. He would certainly have represented far more of a threat from outside the administration, where he would be free to assail the president. Moreover, the original premise behind Stevenson's appointment as UN ambassador, that this would placate those liberals who doubted Kennedy's own commitment to liberal causes, remained valid. But an attack on Stevenson via the *Saturday Evening Post* could destroy his credibility and wreck any plans he might conceivably have to challenge JFK by running again for the Democratic presidential nomination in 1964.

Kennedy's use of Alsop and Bartlett to besmirch Stevenson's reputation, after he had done such yeoman service in the UN during the missile crisis, was cynical, vindictive, and vicious. It adds weight to historian Thomas C. Reeves' charge that Kennedy lacked character. Nevertheless, the *Post* article's long-term influence has been significant. Stevenson was the only American official to articulate a carefully conceived alternative to the strategies of a military attack upon or a blockade of Cuba. Yet his performance has usually been treated perfunctorily by historians, and his views have often been distorted. He deserves a fuller and fairer evaluation.[14]

Stevenson learned of the Soviet deployment of missiles in Cuba only a few hours after the president. On 16 October he took the 9:00 a.m. shuttle from New York to Washington to participate in a State Department press conference and to attend a White House luncheon for the crown prince of Libya. He intended to return to New York later that same day; but his plans would soon change. After the White House reception, which Kennedy also attended, the president had a private word with him. Upholding the pledge he had made after the Bay of Pigs to keep him informed of all important foreign policy developments, he told Stevenson about the situation in Cuba, showed him the U-2 photographs of the missile sites, and indicated that his preference was for an air strike. Stevenson disagreed, insisting that the president should "not go to an air strike until we have explored the possibilities of a peaceful solution." He added that Kennedy should keep to his schedule of campaign appearances across the country for the upcoming congressional elections. To cancel them suddenly "would give alarm." The president agreed and asked Stevenson to remain in Washington to participate in the ExComm meetings.[15]

In preparation for his first of those sessions, Stevenson made extensive notes that represented his preliminary ideas on how the United States should react to the missile deployment in Cuba. Like his ExComm colleagues, he viewed the missiles as a grave threat that had to be removed, but he believed that the best way to proceed was to dispatch private emissaries to Castro and Khrushchev. The emissaries would present the evidence proving the presence of missiles in Cuba, and then issue an ultimatum: Unless the missiles were withdrawn promptly, the United States would take military action to destroy them.[16]

Stevenson wanted JFK to convene an OAS meeting perhaps the day after the ultimatum in order to inform the Latin American governments about the installation of missiles in Cuba and of Kennedy's proposed response. The president also needed to think about briefing Britain, France, West Germany, and then the rest of NATO. The notification of the NATO powers troubled Stevenson: "Will such notice start [a] long wrangle and delay our action dangerously? If [there is] no such notice, will [our] allies desert us?"[17]

Stevenson discussed the need for two presidential addresses in his notes. Kennedy should use the first to state the facts about the missiles in Cuba and to reassure the public that American intelligence was continuously monitoring the situation. He should also say cryptically that "further steps are being taken" to uphold his September pledge to take action if nuclear weapons were put in Cuba. If the ultimatums failed to induce Khrushchev and Castro to withdraw the missiles, Kennedy should make a second statement. This, Stevenson implied, should warn of imminent military action. An air strike limited to the missile sites could be executed immediately after that address. Alternatively, the second speech could simply condemn the Soviet missile deployment in Cuba and "leave [the] time of further [American] action in doubt."[18]

The views articulated by Stevenson in these notes ran counter to the image presented in the Alsop-Bartlett article. His basic position was that Khrushchev and Castro must remove the missiles from Cuba or else a limited air strike on the island would probably have to be carried out. McGeorge Bundy has written that Stevenson's support for a diplomatic approach in the missile crisis was made within "the context of explicit support for military action if necessary." On 17 October that was certainly the case.[19]

Stevenson's notes, however, did illustrate other aspects of his thinking, ones which would soon come to set his ideas apart from those of his colleagues. Perhaps most significantly, he displayed a willingness to examine the crisis from the Soviet and Cuban as well as the American viewpoint. In discussing Castro, for instance, he asked "why is he a danger to [the] US, if [the] US which has far more missiles is not a danger to him?" If the United States felt justified in assailing bases in Cuba, then an "attack on NATO bases [by the Soviet Union is] equally justified." Kennedy, in addition, had to "be prepared for [the] argument that if we have [a] base in Turkey, etc., they have [the] right to have [a] base in Cuba."[20]

The more Stevenson contemplated the dangers of the situation, the more willing he became to consider concessions as an inducement to Khrushchev to remove the missiles. His thinking evolved rapidly, and later that same day he furnished the president with a policy memorandum. The differences between these ideas and the ones he expressed in his notes were significant.[21]

Stevenson reiterated his plan to dispatch emissaries to Castro and Khrushchev, and once again discussed the need for JFK to make an early public statement. This time, however, he made a proposal that had not been present in his earlier notes. "The national security must come first," he acknowledged. *"But the means adopted have such incalculable consequences that I feel you should have made it clear that the existence of nuclear missile bases anywhere is* NEGOTIABLE before we start anything" – an obvious reference to the American missile sites in Turkey and Italy. But Stevenson added that "we can't negotiate with a gun at our head" and "if they won't remove the missiles [from Cuba] and restore the *status quo ante* we will have to do it ourselves." The gist of his argument was that the United States should still give notice to Moscow and Havana that a military strike on Cuba would take place if the missiles were not withdrawn. To make Khrushchev and Castro more willing to remove them, though, Kennedy should promise to negotiate the dismantlement of American missile sites in Turkey and Italy, once the weapons in Cuba had been withdrawn. The mutual cession of bases could form part of a general disarmament treaty.[22]

The ambassador displayed far greater concern in that memorandum than in his earlier notes over the possibility that the missile crisis might result in a devastating nuclear conflict. "To start or risk starting a nuclear war is bound to be divisive at best," he warned, "and the judgments of history seldom coincide with the tempers of the moment." Accordingly, he now placed greater emphasis on the essentiality of negotiation: "it should be clear as a pikestaff that the U.S. was, is and will be ready to negotiate the elimination of bases and anything else." After condemning the Soviet decision to emplace missiles in Cuba and insisting that Kennedy must not accept that deployment, he added at the end of his memorandum an important maxim: "blackmail and intimidation *never,* negotiation and sanity *always.*"[23]

The president was not receptive to those arguments. According to Sorensen, Stevenson's memorandum "annoyed" JFK. Withdrawing the Jupiter missiles from Turkey, Kennedy feared, might fracture the NATO alliance because it would indicate that the United States was prepared to betray European interests in order to protect its own. JFK also thought that the ambassador's proposals were too defensive. Instead of offering concessions, Kennedy felt, as Sorensen recalled, that "we should be indicting the Soviet Union for its duplicity and its threat to world peace."[24]

At 4:00 p.m. on Wednesday, 17 October, Stevenson took the air shuttle to New York to attend the general debate at the United Nations the next day. He returned to Washington on 19 October. By then the consensus in support of the blockade had emerged largely as a result of the efforts of Robert Kennedy and McNamara. Stevenson's thinking, though, had developed beyond the notion of just imposing a blockade. He was convinced that the best way to end the crisis was to establish a quarantine and simultaneously to offer the Soviets a *quid pro quo.*[25]

Rejoining ExComm after his two day hiatus, Stevenson entered George Ball's State Department conference room at around 6:30 p.m. on 19 October. A long meeting was drawing to a close, with Robert Kennedy once again promoting the blockade. When Rusk asked Stevenson if he had any opinions, he replied, "Yes, most emphatic views." But he stated, in probable reference to the attorney general's ardent support for the quarantine, that given "the course the discussion was taking he didn't think if was necessary to express them" at that point. Asked whether he espoused the blockade, he said that he did. He thought it important, however, to "look beyond the particular immediate action of blockade; we need to develop a plan for solution of the

problem – elements for negotiation designed to settle the
current crisis in a stable and satisfactory way and enable us
to move forward on wider problems." He added that he was
"working on some ideas for a settlement."[26]

Stevenson articulated those ideas on Saturday, 20 October, in both a memorandum to JFK and that afternoon's
ExComm meeting. In the memorandum he described a
"Political Program" to be announced by the president and
developed by himself in the UN Security Council at the same
time as the imposition of the blockade. Such an approach
would convince the international community, which might
otherwise view the quarantine as needlessly provocative, that
the United States was intent on reaching a peaceful settlement. To that end, Stevenson called for a Soviet-American
dialogue "to find, through negotiation, [a] permanent solution to the problem." Specifically, he suggested the introduction in the Security Council of a resolution calling for
the immediate dispatch of UN observation teams to the missile
sites in Cuba, Italy, and Turkey. Those teams "would insure
that no surprise attack could be mounted in any of these
countries pending a permanent solution to the problem of
foreign missile bases."[27]

In devising that "permanent solution," Stevenson argued
for the removal of all Soviet missiles and military personnel
from Cuba in exchange for the simultaneous withdrawal of
American bases from Guantánamo, Turkey, and Italy. The
reciprocal disengagements would be considered within the
framework of "nuclear and general disarmament." The United
States, along with the other nations of the Western Hemisphere, should assuage Soviet fears of an impending attack
on Cuba by agreeing "to guarantee the territorial integrity"
of the island. The UN could send an emergency force to
Cuba to reassure Khrushchev and Castro that no invasion
would take place.[28]

Stevenson reiterated and amplified those ideas at what
proved to be the most acrimonious ExComm session of the
entire missile crisis period. For much of that meeting, the
ambassador remained taciturn as the consensus in favour
of the blockade solidified. Then, as the discussion seemed
to be winding down, he spoke. As in his memorandum, he
proposed that Kennedy couple the announcement of the

blockade with the introduction in the Security Council of a resolution on the missiles in Cuba. Stevenson also recommended that the United States obtain prior support for the blockade from the OAS. His arguments on the need to blockade Cuba and on the utility of working through international organisations elicited general agreement from ExComm officials. Indeed, JFK did make effective use of the Security Council and the OAS later on in the missile crisis.[29]

The response of Stevenson's colleagues was far more critical, however, when he described the concessions that should be offered to persuade Khrushchev to withdraw militarily from Cuba. Stevenson stated that Kennedy must be willing to remove the missiles from Turkey and Italy, evacuate the Guantánamo base, and arrange for a noninvasion pledge among the nations of the Western Hemisphere with regard to Cuba. Dillon, McCone, and former Secretary of Defense Robert A. Lovett were furious. As Ball put it, they "intemperately upbraided Stevenson." Robert Kennedy recorded in his notes for the meeting that, "We had a rather strong argument with him." And JFK himself, according to the NSC minutes, "sharply rejected the thought of surrendering our [Cuban] base. . . . He felt that such action would convey to the world that we had been frightened into abandoning our position." The president conceded that he might have to remove the missiles from Turkey and Italy if the Soviets raised the issue, but he was only prepared to do this "in the future." Stevenson repeated that Kennedy would have to accept a *quid pro quo* if the crisis was to be resolved, contending that "the present situation required that we offer to give up such bases in order to induce the Russians to remove the strategic missiles." Stevenson soldiered on, but to no avail. He was able to convince neither Kennedy nor any other officials of the need for a quick diplomatic solution to the crisis before it escalated into military conflict.[30]

What was so striking about this ExComm meeting was the extent to which Stevenson was ostracised. This was due not only to the hostility of those officials who were there; it was a reflection of who was not there as well. Those liberal Democrats who might have lent support to Stevenson, such as Bowles, Goodwin, Schlesinger, and Mennen Williams, were absent. Kennedy's general view of liberals – that they helped the progressive image of his administration but were usually naive and impractical – probably dictated his decision not to include those aides in the ExComm sessions, or not even to consider doing so. The result was that Stevenson had to make his case in ExComm alone, and, consequently, his arguments did not acquire the sort of legitimacy they would have enjoyed had they been embraced by others.

Stevenson's lonely struggle continued on the evening of 20 October, when he attended a party thrown by veteran Democrat James Rowe. Speaking to Ken O'Donnell, an unrepentant Stevenson insisted the course now preferred in ExComm was not the best. "I know that most of those fellows will probably consider me a coward for the rest of my life for what I said today," he told O'Donnell. "But perhaps we need a coward in the room when we are talking about a nuclear war."[31]

Meanwhile, JFK and his advisers, especially Robert Kennedy, took steps to keep Stevenson on a tight rein at the United Nations. At the end of the 20 October ExComm meeting, the attorney general walked out on to the Truman Balcony with O'Donnell and the president. As O'Donnell recalls, Robert Kennedy was "furious." He felt Stevenson's performance in ExComm showed that he was "not strong enough or tough enough to be representing us at the UN at a time like this." To make sure the ambassador did not deviate from administration policy in the UN, he suggested that a Republican, either John McCloy or Herman Phleger, be sent to New York to accompany him. Robert Lovett, who talked with Stevenson that weekend, was also troubled by his ideas on Cuba. He advised the president to dispatch McCloy to New York to keep an eye on the ambassador. Kennedy considered the possiblity of sending Lovett himself, but opted instead for McCloy. He also asked Schlesinger to help prepare the addresses Stevenson would have to make at the UN. As Schlesinger was heading for his plane to New York, Robert Kennedy took him aside. "We're counting on you to watch things in New York," he explained. "That fellow is ready to give everything away."[32]

For Stevenson, the events of 20 October were undoubtedly traumatic. He had frankly presented what he believed to be the safest way of defusing the crisis, and his colleagues had responded by launching an unrestrained attack on him. According to Elie Abel, "The bitter aftertaste of that Saturday afternoon in the Oval Room stayed with him until his death." In the short-term, the browbeating that Stevenson received dented his confidence. On the next day, Sunday, 21 October, he produced a memorandum that described another "political program" to be presented by JFK at the same time that he announced the blockade. Many of the ideas the ambassador had expressed the day before were again present, but there were also significant changes. Those modifications were concessions that a subdued Stevenson made in order to placate his ExComm critics.[33]

The ambassador did reiterate his belief that there should be reciprocal Soviet-American concessions. The United States, in exchange for the removal of the Soviet military threat from Cuba, should both evacuate the Guantánamo base and pledge not to invade Cuba. But he now dropped the proposal that the bases in Turkey and Italy should be dismantled. That "would divert attention from the Cuban threat to the general problem of foreign bases." Stevenson also advocated the "neutralisation" of Cuba. He first mentioned that concept in ExComm on 19 October, without fully explaining its meaning. He had probably used it to make the point that Cuba would become militarily neutral after the Soviets removed their missiles and troops and the United States evacuated Guantánamo. But in his 21 October memorandum he employed the concept of neutralisation in a broader sense in order to express the hope that the removal of Soviet support for the Cuban leader would spark the "early overthrow" of the Castro government.[34]

Despite the inclusion of these obvious sops to hardline sentiment, John Kennedy still found Stevenson's suggestions unpalatable. The president would use his speech before the nation to alert the American people to the missile threat in Cuba and to announce the blockade. But he would not present any programme of mutual Soviet-American concessions, as his UN ambassador desired.

The reasons for Kennedy's rejection of Stevenson's advice on Cuba can be found in their differing approaches to foreign policy. Stevenson placed less emphasis on the use of military force and more stress on compromise through negotiation. Kennedy, on the other hand, always believed that the foundation of a sound foreign policy was the possession of immense military power and the willingness to use it. His reading of history, especially of the appeasement of Adolf Hitler in the late 1930s, convinced him of the importance of toughness rather than compromise in dealing with crisis situations.

Another possible factor behind Kennedy's dismissal of Stevenson's recommendations on Cuba was that on a personal level he detested his UN ambassador. More precisely, JFK's attitude towards Stevenson was a *mélange* of competitiveness and contempt. The sense of rivalry was rooted in Kennedy's own natural competitiveness, his particular desire to win the 1960 Democratic presidential nomination, and his understanding that the Illinoisan was his principal rival in the quest for that nomination. As JFK won primary after primary in 1960, with an apparently supine Stevenson on the sidelines, the spectre that haunted him was the possibility that the Democratic National Convention – despite his success in the primaries – would still bestow the nomination on Stevenson, as it had in 1952 and 1956. To avert that scenario, Kennedy tried throughout the late spring and summer of 1960 to persuade Stevenson to support his candidacy in public. JFK indicated that he would in return appoint him secretary of state, should he be elected president. Stevenson refused the offer, in part because he still hoped, despite his professions of disinterest, to garner the Democratic nomination himself. But he also declined because he did not consider Kennedy a worthy candidate. "My difficulty," he told Barbara Ward at the time of the Wisconsin primary, "is that I don't think he'd be a good president. I do not feel that he's the right man for the job; I think he's too young . . . and I cannot in conscience throw my support to someone whom I do not really think is up to it."[35]

Kennedy, as Arthur Krock detected in a 24 May 1960 telephone conversation, became increasingly irritated by Stevenson's tactics. The day after the Oregon primary, he exploded in a private meeting with the twice presidential candidate. "Look," he told Stevenson, "I have the votes for the nomination and if you don't give me your support, I'll have to shit all over you." The former governor was livid. "I should have told the son-of-a-bitch off," he later confided in George Ball, "but, frankly, I was shocked and confused by that Irish gutter talk." Despite that barrage, Stevenson would not oblige JFK. At the Democratic Convention in Los Angeles, Stevenson not only refused to make the nominating speech for Kennedy, he also tried at the last moment to secure the nomination for himself. That last endeavour included an unsuccessful attempt to persuade the Illinois delegation to transfer its votes from JFK to himself – a performance that heightened Kennedy's anger.[36]

The Kennedy–Stevenson rivalry also related to the enthusiastic support the Illinoisan received from the liberal set and Kennedy's desire to transfer that allegiance to himself. Many liberals viewed JFK with skepticism. The issue of McCarthyism was generally viewed as the key test of a Democrat's commitment to liberalism, and Kennedy's record was suspect. Not only did he fail to vote in the 1954 Senate decision to censure McCarthy (although Kennedy was in hospital, he could easily have registered his vote), he was in fact a personal friend of the Wisconsin senator. Mary Pitcairn Keating, who knew both men, recalled that Kennedy was "fascinated by Joe McCarthy." Whereas Kennedy's liberalism was questionable, Stevenson's credentials were impeccable. Indeed, to many Democrats, he was the authentic heir to Franklin Roosevelt.[37]

Kennedy had tried to wrest that mantle from Stevenson during the late 1950s and into 1960 – with some success. Such liberals as Mennen Williams, Chester Bowles, and Arthur Schlesinger, all of whom had been fervent Stevenson supporters, came out in favour of the Kennedy candidacy. But JFK suffered constant reminders of the support Stevenson still enjoyed in liberal quarters. Bowles, for instance, told him he would only become his foreign policy adviser in the 1960 campaign after he had made sure Stevenson did not intend to run again for president. Even after winning the Democratic nomination, Kennedy had to listen to the likes of Eleanor Roosevelt lecture him on the necessity of working in close collaboration with Stevenson (and Bowles) and of demonstrating ideological soundness by quoting from Stevenson in his speeches.[38]

Kennedy's hostility towards Stevenson, therefore, was intensified by the particular need he felt to redirect liberal sentiment away from Stevenson and towards his own candidacy, as well as by the general contest for the 1960 Democratic nomination. After the election he felt compelled to include Stevenson in his administration in order to placate liberal opinion, but at the same time did not wish to appoint his rival to an important office such as secretary of state or defense. He solved that conundrum by giving Stevenson what was generally viewed as the ceremonial and relatively powerless position of United Nations ambassador. Throughout JFK's presidency, Stevenson remained, as one Kennedy confidant noted, "a man whose popularity with liberal Democrats Kennedy resented."[39]

Contempt, as well as competitiveness, characterised JFK's view of Stevenson. As a result of Stevenson's defeats at the hands of Eisenhower in 1952 and 1956, John and Robert Kennedy regarded him as a loser. Bobby had worked on Stevenson's staff during his 1956 bid for the presidency, and was shocked by what he felt to be an appallingly disorganised campaign. Disgusted by its ineptness, he voted for Eisenhower on election day. In fact, the Kennedys came to associate Stevenson with a particular group of liberals who, in their opinion, placed inordinate emphasis on the articulation of high principles and insufficient stress on success. For these liberals, Robert Kennedy argued, "action or success makes them suspicious, and they almost lose interest. That's why so many of them think that Adlai Stevenson is the "Second Coming." He never quite arrives there; he never quite accomplishes anything."[40]

Not only did the Kennedys regard Stevenson as a loser, they also thought of him as effeminate. Stories of Stevenson's homosexuality had circulated during the 1950s. FBI chief J. Edgar Hoover, around whom similar rumours swirled, was chiefly responsible for propagating those canards. Hoover was determined to prevent Stevenson's election as president, and so in the 1952 campaign he disseminated information on Stevenson's sexual propensities to Nixon and McCarthy, as well as the press. After the 1960 election, the president-elect requested security checks on all the people that he intended to appoint to senior positions in his administration. The FBI director's December 1960 report on Stevenson included the allegation that he was part of an elite New York gay group in which he went by the name of "Adelaide."[41]

Although few took these charges seriously, Kennedy did. Even before becoming president, he had privately said of Stevenson, "He must be a switcher." George Smathers recalled conversations with JFK in which, "We sometimes talked about the fact that he [Stevenson] just wasn't masculine enough for Jack Kennedy." Robert Kennedy once commented that to he and his brother, Stevenson's manoeuvres at the 1960 Democratic convention seemed to be "the actions of an old woman." The irony was that after JFK's assassination Stevenson tried to court Jackie Kennedy. The important point, though, is that the Kennedys' perception of Stevenson as effeminate probably increased their disrespect for him.[42]

For all these reasons, JFK detested Stevenson. Robert Kennedy later revealed the depth of that antipathy, recalling that his brother "didn't like Adlai Stevenson. [Stevenson] used to drive him out of his mind." The president used to "hate to have him around," and he would "talk about him frequently – what a pain in the ass he was." Kennedy's contempt for Stevenson probably influenced his reaction to the advice offered by the ambassador during the missile crisis. Of course, JFK was far too shrewd a politician to reject Stevenson's suggestions on Cuba simply because he loathed him. Still, his perception of Stevenson as effeminate, a loser, and an overly-principled liberal probably served to reinforce his belief that the ambassador's recommendations were "soft."[43]

Yet perhaps Kennedy should not have dismissed Stevenson's proposals so quickly. The essentials of the final settlement to the missile crisis – Soviet removal of the missiles in Cuba in return for an American noninvasion pledge and withdrawal of the Jupiters from Turkey – had all been advocated by Stevenson on 20 October, and, among ExComm officials, by him alone. Had Kennedy implemented some form of the ambassador's programme, it may have been possible to resolve the crisis several days before 28 October.

There were two important differences between Stevenson's proposed settlement and the one that ended the confrontation over Cuba. The abandonment of Guantánamo was a concession that Kennedy did not ultimately have to make, and the trade of missiles in Cuba for Jupiters in Turkey, a clandestine component of the final settlement, was a public part of the Stevenson plan. The Guantánamo idea was an example of Stevenson's proclivity to analyse problems in excessively theoretical terms. He was probably thinking here about the concept of neutralisation. If Kennedy was to argue that the Soviets had to withdraw militarily from Cuba because the island should be neutral, and not a military base for the superpowers, then the United States, strictly speaking, should evacuate Guantánamo. In terms of practical politics, however, the proposal was naive. To cede Guantánamo under the pressure of the Soviet missile deployment in Cuba would have left Kennedy vulnerable to the charge of appeasement. The Stevenson plan and the one that finally defused the crisis were, nevertheless, very similar. Though not entirely satisfied with Stevenson's recommendations, the president could have adapted them to suit his own tastes. The Guantánamo proposal could have been discarded, and the Jupiter swap recast as a secret *quid pro quo*. By refining Stevenson's ideas, Kennedy might have produced a settlement acceptable to both Khrushchev and American public opinion, thereby securing an early resolution to the crisis.[44]

The distaste of ExComm officials like Dillon, Lovett, McCone, and Paul Nitze for Stevenson's proposals probably derived from the simple fact that they involved concessions. To men conscious of the lesson of the 1930s – that dictators must never be propitiated – the notion of yielding anything to a Soviet leader was repugnant. Nitze later acknowledged that the reason he was "outraged" at the 20 October meeting was because Stevenson's ideas represented an "attempt at total appeasement."[45]

It was obvious, however, that the *sine qua non* of a settlement for both Khrushchev and Kennedy was that they emerge from the crisis with their credibility intact. Each had to walk away with something tangible. Hence, the situation had to be examined to some extent from the Soviet point of view. Stevenson's proposed settlement had that virtue, albeit too abundantly. Moreover, it was dangerously anachronistic to conceptualise the missile crisis, as officials like Nitze did, in terms of the late 1930s. That analogy was not sound because the necessity of avoiding conflict between the great powers was far greater in the nuclear age, when mutual annihilation was possible, than in the pre-nuclear epoch. As one pundit observed:

> Translating the old rule [of making no concessions and being prepared to take military action] into nuclear terms would mean that Americans are ready to destroy their country if they feel that its security is threatened. A principle well-established in the world of 1940 became a complete *non-sequitur* in the world of 1962.[46]

For some ExComm officials, like the Kennedys themselves, it was not so much the idea of concessions that was unacceptable, but more the notion that the president should proffer them as part of his initial response. JFK and RFK both thought they might ultimately have to offer inducements to the Soviets to end the crisis, but those inducements should come only after they had first demonstrated an uncompromising determination to eject the missiles from the island. "We will have to make a deal in the end," the attorney general told Schlesinger, "but we must stand firm now." The president made the same observation during the 20 October ExComm meeting. Khrushchev, the Kennedys implied, would only be willing to suffer the embarrassment of withdrawing the weapons from Cuba after being confronted with an American posture of unflappable resolution.[47]

Stevenson, however, made the implicit and perhaps compelling point that the president needed to strive for a quick settlement because the crisis could result in war through either escalation or accident. In the end, both scenarios might have materialised. By the time Kennedy and Khrushchev struck a deal on 28 October, the United States was possibly within twenty-four or forty-eight hours of initiating military action against Cuba. Accidents did nearly derail Soviet-American efforts to defuse the crisis. The 27 October downing of an American U-2 over Cuba by a Soviet surface-to-air missile and the unintentional entry on the same day of another United States reconnaissance plane into Soviet airspace showed how easily events might spiral out of control. Neither incident occurred at the behest of Kennedy or Khrushchev, but both heightened the suspicion of each towards the other, thereby exacerbating the crisis. Stevenson geared his suggestions towards reaching an early settlement before accidents or escalation produced a superpower war.

ExComm officials may also have found the ambassador's recommendations unsatisfactory because they thought there was nothing, with the blockade as yet unestablished, compelling the Soviet premier to accept the *quid pro quo* Stevenson described. They may have overlooked, as historians often do, that he *never* suggested a diplomatic trade as an alternative independent of the blockade and military options. He always maintained that the quarantine and diplomatic alternatives should be pursued simultaneously. Under the Stevenson plan, Khrushchev would be mulling over the *quid pro quo* with the knowledge that a blockade was being established around Cuba and that subsequent military action would probably be initiated should he reject the trade. The Illinoisan understood only too well that the Soviet leader would not decide capriciously to remove the missiles from the island unless he was subject to the sort of coercive pressure that a blockade would apply. Even if Khrushchev rejected Stevenson's diplomatic solution, the blockade would be in place and no tactical disadvantage incurred. A negotiated settlement could still be reached at a later point in the crisis.[48]

Although John and Robert Kennedy and the other ExComm officials raised what on first appearance might seem like reasonable objections to Stevenson's plan, their criticisms were not generally cogent. For the ambassador to examine the crisis from the Soviet as well as the American viewpoint, and to construct a settlement that involved some concessions to Khrushchev was not naive; it was realistic. His plan was far more shrewd, sensible, and carefully crafted than his colleagues and historians have recognised. There is, therefore, a need for a fairer appraisal of Stevenson's role during the first week of the missile crisis, one not based on the uncharitable evaluation made originally by President Kennedy through the proxies of Alsop and Bartlett. In fact, when the sagacity of Stevenson's recommendations are considered alongside his sparkling performance at the UN Security Council meeting on 25 October, it might well be concluded that the former governor of Illinois was the unsung hero of the missile crisis.

8 Dénouement

In the days from 22 to 28 October, the public phase of the confrontation over Cuba, John Kennedy handled the missile crisis with increasing dexterity. Initially determined to force Khrushchev to withdraw the missiles from Cuba without offering any concessions, he became – from 25 October onwards – more flexible, conciliatory, and conscious of the need to avoid a military engagement in the Caribbean. The increasing maturity that JFK displayed was particularly evident on 27 October, the critical day of the crisis.

Monday, 22 October, was a frenetic day for Kennedy. At 3:00 p.m., four hours before he was scheduled to address the nation, he talked to his ExComm advisers in the White House Cabinet Room. Emphasising the importance of unity in dealing with the public, JFK stated that, "Everyone should sing one song." He proceeded to enumerate the reasons which should be given, in explaining the necessity for the quarantine, to those who pointed out that the United States had been vulnerable for some years to an ICBM attack from the Soviet Union anyway. He mentioned the pledges he had made in September to take action if offensive missiles were placed in Cuba. "We have to carry out commitments," Kennedy averred, "which we had made publicly at that time." Also to be stressed was the unprecedented nature of the build-up in Cuba, with this being the first time Khrushchev had deployed missiles outside Soviet territory, and the United States had to demonstrate its unwillingness to accept that departure from previous Soviet policy. Another important factor, Kennedy added, was the danger that a failure on his part to respond would damage the United States position throughout Latin America because it would then appear as though "the Soviets were increasing their world position while ours was decreasing."[1]

JFK and his advisers continued to consider their response to public queries about various aspects of the Cuban situation during the rest of the meeting. They framed answers to potential questions about the administration's failure to react more quickly to the missile deployment, why evidence proving the existence of offensive missiles on the island had taken so long to garner, and whether an invasion of Cuba was being prepared. As well as eliciting ideas on how best to handle the press and mould public opinion, Kennedy posed two questions, asking his advisers to provide answers by the following day: First, how should he respond if the Soviets shot down an American intelligence-gathering U-2 plane with a SAM? Second, and the really crucial question, "If the missile development in Cuba continues [after the establishment of the quarantine], what is our next course of action?"[2]

Perhaps the most important aspect of Kennedy's comments during this ExComm session was the reference to the public promises he had made on Cuba in September, a factor which JFK would continue to highlight during the next few days. To a large extent, the emphasis he placed on his September commitments determined his basic position from the time he announced the blockade to 25 October. In September he had told the American public he would remove any surface-to-surface missiles placed in Cuba, and he had not qualified this by saying he might have to compromise in order to make that happen. Kennedy's awareness of this was the factor which probably convinced him, at the start of the second week of the missile crisis, of his political need to have Khrushchev back down and remove the missiles without offering any concessions in return. McGeorge Bundy has argued that JFK's determination to remove the missiles was "necessarily based on his respect for American public opinion," and his concomitant perception that the public would never accept missiles in Cuba. Kennedy's declarations in September making clear his own refusal to tolerate nuclear weapons in Cuba made his awareness of the role played by American public opinion during the crisis even more acute.[3]

After the ExComm meeting and two hours prior to his television address, Kennedy briefed a group of stunned congressional leaders about the situation in Cuba and the quarantine that would be imposed. One senator audibly groaned and, as Rusk recalls, "fell over on the table with his head in his hands and stayed there for a while." "Thank God I am not the president of the United States!" declared another. Some of the most distinguished took exception to the blockade. Both William Fulbright and Georgia Senator Richard B. Russell felt it would be inadequate and argued that military action was appropriate. "The President had warned them [the Soviets] in September," Russell said, "and no further warning was necessary." In diametric opposition to the moderation he had displayed in opposing the Bay of Pigs plan, Fulbright now called for the use of force. He suggested that a quick attack on the Soviet bases in Cuba would be less threatening to Khrushchev than a blockade enforced against his ships. Kennedy disagreed with Fulbright, claiming that "an attack on these bases, which we knew were manned by Soviet personnel, would involve large numbers of Soviet casualties and this would be more provocative than a confrontation with a Soviet ship." The meeting ended only twenty-five minutes before his address to the nation. If his equanimity had been unsettled by the general lack of support offered by the leadership on Capitol Hill, Kennedy would show no signs of it.[4]

While JFK was listening to the congressional reaction, Dean Rusk went to speak to Dobrynin at the State Department. After handing the Soviet ambassador a copy of the president's speech as well as a letter from Kennedy to Khrushchev, Rusk bitterly observed that "it was incomprehensible to him how leaders in Moscow could make such [a] gross error of judgment as to what [the] US can accept." Dobrynin, in a state of shock because Khrushchev had not informed him about the missiles in Cuba, returned the complaint, predicting that the blockade would "very strongly aggravate [the] international situation." He also expressed his surprise at Kennedy's failure to broach the question of missiles in Cuba with Gromyko during their 18 October meeting. Rusk, Dobrynin would later recall, was "clearly in a state of nervous tension [during the conversation] although he was doing his best to conceal it."[5]

In Moscow Ambassador Kohler delivered the private message from Kennedy to Khrushchev at the Kremlin, thereby initiating a frenetic correspondence between the two leaders over the next few days. Kennedy expressed concern in his 22 October letter that Moscow "would not correctly understand the will and determination of the United States in any given situation." He also reminded Khrushchev of the point he had made at the Vienna summit that the purpose of American policy was to prevent any Soviet-induced modifications in the international balance of power, including changes in the status of Berlin. Recounting the events of the past few weeks, Kennedy recalled the promises he had made on Cuba in September as part of that policy. He also mentioned the congressional resolution passed in support of those commitments. As a thinly veiled warning to Khrushchev, he made clear that the initiation of the quarantine represented only "the minimum [pressure] necessary to remove the threat to the security of the nations in this hemisphere." The implication was that Soviet failure to remove the "offensive" missiles would necessitate additional American action.[6]

Kennedy revealed to the American public – and the world – the true nature of the Soviet build-up in Cuba in his television address at 7:00 p.m. After describing the categories and range of the missiles on the island, he indicated yet again the importance he attached to the upholding of his September pledges. The surface-to-surface missiles, he declared, not only contravened the 1947 Rio Pact, the Western Hemisphere's tradition of preventing extra-continental penetration of its own domains, the recent congressional resolution on Cuba, and the UN Charter, but also "my own public warnings to the Soviets on September 4 and 13." In discussing the promises not to put offensive missiles in Cuba made in a 11 September Soviet government statement and by Foreign Minister Gromyko on 18 October, Kennedy also charged Moscow with duplicity.[7]

The president cited the example of the 1930s in explaining the rationale behind his decision to respond to the Soviet missile deployment. That decade "taught us a clear lesson: aggressive conduct, if allowed to go unchecked and unchallenged, ultimately leads to war." To avoid repeating the mistakes of appeasement, Kennedy announced a programme of "*initial* steps to be taken immediately." The most important was the imposition of a naval quarantine around Cuba to prevent the entry of "all offensive military equipment." The United States would also expand its surveillance of the

Soviet build-up in Cuba; regard a missile attack from Cuba on any nation in the Western Hemisphere as an assault on the United States necessitating "a full retaliatory response upon the Soviet Union"; reinforce Guantánamo but simultaneously evacuate the dependents of military personnel from the base; and convene meetings of the UN and the OAS. Kennedy called upon Khrushchev directly to remove the missiles from the island in order to defuse the situation. During the remainder of the address, he explained his determination to respond to Soviet challenges at all points. He mentioned, in particular, his support for "the brave people of West Berlin." That reference was not merely a footnote to the main body of Kennedy's address. Much of JFK's concern during the next few days would centre on the possibility that the Soviets would respond to the American quarantine of Cuba by moving on West Berlin.[8]

Kennedy's fears about Berlin were probably exaggerated. During the missile crisis, Deputy Foreign Minister Vasily V. Kuznetsov reminded Khrushchev that he could retaliate to the American blockade of Cuba by applying pressure to West Berlin. Oleg Troyanovsky, special assistant for international affairs, recalls that Kuznetsov's comment "provoked a sharp, and I would say violent, reaction by Khrushchev. The latter said in a peremptory manner that he would do without such advice. It prompted a conclusion that we had no intention to add fuel to the conflict, the more to expand its geographic boundaries."[9]

No American could have been more exhilirated by Kennedy's speech than Kenneth Keating. There had always been the suspicion throughout the fall that the senator was little better than a charlatan who manufactured evidence or obtained it from unreliable Cuban émigrés, and made charges that were utterly false. Now America knew he had been right all along. Keating aide Richard Nathan was with the senator on 22 October when Kennedy made his address. Keating was campaigning for congressional candidates in upstate New York, and he was scheduled to give a speech in Utica that evening. Before he started his talk, journalist James Reston called to apologise. The *New York Times* had not taken his claims seriously, and it was now clear that they should have. Arranging for Nathan to give the speech in his place,

Keating immediately flew to New York City to appear on national television. Nathan recalls that Keating was "very excited."[10]

Kennedy's public acknowledgement that there were offensive missiles in Cuba, however, was a double-edged sword for Keating. On the one hand, it was a personal vindication. His allegations throughout the fall had been proven accurate. On the other, Kennedy's address immediately marginalised him. For the public, the issue of Keating, his sources and motives, the veracity of his charges, was no longer important. The question of whether JFK and Khrushchev could avert nuclear war over Cuba had obviously superseded it. In this way, 22 October represented the high point of Keating's campaign on Cuba and signified its end.

The initial Soviet response to Kennedy's address was to disregard the quarantine, press ahead with the military build-up in Cuba, and prepare for a protracted crisis. Defense Minister Malinovsky announced on 23 October that a decision had been made to increase "the combat readiness and vigilance of all [Soviet] troops." The demobilisation of various types of outmoded military equipment was suspended, and all furloughs for Soviet personnel were postponed. On the same day Marshal Andrei A. Grechko, commander in chief of the Warsaw Pact, called a meeting of officers from the various Eastern European countries. Grechko instructed them to heighten the military readiness of their forces. Moreover, twenty-seven Soviet bloc ships, according to American intelligence, continued en route for Cuba. Of those, probably as many as nineteen carried equipment connected with the military build-up on the island. Most ominous was the exchange on the evening of 23 October between Soviet military attaché Vladimir Dubovik and a group of reporters during a party at the Soviet embassy in Washington. Dubovik told the journalists that the commanders of the ships heading for Cuba were under orders to disregard the blockade and remain on course for the Caribbean island. "I have fought in three wars already," he brazenly added, "and I am looking forward to fighting in the next."[11]

Khrushchev himself showed no signs of flinching. In a letter received in Washington just before midday, he told Kennedy that the establishment of a blockade was "aggressive" and a "threat to peace." He reiterated his contention that the missiles deployed in Cuba, "regardless of the classification to which they may belong, are intended solely for defensive purposes." Offering no concessions, Khrushchev instead called on Kennedy to revoke his recent decisions, which, he indicated, could have "catastrophic consequences for world peace." To demonstrate his unflappability under pressure, Khrushchev nonchalantly attended the theatre on 23 October with a group of high-ranking officials' that included Leonid Brezhnev and Alexei N. Kosygin.[12]

As with Khrushchev's letter, Kennedy's reply, dispatched only seven hours later, made no attempt to formulate a settlement to the crisis and was simply based on the assumption that the Soviets must back down first. The president argued that the origins of the current confrontation lay in Khrushchev's surreptitious installation of offensive missiles in Cuba, and he advised the Soviet leader to respect the blockade. Revealing his fears over escalation, he did suggest, however, that "we both show prudence and do nothing to allow events to make the situation more difficult to control than it already is."[13]

The issue of how the United States should react to a Soviet attack on a U-2 plane flying over Cuba, raised by JFK the previous day, was settled during the two ExComm meetings on 23 October. Eight aircraft would be ordered to strike the particular site from which the Soviet SAM had shot down the U-2. If the president was unavailable and the evidence indicating such an assault on an American plane was indisputable, McNamara would be responsible for authorising retaliatory action. Should the Soviets continue to use their SAMs to attack U-2s after the United States had responded in this way, then Kennedy would approve a broader strike aimed at destroying all SAMs in Cuba.[14]

No attempt was made, though, to even broach the second question that Kennedy had asked ExComm on 22 October about the appropriate American response to a Soviet decision to ignore the blockade and to continue work on the missile sites in Cuba? The assumption or hope was that Moscow would simply yield under the pressure from the blockade (and possibly its extension to include petroleum, oil, and lubricants (POL)) without requesting any concessions in return.[15]

Discussion centred instead on such issues as the mechanics of initiating the quarantine, the steps being taken to advance military preparations, and future reconnaissance missions over Cuba. The wording for Proclamation 3504, declaring the establishment of the blockade, was approved and issued later that day. Kennedy reviewed and authorised an Executive Order extending the tours of duty for various military personnel. Preparations for invasion, McNamara announced, were being expedited. Six low-level reconnaissance flights designed to obtain updated information about activity at the missile sites were scheduled. Attention was also paid to Berlin. During the morning ExComm meeting, Kennedy showed concern over the possibility that Khrushchev would retaliate to the blockade around Cuba by taking similar action against Berlin. He asked McCone to analyse and compare the effects of the quarantine on Cuba with a possible Soviet blockade of Berlin, and he suggested that Paul Nitze be appointed head of an ExComm subcommittee on Berlin.[16]

Much of the discussion on 23 October, as on the previous day, focused on ways of selling the blockade to the press and the American people. During the ExComm session in the morning, there was a debate on how best to brief journalists and members of Congress. Various officials were instructed to examine the matter further. JFK himself worked indefatigably outside of ExComm to win the support of Henry R. Luce, head of the Time Inc. empire. In the morning, the president phoned Luce, who was at Chicago airport, and invited him to the White House. Later in the afternoon, Kennedy briefed the media tycoon, and also Otto Fuerbringer, managing editor of *Time*, about the ongoing crisis. He then had McNamara and McCone show Luce aerial reconnaissance photographs at the Pentagon. Obligingly, Luce devoted several pages of the next edition of *Time* to the presentation of many of those photographs in order, as Luce recalled, "to explain the whole situation."[17]

Several other episodes of note took place on 23 October. In the afternoon, American officials talked to a group of Western European ambassadors. The meeting demonstrated that a negotiated removal of the Jupiters in Turkey for the missiles in Cuba was not what the Kennedy administration had in mind at this point. When the French ambassador mentioned the unfortunate comparison that many would make between the weapons in Turkey and Italy and the missiles in Cuba, American officials tried to explain why the analogy was not sound rather than exploring whether such a trade, even as a last resort, was feasible.[18]

An OAS meeting, opening in the morning and reconvening in the afternoon, produced promising results for Kennedy. Rusk introduced a resolution calling for "the immediate dismantling and withdrawal from Cuba of all missiles and other weapons of offensive capability," and also asked OAS members to take any military steps that would help to remove the missiles. Despite some initial hesitation from the Brazilian and Mexican delegates, the secretary of state managed to secure unanimous approval for the resolution.[19]

A meeting between Robert Kennedy and Dobrynin, arranged by RFK at his brother's behest, took place at 9:30 p.m. in the ambassador's office on the third floor of the Soviet embassy. During their discussion, Bobby emphasised American anger at the Soviets for the deceitful manner in which they had installed missiles in Cuba. Referring to Moscow's promises that no offensive weapons would be deployed, he explained it was on the basis of those assurances that his brother had told the American people no action against Cuba was required. Now the president "had been deceived, and that had devastating implications for the peace of the world." When Dobrynin denied the presence of missiles in Cuba, Robert Kennedy advised him to phone Moscow so he could get the facts straight. As the attorney general departed, he asked whether Soviet ships were still under orders to ignore the quarantine and continue on to Cuba. His government, Dobrynin replied, had not briefed him on this but he did know that a month earlier an order had been given to Soviet vessels to disregard any blockade that the United States established. Bobby Kennedy reported immediately on his conversation to JFK and David Ormsby Gore. According to the British ambassador, the attorney general said he had left Dobrynin "looking ashen."[20]

By 23 October, the Kennedy administration had succeeded in lining up NATO allies, as well as the OAS, behind the blockade of Cuba. While Ambassadors Bruce and Dowling briefed Macmillan and Adenauer respectively on 22 October, Dean Acheson was making his most valuable contribution to the American cause during the missile crisis by gaining the support of the habitually intractable de Gaulle. After meeting that morning in Paris with the American mission to NATO, Acheson went to the Elysée Palace for talks with the French leader. To avoid attracting attention from the press, the French made arrangements to escort Acheson surreptitiously into the Elysée through a back door rather than the main entrance.[21]

Acheson entered de Gaulle's office at exactly 5:00 p.m., accompanied by a French interpreter and Cecil Lyon, the US chargé d'affaires in Paris. The CIA's Sherman Kent remained outside with photographic evidence of the missiles in Cuba. The French leader rose from his desk to shake hands. "Your President," he declared, "has done me great honor by sending so distinguished an emissary." Acheson simply bowed in response. Getting down to business, he handed de Gaulle a letter from Kennedy, as well as the opening portion of the president's speech to be delivered later that evening. The Frenchman, after reading both communications, said that he "would welcome further elucidation." Acheson prefaced his remarks by explaining that the purpose of the meeting was only to inform de Gaulle on a decision already taken rather than to solicit his opinions on how to respond to the missiles in Cuba. According to Lyon's record of the meeting, he then:

> outlined [the] background of [the] present situation in Cuba, [the] reason for [the] President's proposed action, going into considerable detail, emphasizing that maximum build-up had occurred within [the] past week, and saying that he had Mr. Sherman Kent with him who was prepared to brief President De Gaulle in more detail.

De Gaulle said that he did not need to see Kent's photographs for the time being. "A great nation like yours would not act if there were any doubt about the evidence, and, therefore, I accept what you tell me as a fact without any proof of any sort needed."[22]

The two elder statesmen then discussed Khrushchev's probable reaction to the quarantine, and agreed that he would probably not force the blockade. When de Gaulle asked how Khrushchev might retaliate, Acheson said by moving on Berlin or perhaps Turkey, although he considered both those scenarios unlikely. De Gaulle went on to pose the really difficult question: How would Kennedy get the missiles out of Cuba if Khrushchev decided not to respond at all to the quarantine? No one had supplied Acheson with an answer to that query in the briefing he had received at the State Department before leaving Washington; so, extemporising, he explained that, "We will immediately tighten this blockade and the next thing we would do is to stop tankers – and this will bring Cuba to a standstill in no time at all." "That's very good," de Gaulle interjected. "If we have to go further," Acheson added, "why, of course, we'll go further."[23]

De Gaulle thanked Acheson for the briefing. Although "this had been done after [the] decision had been made," he "nevertheless [*sic*] appreciated being informed," and he asked Acheson to convey his gratitude to Kennedy. De Gaulle went on to stress the importance of close contact between the French and American governments in the days ahead. The two elder statesmen then called for Sherman Kent, who proceeded to spread the greatly enlarged CIA photographs across de Gaulle's desk. The French leader, impressed by the detail of photographs taken from an altitude of 65 000 feet, revealed his military expertise by asking several germane questions. "You could see the soldier really taking over at this point," Acheson recalled.[24]

Their talk ended cordially. A strong sense of mutual respect had suffused the meeting, and, at its close, de Gaulle gave Acheson what he had wanted – his backing. "You may tell your President," he stated, "that France will support him in every way in this crisis." Walking Acheson to the door, de Gaulle, who now broke into English for the first time, said, "It would be a pleasure to me if these things were all done through you." Acheson, who liked his ego stroked as much as anyone and more than most, was no doubt flattered. In a letter written six weeks after that meeting, he returned the compliment:

De Gaulle could not have been better. He has a magnificent inner calm and serenity which makes all the nervous affectations of social talk unnecessary as well as any urge to make an impression or to charm. His dignity is real, like General [George C.] Marshall's. We could not have had a more satisfactory talk.[25]

Although de Gaulle had impressed Acheson and assured him of French support, he held more reservations about American policy than he had indicated to the former secretary of state. These he conveyed to Harold Macmillan who passed them on to his cabinet. On 23 October the prime minister explained to the cabinet that de Gaulle "was skeptical about the effectiveness of the Cuban blockade and considered that the Soviet build-up in Cuba might be designed to secure the withdrawal of United States bases in Europe." But de Gaulle acknowledged, Macmillan further reported, that the Kennedy administration "could not have been expected to ignore the Soviet threat."[26]

Acheson, meanwhile, followed his session with de Gaulle by briefing the North Atlantic Council. For two hours, he spoke in defence of Kennedy's decision to blockade Cuba. Despite some grumblings about lack of consultation, there was, as one American official wrote, a "satisfactory recognition of [the] importance [of the] need for allied solidarity." The same observer felt that although the NATO representatives "had received no authority from [their] governments for comment, ... I anticipate [that] perm[anent]-rep[resentative]s will make strong recommendations to their capitals in favor of holding together on this issue." As Acheson left the NATO Council meeting, he ran across a *New York Times* correspondent and another American journalist. Both were surprised to see Acheson, who was still moving around Paris incognito. When they said that they had heard "something hot is coming out of Washington," the veteran Democrat assured them they had not been misinformed.[27]

Although Acheson had laboured hard in Paris, his European sojourn was not yet over. Adenauer was proving difficult for Ambassador Dowling to win over, and so Kennedy asked Acheson, who enjoyed a personal rapport with the German chancellor, to head to Berlin on the morning of 23 October to add weight to the American case there. When Acheson and Dowling talked to Adenauer later that same day, the chancellor argued that the blockade "would be insufficient to check [the] Soviets." He also felt that Kennedy needed to "consider all possible actions for [the] elimination of [the] Castro regime and Soviet influence in Cuba, including rapid tightening of quarantine restrictions." Acheson then moved the discussion to the question of what policy options had been available to JFK, and explained why the blockade had been the preferred alternative. Adenauer, according to Dowling, "listened most attentively, and at the end seemed reassured but he was obviously still convinced of the necessity for further firm measures at [an] early date to achieve our purpose." At the root of Adenauer's objections was the fear that the Soviets would use the blockade of Cuba as a pretext to move on West Berlin. As much as was possible, Acheson succeeded in persuading him that the blockade had been the appropriate policy choice. He later acknowledged, though, that Adenauer had given him "a terrific workout." Later in the day, a presumably weary Acheson met with Adenauer's defence minister, Franz Josef Strauss.[28]

Acheson finally returned to Washington on the afternoon of 24 October. He spoke to Rusk immediately and Kennedy the next day, filling them in on the details of his talks with de Gaulle and Adenauer. Acheson used those meetings to point out that the missiles were still in Cuba, work on them was continuing apace, and the time when they could be safely destroyed was running out. The air strike, therefore, "remained the only method of eliminating them." JFK and Rusk were apparently unmoved by Acheson's plea for military action.[29]

As the former secretary of state flew over the Atlantic on 24 October, the confrontation between Kennedy and Khrushchev reached boiling point. Soviet ships were nearing the naval blockade which the United States had just imposed around Cuba. As the vessels approached the quarantine line, the Kennedy brothers talked across the table during that morning's ExComm meeting. "It looks really mean, doesn't it?" observed the president. Bobby Kennedy replied that JFK had been given no alternative but to take steps to remove the missiles. "If you hadn't acted," he added, "you would have been impeached." The president concurred:

"That's what I think – I would have been impeached."[30]

Shortly after 10:00 a.m., McNamara announced that two Soviet ships, the *Gagarin* and the *Komiles*, were now very close to the quarantine line. A little later it was reported that a Soviet submarine had moved between those two vessels. Consequently, the decision was made to enforce the blockade against the submarine and two ships with the help of an aircraft carrier and helicopters equipped with antisubmarine weaponry. The *Essex* was instructed to signal the Soviet submarine to surface. If it did not, depth charges with an explosive would be used to force compliance. As the point of no return approached, the president's thoughts turned to the European theatre. "We must expect that they will close down Berlin," he observed, "make the final preparations for that."[31]

As the ExComm members waited with bated breath, an official entered the room at 10:25 a.m. with a note for McCone. The CIA director read it and then announced, "Mr. President, we have a preliminary report which seems to indicate that some of the Russian ships have stopped dead in the water." "We're eyeball to eyeball," Rusk commented to Bundy, "and I think the other fellow just blinked." In a note which was undated but presumably written at that moment, Lyndon Johnson observed that Moscow "was prepared to pay quite a price for time. Ships Returning." Seven minutes later it was confirmed that six Soviet vessels had either stopped or reversed course and set off back for the Soviet Union. Khrushchev's strategy had been one of classic brinksmanship. He held his nerve until the very last moment – and only then had he backed down.[32]

Kennedy responded prudently to this promising development. He ordered his military to avoid intercepting a Soviet ship for at least one hour until better information on the naval stand off had been obtained, and he subsequently decided to permit the *Bucharest*, a Soviet tanker, to pass through the blockade because it did not appear to be carrying any military equipment. Some administration officials wished to board the vessel to make clear the depth of American resolve. But the president refused, arguing that, "We don't want to push him [Khrushchev] to a precipitous action – give him time to consider."[33]

Kennedy and Khrushchev had managed to avert a direct military engagement but they were no closer to ending the crisis. In that morning's ExComm discussion devoted to matters apart from the narrowly-avoided clash on the seas, there was no attempt to conceptualise how the crisis might be resolved. Instead Kennedy and his advisers focused upon the improvement of government communications throughout the world, especially in the Caribbean, and also upon the public presentation of the administration's position. For instance, JFK instructed both the State Department and the United States Information Agency (USIA) to promote "understanding in Europe of the fact that any Berlin crisis would be fundamentally the result of Soviet ambition and pressure," and also to convey the idea that it would have been more dangerous for Berliners had the United States taken no action to meet Khrushchev's challenge in Cuba. Demonstrating the importance he attached to the packaging of his blockade policy, Kennedy instructed a senior member of the USIA to attend every ExComm session. At a meeting with congressional leaders in the late afternoon, the president again failed to explain how the crisis might be defused. His assessment was that "we must now wait until the confrontation of the ships and . . . the next 24 hours will bring out important developments."[34]

Khrushchev shared Kennedy's outlook on 24 October. Although the Soviet leader was prepared to take steps to avoid a military engagement in the short-term, he was not willing to develop a feasible settlement to the crisis. His assumption, at least at this point, was that the confrontation could only end once Kennedy had decided to lift the quarantine and accept the presence of missiles in Cuba. In a long conversation that day with American businessman William E. Knox, Khrushchev was unrepentant. The stand taken by Kennedy on Cuba, he argued, was related to his concerns about the upcoming congressional elections. Suggesting a youthful immaturity in Kennedy's handling of the Cuban situation, he mentioned JFK's age and noted that his own son was older than the president. Khrushchev also described the blockade as illegal, maintained that the military build-up in Cuba was "defensive," and observed the double-standard involved in Soviet tolerance for nearby countries it did not like such as Italy and Greece, and America's refusal to countenance the current Cuban government. Khrushchev took the opportunity of his talk with Knox to indulge his penchant for brinksmanship. If the United States should attack Cuba, he blustered, "Guantanamo would disappear the first day."[35]

Khrushchev also showed no signs of accommodation in his 24 October message to Kennedy, although the tone of the letter did reveal some concern over the increasing intractability of the crisis. He argued that Soviet-Cuban relations were none of America's business, charged Kennedy with trying to intimidate Moscow into submission, and claimed that the blockade was illegal. As in his conversation with Knox, Khrushchev accused the president of establishing the quarantine "because of considerations of the election campaign." Most importantly, he told Kennedy that he would not order the captains of the Soviet ships en route for Cuba to observe the blockade.[36]

A goverment statement, issued the same day through Tass, was even more dogmatic. It reiterated the argument that the Soviet build-up in Cuba was intended to prevent a repetition of the Bay of Pigs invasion, and it warned that if Kennedy started a war over Cuba, the Soviet Union would "strike a most powerful retaliatory blow." In a letter to Bertrand Russell, written in response to his plea for compromise over Cuba, Khrushchev said he could not back down because that would serve only to encourage aggression. He did embrace, however, the idea of a Kennedy-Khrushchev summit to help resolve the crisis.[37]

On Thursday, 25 October, Kennedy continued to avoid any action that might provoke a hostile Soviet response. He decided to follow McNamara's advice and not intercept the *Volker Freundschaft,* an East German passenger ship. To force the ship to comply with the quarantine, the secretary of defense argued, might injure innocent people unconnected with the Soviet build-up in Cuba. Accordingly, Kennedy gave orders to allow the ship to pass. He also urged his advisers to make sure there was no incident on the seas until they had learned of Khrushchev's reaction to the proposals just made by UN Secretary General U Thant.[38]

JFK finally began to show signs on 25 October of recognising that the pressure from the blockade might not be sufficient to persuade Khrushchev to back down. In the morning, he asked his ExComm colleagues "to make appropriate arrangements for preparing alternative courses of action for discussion with him at a later meeting." During a late afternoon session, Kennedy sat with a folder containing drafts of the "Airstrike," "Political Path," and "Progressive Economic Blockade" alternatives that had been prepared by administration officials. The political option explored the value of negotiations with the Soviets under UN auspices or with Khrushchev at a summit. The economic alternative involved the extension of the blockade to cover POL.[39]

There was still, however, a paucity of discussion in the 25 October ExComm meetings of those alternatives and of how the crisis might be defused should the Soviets not yield to Kennedy's demands. There appears, for example, to have been no exploration of the American-bases-in-Turkey issue – on whether it was likely the Soviets would raise that subject and if, in the final analysis, it would be an acceptable *quid pro quo* to remove the Jupiters and the missiles from Cuba. That was in spite of the fact that Walter Lippmann had suggested just such an arrangement in his syndicated column on the morning of the twenty-fifth. Even Rusk, who was asked specifically about the negotiability of the Jupiters in a background press conference on 25 October, neglected to broach the subject in ExComm. In discussing a possible "political track," the secretary of state talked about negotiations in the UN and the possibility of prompting another government to propose a denuclearised zone in Latin America, a plan that would include the removal of missiles from Cuba. But he did not mention a diplomatic deal involving the Jupiters.[40]

In his message to Khrushchev on 25 October, Kennedy, as with all the correspondence between the two leaders since the announcement of the blockade, simply defended his position, condemned his adversary's, and introduced no terms of settlement to the crisis. What the letter did demonstrate was the extent to which Kennedy still felt compelled to remove the missiles from Cuba not only or even primarily because of the strategic threat they posed, but also in order to uphold his pre-crisis public pledges. Retracing the developments of the last two months, the president observed that in response to reports of a military build-up in Cuba, he made clear in September the unacceptability of an offensive missile deployment on that island. Khrushchev had reassured him both in public and private that no such weapons would be installed. By deploying surface-to-surface missiles, the Soviet leader had deceived the United States. Hence, Kennedy contended, it was Khrushchev and not he "who [had] issued the first challenge." JFK ended the message by urging his Soviet counterpart to take the steps needed to end the crisis.[41]

Behind the scenes, however, Kennedy was acting in a rather more conciliatory vein by 25 October, making arrangements for a possible *modus vivendi* with Khrushchev. Enlisting the help of Rusk, the president developed a contingency plan whereby Andrew Cordier of Columbia University would ask U Thant to propose publicly that UN commissions be sent to Cuba and Turkey to keep watch on Soviet and American missile sites. Cordier was an old friend of Rusk, and was in a position to contact U Thant at very short notice. Rusk dictated the message to Cordier over the phone and instructed him to deliver it to the secretary general if Kennedy gave the go-ahead.[42]

Dean Rusk revealed the existence of the Cordier ploy in 1987 at a conference held in Hawk's Cay, Florida, to commemorate the twenty-fifth anniversary of the missile crisis. Rusk did not attend but McGeorge Bundy read out a letter from him. In it, the former secretary of state claimed that JFK hatched the Cordier plan on 27 October and that it would have involved Cordier asking U Thant to call for the withdrawal of the Jupiters and the missiles in Cuba. Some historians have regarded Rusk's revelation as proof that at the end of the missile crisis Kennedy would have opted for a negotiated settlement rather than a military attack on Cuba.[43]

Rusk's memory, though, was faulty, as a recently released document from British archives demonstrates. On 25 October Sir Patrick H. Dean, the permanent United Kingdom representative to the UN, dispatched a top secret telegram to the Foreign Office in which he wrote:

I have heard from a most reliable source that Cordier (lately United Nations Under-Secretary) has been in touch with top level persons in the United States Government about U Thant's statement on Cuba. Cordier says that if a United Nations Commission could be introduced to keep a watch on Russian bases in Cuba under satisfactory guarantees, the United States might be prepared to consider allowing a similar United Nations Commission to look at some bases elsewhere, e.g. the United States bases in Turkey.

This plainly refers to the Cordier ploy described by Rusk at Hawk's Cay. But the date of the telegram shows it was not devised on 27 October, as Rusk alleges, but two days before that. And, further, the British documentary evidence suggests that the plan involved sending UN observers to Cuba and Turkey, and not, as Rusk also asserted, the actual withdrawal of the missiles.[44]

The Cordier ploy in itself does not indicate that at the dénouement of the crisis Kennedy would have resisted military action and compromised had Khrushchev not backed down. The plan, as Dean described it, would not have ended the crisis because it did not call for the removal of the missiles from Cuba, and it was impractical anyway as Castro would certainly have prevented UN observers from being stationed on Cuban soil, as he in fact did after the missile crisis. None the less, the Cordier ploy indicated that by 25 October Kennedy had started to recognise that a settlement of the crisis would require American concessions.

The Cordier initiative was only one example of the increasingly active role played by the United Nations as a forum for Soviet-American sparring over Cuba. Most famously, it was the arena in which Adlai Stevenson clashed with Ambassador Zorin. Stevenson had been busy since the emotional confrontation with his ExComm colleagues on 20 October. He had left Washington for New York by shuttle late on the evening of 21 October and had remained there for the rest of the crisis, labouring at the UN, except for a quick trip back to Washington on 26 October.[45]

The United Nations became involved in the crisis over Cuba on the afternoon of 22 October. When U Thant learned from his military adviser that JFK was preparing an import-

ant public address on Cuba, he asked to see Stevenson. By
the time he arrived at U Thant's office at 4:30 p.m., the
White House had already announced that the president would
be speaking to the nation that evening. Stevenson told U
Thant that the speech would be on Cuba and that it would
be tough. After watching Kennedy's address on television,
Stevenson delivered a request to U Thant for an emergency
meeting of the Security Council. Soviet and Cuban officials
made the same request the next morning. The Security
Council's first session on the crisis was scheduled for the
late afternoon of 23 October.[46]

Stevenson addressed that Security Council meeting at
length, using a speech written by Schlesinger and other aides.
The ambassador was nothing if not a good team player, and
despite his private reservations about the strategy that Kennedy
had adopted on Cuba, he faithfully adhered in public to
the administration line; and he did so in this speech. In
what was a classic rendition of American Cold War philosophy, Stevenson surveyed the history of international relations since 1945. Whereas the Soviet Union had been
consistently aggressive, the United States had displayed an
unswerving loyalty to the ideals of the United Nations. As
for the Cuban Revolution, what made it unacceptable to
Washington was not that a revolution had taken place, not
that Castro had carried out sweeping reforms, not that social-
ism had come to Cuba as a result, and not that the government in Havana was a dictatorship. Rather, it was the way
Castro had associated with the Soviet Union. "The crucial
fact," Stevenson asserted, "is that Cuba has given the Soviet
Union a bridgehead and staging area in this hemisphere . . .
that it has made itself an accomplice in the communist enterprise of world dominion."[47]

Stevenson emphasised the need to avoid 1930s-style appeasement and to maintain American credibility in explaining why the missiles in Cuba had to go. "If we do not stand
firm here," he argued, "our adversaries may think that we
will stand firm nowhere." He went on to explain that the
American resolution before the Security Council called for
an immediate removal of Soviet missiles monitored by UN
observers dispatched to Cuba. Once the withdrawal had taken
place, the blockade would end. At the end of his address,

Stevenson was able to report that the OAS had just passed a resolution demanding the dismantlement of the missiles in Cuba and pledging military collaboration between member states to bring that about. Predictably, Stevenson's speech was followed by long, denunciatory responses from Ambassador Zorin and the Cuban representative, Mario García-Inchaustegui.[48]

After the Security Council adjourned, American officials walked the corridors eliciting what proved to be a very mixed reaction from the various UN delegates. Stevenson, meanwhile, spoke to the press. He noted that Zorin had not denied there were missiles in Cuba and so had in effect acknowledged their presence. Hence, the Soviet Union had "itself fully confirmed to the Security Council the urgent necessity" of the blockade. Stevenson recommended that the Security Council and the international community in general disregard all the protestations of innocence that the Soviets would undoubtedly make. The next day he concentrated on working the African and Asian ambassadors to the UN, many of whom expressed their concern over the blockade at that morning's Security Council meeting. Stevenson encouraged them to convey their fear that the quarantine would lead to a war on the seas to the Soviets in the hope that this would encourage Khrushchev to respect the blockade.[49]

The climax of the UN debate on Cuba came on 25 October when Stevenson confronted Zorin in the Security Council. In his address that day, the American ambassador talked of the threat to peace caused by the installation of missiles in Cuba and the consequent need for the United States to respond by establishing a blockade. He added that he did have photographic evidence of the missiles in Cuba. In response, García-Inchaustegui stated that the weapons on the island were for defensive purposes only and that their deployment was justified by the unceasing American campaign of aggression against Cuba. Zorin, whose mental faculties were reputed to be fading by this point in his career, characterised Stevenson's address as tentative in comparison with his 23 October speech. He also claimed that the only evidence the United States had was "falsified information."[50]

Stevenson, incensed by Zorin's accusation, insisted he did have proof, and went on to challenge his Soviet counterpart directly: "Let me ask you one simple question: Do you, Ambassador Zorin, deny that the USSR has placed and is placing medium and intermediate-range missiles and sites in Cuba? Yes or no? Don't wait for the translation, yes or no?" Zorin replied that he was "not in an American court-room" and so would not "answer a question that is put to me in the fashion in which a prosecutor puts questions." Stevenson pointed out that the Soviet ambassador was in "the courtroom of world opinion" and once again pressed him for a direct answer. After further evasions from Zorin, he declared that he was ready "to wait for my answer until hell freezes over," a statement destined to become the most famous utterance of the entire missile crisis period. Stevenson said he was "also prepared to present the evidence in this room," and proceeded to do just that, revealing the intelligence photographs of the missile sites that had been taken, and supplying the other UN representatives with interpretive explanations of them.[51]

It was spectacular theatre. It was Stevenson at his best. And his assured and eloquent performance did much to galvanise world opinion behind the United States. Although this was Stevenson's most memorable contribution to the American cause during the second week of the missile crisis, it was by no means his only one. On 26 and 27 October he would play an equally important and generally overlooked behind-the-scenes role in shaping Kennedy's diplomacy.

The United Nations also became more centrally involved in the crisis as a result of U Thant's energetic endeavours. Following pressure from around forty non-aligned UN delegations to intervene, he dispatched identical letters to Kennedy and Khrushchev on 24 October, suggesting that the United States suspend the quarantine and the Soviet Union cease weapons shipments to Cuba for two or three weeks in order to provide a block of time for a settlement to be reached. While Khrushchev responded enthusiastically to the proposal, Kennedy, though encouraged by Stevenson not to reject it out of hand, told the secretary general that "the existing threat was created by the secret introduction of offensive weapons into Cuba, and the answer lies in the removal of such weapons." Without endorsing U Thant's plan in the way Khrushchev had, JFK indicated that Stevenson would discuss it with the secretary general.[52]

Following this up, U Thant dashed off new messages to the American and Soviet leaders on 25 October. He asked Khrushchev to keep his ships away from the quarantine line for "a limited time only," and urged Kennedy to "do everything possible to avoid direct confrontation with Soviet ships in the next few days." This, U Thant hoped, would furnish the time in which "the modalities of a possible agreement" could be discussed. Kennedy replied the same day, saying that he would abide by U Thant's stipulations providing Khrushchev did the same. On 26 October the Soviet leader accepted U Thant's offer but with the proviso that this arrangement "must be a purely temporary one."[53]

In the ExComm meeting on Friday, 26 October, JFK continued to advocate the application of pressure on the Soviets while avoiding action that might evoke a hostile response from Khrushchev. Although he authorised air reconnaissance missions during daylight hours, he did not endorse McNamara's idea of using night flights to collect intelligence through the use of flares because he thought that might provoke the Soviets and Cubans. Another example of Kennedy's predilection for only limited pressure was his decision to stop and board the *Marucla,* the first ship to be intercepted in the blockade. On the one hand, this conveyed to Khrushchev America's determination to enforce the quarantine. On the other, the fact that the vessel was owned by Panama and registered from Lebanon meant that although it had departed from Riga under a Soviet charter, it was unlikely its interception was sufficiently challenging to make Khrushchev consider a stern response. At 6:51 a.m. on 26 October an American party boarded the *Marucla,* did not find any prohibited weapons on board, and allowed the vessel to pass. Khrushchev ordered no retaliation to the incident.[54]

As the ExComm discussion proceeded on 26 October, it was finally acknowledged that the blockade might not be enough to compel the Soviets to remove the missiles from Cuba. In addition to carrying out military action if the quarantine failed, the other clear alternative was the extension of the blockade to include POL. Rusk did not wish to embargo POL for at least one more day, and Secretary Dillon preferred direct military action against the missiles rather than a mere embellishment of the quarantine. But McNamara indicated his support for that alternative, as did Ball. The president also talked of the possibility of making a decision "to embargo fuel." In notes taken at the meeting, Lyndon Johnson wrote, "Tomorrow Extend Blockade P.O.L." Bundy accurately reflected prevailing sentiment when towards the end of the discussion he observed that if the negotiations at the UN did not provide a quick settlement, "our choice would be to expand the blockade or remove the missiles by air attack."[55]

In many ways, the 26 October ExComm meeting mirrored the 20 October session. Stevenson, who had been preoccupied in New York during recent days, took the shuttle down to Washington first thing in the morning. Once again he raised an issue on which discussion in ExComm had been strangely muted ever since that acrimonious 20 October meeting – namely, the Jupiters in Turkey. On this occasion Stevenson offered his colleagues what would prove to be a highly accurate prediction. In the negotiations for the removal of missiles from Cuba, Khrushchev would "ask us for a new guarantee of the territorial integrity of Cuba and the dismantlement of U.S. strategic missiles in Turkey." The vice-president's notes say that Stevenson also mentioned the American missiles in Italy.[56]

As in the 20 October meeting, McCone expressed his complete disagreement "with Ambassador Stevenson's linking of Soviet missiles in Cuba to U.S. missiles in Turkey." Without being specific, he went on to say that "we must keep up the momentum so far achieved by the quarantine." Kennedy, in an untypical defence of Stevenson, responded to McCone by arguing that "we will get the Soviet strategic missiles out of Cuba only by invading Cuba or by trading. He doubted that the quarantine alone would produce a withdrawal of the weapons." But after further discussion, the president acknowledged that "there appeared to be little support for Ambassador Stevenson's plan." At 1:30 p.m. Stevenson hurried back to New York.[57]

The ambassador was not the only one of Kennedy's advisers to be thinking along those lines. On 26 October Averell Harriman, in a memorandum to Ball, argued the case for the Brazilian resolution in the United Nations that called for the denuclearisation of Latin America, including the removal of the missiles from Cuba. If that failed, Harriman proposed a settlement in which Washington and Moscow agreed to consider installing missiles in other countries only if they were already nuclear powers. The United States, therefore, would have to remove its missiles from Turkey and Italy but could still deploy them in Britain or on the seas (with Polaris submarines, for example). Moscow would have to withdraw its nuclear weapons from Cuba. If the Soviets did not agree to the plan, Kennedy, Harriman added, would have to extend the blockade to POL.[58]

Overriding the importance of all these developments on 26 October was Khrushchev's transmission of a long letter to Kennedy. Received by the State Department in four portions over a three-hour period beginning at 6:00 p.m., this message represented a departure from the previous Kennedy–Khrushchev correspondence over the past four days. As part of the game of bluff and counter-bluff, the two leaders had assumed an assured deportment, dissembling their own fears about the likelihood of a nuclear war over Cuba. This message, though, was suffused with an earnest, almost imploring tone. Frankly describing his concerns over the possibility of a catastrophic nuclear confrontation, Khrushchev wrote that he had "participated in two wars and [I] know that war ends when it has rolled through cities and villages, everywhere sowing death and destruction."[59]

More importantly, this was the first message in which one of the leaders did not write on the assumption that he could end the crisis without having to compromise. Khrushchev repeated the argument that the deployment in Cuba was defensive, motivated by a desire to prevent another Bay of Pigs invasion, and he implied that concern over the outcome of the congressional elections lay behind Kennedy's establishment of the blockade. Nevertheless, the Soviet premier did offer a plan designed to resolve the crisis. Towards the end of the message, he indicated that a promise from Kennedy to refrain from attacking Cuba "would immediately change everything." The president should thus "declare that the United States will not invade Cuba with its forces and will not support any sort of forces [presumably Cuban exile groups] which might intend to carry out an invasion of Cuba."

In exchange, Khrushchev implied, the Soviet Union would remove its missiles from Cuba. "These thoughts," he concluded, "are dictated by a sincere desire to relieve the situation, to remove the threat of war."[60]

A cable transmitted by the Soviet embassy in Washington to Moscow on 25 October may explain in part why Khrushchev sent this letter to Kennedy. The embassy reported that the atmosphere in Washington was very tense and that the American press was emphasising the predilection of various administration officials for an air strike on Cuba. The cable noted that these stories might be contrived so as to put extra pressure on the Soviet government, but argued that because Kennedy had staked his political reputation on a victory over Khrushchev "we cannot entirely rule out, above all if we take account of his entourage, the possibility of his making such reckless moves as a bombing raid on the Cuban missile bases or even an invasion of Cuba although this is clearly less likely." The embassy also reported that Rusk had stressed in a State Department press briefing the administration's resolve to do whatever was required to remove the missile sites. This cable may have caused Khrushchev to feel that an American attack on Cuba was close at hand, and hence his conciliatory 26 October letter was needed in order to secure a quick settlement to the crisis before such an assault was launched.[61]

What seemed to suggest that Khrushchev's offer might be part of a co-ordinated strategy was the approach made on 26 October by Aleksandr S. Fomin, Soviet embassy counsellor and the leading KGB official in Washington. During a lunch which he had arranged with ABC news correspondent John Scali at the Occidental Restaurant on Pennsylvania Avenue, Fomin suggested the same *quid pro quo* that Khrushchev had described in his long letter. The United States would promise not to invade Cuba; the Soviets would withdraw their surface-to-surface missiles under UN supervision and Castro would pledge never to accept these sorts of weapons again. (Fomin, it should be noted, has recently made the unconvincing allegation that this settlement was proposed by Scali, not himself.) When Scali informed the State Department of the conversation after lunch, Rusk instructed the correspondent to tell Fomin that the proposal sounded feasible but that it would have to be arranged quickly because time was running out. That answer, Scali was to say, came from "the highest levels." At the time the assumption seems to have been made in the Kennedy administration that Fomin's offer had been approved by Khrushchev, but this was not the case. Fomin, who had never actually spoken to Khrushchev, had made the offer on his own initiative, independently of the Soviet leader, with only Dobrynin having direct knowledge of his intention to talk to Scali.[62]

An emergency ExComm meeting was convened in the late evening of 26 October to appraise and frame a response to Khrushchev's message. After much discussion, it was decided to refer the letter to the State Department for further analysis and to re-evaluate the letter in ExComm the following morning. Most striking was the administration's failure to embrace Khrushchev's offer immediately and to dash off a letter of acceptance. This suggests that the concession which the Soviet leader had requested – a pledge not to invade Cuba – was one the president and at least some of his advisers were reluctant to make. Kennedy's comments during the ExComm meeting earlier on 26 October, especially his discussion of the Brazilian proposal on the denuclearisation of Latin America, indicate that he was indeed wary of making such a commitment. One component of the Brazilian plan was the provision that each participant agree to respect the territorial integrity of all Latin American nations. Having noted that, JFK asked "whether we could commit ourselves not to invade Cuba." After the Bay of Pigs, the idea that the United States might have to attack Cuba had persisted in the Kennedy administration, as evinced by the development of contingency plans for military action against the Caribbean island. Kennedy's response to Khrushchev's long letter showed that this was an alternative he was reluctant to abandon.[63]

Dean Acheson, meanwhile, was still on the scene. He avoided the ExComm sessions but did spend time in the State Department at Rusk's request. As Khrushchev's 26 October message came through, he drank Scotch with Rusk in the Secretary's seventh-floor office. Acheson was not impressed by Khrushchev's letter and he thought it would be premature to accept the Soviet leader's offer. Khrushchev, he argued, would never actually go through with it, and, anyway, it was important to keep the pressure on the Soviet premier now that he was on the retreat. "So long as we had the thumbscrew on Khrushchev," Acheson recalled, "we should have given it another turn every day."[64]

The relationship between General Lansdale's Operation Mongoose and the administration's response to the missiles in Cuba was also defined on 26 October. Marshall Carter of the CIA had noted in a memorandum the day before that "Lansdale feels badly cut out of the picture and appears to be seeking to reconstitute the MONGOOSE Special Group operations during this period of impending crisis." Carter went on to conclude that the Mongoose bureaucracy was too cumbersome to handle military operations during the present crisis. On the morning of the twenty-sixth McCone reported these turf battles to ExComm officials. Kennedy felt that "the Lansdale organization should be used and suggested it might serve as a Subcommittee of the NSC Executive Committee." A meeting, attended by the likes of McNamara, McCone, Lansdale, and Robert Kennedy, convened in the afternoon to solve the problem. After Lansdale expressed his dissatisfaction with the situation, McCone assured him that the CIA still supported the objective of ousting Castro but explained that in the current situation its primary obligation was to support the needs of the JCS and the military rather than those of the Mongoose planners. During the rest of the meeting, officials acknowledged Lansdale's position as head of Mongoose but at the same time curtailed his authority by transferring, for example, the planning for a post-Castro Cuban government from the Mongoose team to the State Department.[65]

The tension generated by the missile crisis intensified on Saturday, 27 October. Work on the sites in Cuba was continuing apace. A CIA memorandum, describing the situation at 6:00 a.m., noted that four MRBM sites at San Cristobal and two at Sagua La Grande seemed to be fully operational. That, Maxwell Taylor later acknowledged, was a matter of real concern to ExComm officials. The report also revealed that the Cuban military were being mobilised at great speed. Soviet ships were still heading for Cuba, and one of those, the *Graznyy*, was approaching the interception area. More disturbing news arrived. In the morning, the attorney general received a memorandum from J. Edgar Hoover stating that the Soviet mission in New York was preparing to destroy all of its important documentation. As Robert Kennedy later wrote, "there was the feeling that the noose was tightening on all of us, on Americans, on mankind, and that the bridges to escape were crumbling."[66]

What promoted even greater concern than all of this was the public message sent by Khrushchev to Kennedy via Radio Moscow that morning. More formal in tone than Khrushchev's private letter of the previous evening, it also raised the issue of the Jupiters in Turkey. Khrushchev pointed to the double-standard involved in JFK's refusal to accept Soviet missiles in Cuba when at the same time he had missiles stationed in Turkey on the Soviet border. Accordingly, Khrushchev altered the terms of settlement offered in his 26 October message. Only if Kennedy both removed the Jupiters from Turkey and promised not to invade Cuba would he take the missiles out of Cuba and promise to respect Turkey's territorial integrity. The mutual withdrawal of missiles would take place under the supervision of UN Security Council representatives.[67]

To American policy-makers at the time, as well as future historians, Khrushchev's decision to send two different messages within such a short span of time was baffling. The traditional explanation has centred on the tension between the Soviet leader and the hardliners in his government, with the argument being that the latter acted to restrain their overly-accommodating leader and to frame the 27 October message. Various former Soviet officials have cast doubt on the likelihood of that hypothesis. Khrushchev, they have confirmed, was firmly in control of the reins of state in the fall of 1962. While he did listen attentively to the advice of senior officials, it is implausible to suggest that they could have coerced him in this way.[68]

The differences between the two messages perhaps related to the role played by Soviet intelligence and the transmission of information from Soviet officials in Washington to Moscow. Khrushchev received information just prior to sending his 26 October message, such as the 25 October telegram from the Soviet embassy in Washington, indicating that the United States was on the verge of attacking Cuba. That would have encouraged him to rush off his impassioned private letter to JFK. By the time he composed his 27 October message, however, he had probably received intelligence indicating that the imminence of an American assault on Cuba was far less immediate than had previously been thought. Khrushchev perhaps assumed that the situation was less critical on 27 October than it had been the day before and that he could now seek to extract greater concessions from JFK.[69]

To resolve the dilemma created by the differences between Khrushchev's 26 and 27 October correspondence, ExComm decided to respond to the former message and ignore the latter, agreeing to refrain from invading Cuba but not promising to remove the Jupiters from Turkey. In *Thirteen Days*, Robert Kennedy (and perhaps Ted Sorensen who edited the book) claimed that he himself had been the architect of this approach. According to his account, he originated the idea after having read with dissatisfaction a State Department draft (probably written by Ball and Alexis Johnson) for a response to Khrushchev's 27 October message. The president then allegedly asked his brother and Sorensen (who endorsed the attorney general's plan) to leave the room, go to his office, and compose a message to Khrushchev according to their own tastes. With a few revisions, the president accepted the RFK-Sorensen draft and dispatched it to the Soviet leader.[70]

A variety of evidence, however, indicates that Robert Kennedy did not hatch the plan to embrace Khrushchev's private letter of 26 October and disregard his public message of 27 October – a strategy later dubbed the "Trollope ploy." The transcripts reveal that Paul Nitze was the first official to recommend this approach during the ExComm meetings. "What you do," he told JFK, "is to say that we're prepared only to discuss *Cuba* at this time. After the Cuban thing is settled we can thereafter be prepared to discuss anything." In other words, Kennedy should respond to Khrushchev's 26 October letter but not the one that had just been received. Later on, Nitze argued that "you would get support from the United Nations on the proposition, "Deal with this Cuban thing." We'll talk about other things later, but I think everyone else is worried that they'll be included in this great big trade, and it goes beyond Cuba."

McGeorge Bundy gave Kennedy an even more explicit endorsement of the Trollope ploy. "I would answer back," he advised JFK, "saying I would prefer to deal with your – with your interesting proposals of last night [that is, Khrushchev's 26 October message]." When the president stated that it would be difficult to reject Khrushchev's 27 October offer, Bundy disagreed: "I don't see why we pick that track when he's offered us the other track, within the last twenty-four hours. You think the public one is serious?" A little later he urged his colleagues to knock Khrushchev's Turkish proposals "down publicly . . . , separating the issues, keeping the attention on Cuba." If there were heroes on 27 October, then, they were Paul Nitze and McGeorge Bundy, not Robert Kennedy.[71]

Ted Sorensen, in addition to Nitze and Bundy, also expressed his support for the Trollope ploy in that morning's ExComm meeting before Bobby Kennedy had even started to contribute to the discussion. He told JFK that "between the *two* I think it is clear that practically everyone here would favor the private proposal."[72]

Other officials from both inside and outside the ExComm group also responded to Khrushchev's 27 October message by recommending that the president ignore it and deal exclusively with the 26 October letter instead. Dean Rusk, for example, has written that, "Although most people credit Bobby Kennedy, actually Llewellyn Thompson came up with the idea of how to respond to Khrushchev's linking American Jupiters in Turkey to Soviet missiles in Cuba." Harlan Cleveland has said of the plan supposedly formulated by the attorney general that "he was not the only person to whom that occurred as a matter of fact. I was up in New York and telephonically transmitted a suggestion to that effect, also." Francis T.P. Plimpton, a Stevenson adviser at the UN, claimed to have devised the same scheme. When he read Khrushchev's 27 October message, he told other officials, "For Christ sakes, let's accept the first one and disregard the second." Plimpton also recalled that Stevenson, who was in New York at the time, arrived at the same conclusion. Robert Kennedy, Plimpton argued, had received inordinate credit "for an idea that certainly occurred to me, and I'm sure to Adlai and to a lot of other people."[73]

The idea had occurred to Stevenson, who after his brief trip to Washington on 26 October was now back in New York at the UN. On 27 October NSC adviser Michael V. Forrestal passed on to the president a memorandum that included a Stevenson draft for a public statement, and JFK read it out to his ExComm advisers. The statement assured the Soviets that the United States never had "any territorial designs against Cuba." Stevenson also proposed that "we do not consider the Turkish offer . . . as an alternative or an addition to the Khrushchev proposal in his letter." Stevenson was advising Kennedy, in effect, to respond positively to Khrushchev's 26 October proposals and to ignore his 27 October message. In a draft for a letter from JFK to Khrushchev, transmitted by Stevenson to the ExComm group later that day, the ambassador recommended the same approach.[74]

Robert Kennedy, for his part, did come to support the Trollope ploy, but not as quickly as some of his colleagues. By the time he made his first contribution to the ExComm discussions, Bundy, Nitze, Sorensen, and Stevenson had already argued the case for accepting only Khrushchev's 26 October proposals; and when the attorney general did speak, he did not endorse the Trollope ploy. The United States, he said, should not only "give assurances that we are not going to invade Cuba," but should "obviously consider negotiating the giving up of bases in...Turkey if we can assure the . . . Turks and the other European countries for whom these bases were emplaced that there can be some assurances given to them for their own security." In other words, Robert Kennedy was encouraging his brother to embrace Khrushchev's 27 October offer, not to ignore them and accept only the 26 October proposals, as Bundy *et al.* had recommended. Later in the ExComm session, the attorney general once again argued that the United States should "be glad" to give "assurances that we don't intend to invade" Cuba, and be willing to "withdraw the bases from Turkey . . . and allow . . . inspection of Turkey to make sure we've done that." It was only later in the meeting, then, that Robert Kennedy started to espouse the Trollope ploy.[75]

Although the attorney general did not devise this plan of action, he, along with Thompson, did play the crucial role in convincing JFK to implement it. After the Trollope ploy emerged as the strategy of consensus, helped along by Stevenson's draft for a letter to Khrushchev embodying that approach, the president did not feel confident about its potential efficacy. Khrushchev, he maintained, would react by simply raising again the issue of the missiles in Turkey. Thompson interjected to say that he felt the Trollope ploy was worth trying. Robert Kennedy concurred. "It's certainly conceivable," he reasoned, "that you could get him *back*" to the settlement described in his 26 October letter. At that point JFK announced that he was in agreement with Thompson and RFK.[76]

It is clear, then, that several officials independently concluded that the best tactic was to reply to Khrushchev's 26 October letter, promising not to invade Cuba, and disregarding the Jupiter issue raised in the second message. It was not a case of Robert Kennedy hatching a plan that had not occurred to other policy-makers. The recollections of administration officials bear this out. Ros Gilpatric remembered that "there was a general agreement with this course of action." He could not recall Bobby Kennedy playing a special role. Harlan Cleveland put it another way: "a lot of people had thought of it. It was not that exotic a ploy. You answer the mail you want to answer."[77]

Robert Kennedy's role in the actual drafting of JFK's 27 October letter to Khrushchev was also not as dominant as he later claimed. Alexis Johnson recalls that this message was an amalgam of a draft composed by himself and George Ball and what he regarded as a "softer, less explicit" one written by Stevenson. The summary record and transcript for that day's ExComm meetings do indeed refer to a Stevenson draft and also a State Department version. The latter was presumably the one penned by Ball and Johnson. Rusk may also have contributed to the State Department draft because during an ExComm session that day he read out a letter which, he said, he had prepared. Of the two, it appears that Stevenson's draft, more than the State Department's, formed the basis of the final message. "The President," recalled Johnson, "finally took a part of our draft and left out some of the more important points, we felt, together with a part of Stevenson's draft, and this finally formed the letter that was sent."[78]

The transcripts indicate that Kennedy and his advisers used both Stevenson's and the State Department's draft as the starting-point for their discussion on how to compose a reply to Khrushchev's 26 and 27 October letters. Robert Kennedy's contribution to the shaping of the letter to Khrushchev was twofold. First, he did not feel the Stevenson draft offered a sufficiently explicit acceptance of Khrushchev's 26 October offer. Second, he did not wish to mention the missiles in Turkey, as Stevenson had. It was these fraternal objections which prompted the president to ask Robert Kennedy to leave the room and produce the final draft for the letter to Khrushchev. So the attorney general and Sorensen, as the latter recalls, did "pull together a final version" of the message to Khrushchev. But it was highly derivative of the work of State Department officials and especially Stevenson. As the president himself pointed out, there was "no policy difference" between what Stevenson had written and what Robert Kennedy was proposing. Both men advocated an acceptance of Khrushchev's 26 October offer. In addition, the first two paragraphs of the message RFK and Sorensen produced were largely verbatim copies of Stevenson's opening section. Even after Sorensen and Robert Kennedy had composed the final draft, Sorensen solicited Stevenson's approval, which was forthcoming after two minor changes to the text of the letter had been made.[79]

That Robert Kennedy, above all other American officials, created the strategy which ended the missile crisis and thus averted nuclear war is an idea that represents another strand in the tapestry of Camelot mythology. The president placed more faith in his brother than in other advisers, and so Robert Kennedy's support for the Trollope ploy was important because it increased the probability JFK would accept that approach. None the less, the process by which that strategy had been devised was plainly a collaborative one.

In his message to Khrushchev, then, the president called for a resolution of the crisis "along the lines suggested in your letter of October 26th." A permanent withdrawal of the missiles from Cuba under UN supervision, the termination of the blockade, and American "assurances against an invasion of Cuba" would be the salient ingredients in the settlement. Without mentioning the Jupiters in Turkey,

Kennedy hinted that defusing the missile crisis in this way could lead to their removal. "The effect of such a settlement on easing world tensions," he stated, "would enable us to work toward a more general arrangement regarding "other armaments," as proposed in your second letter which you made public." JFK's letter was transmitted to Moscow at 8:05 p.m. and also released immediately to the press.[80]

As the president and his advisers settled on the Trollope ploy as the best way of responding to Khrushchev's 26 and 27 October letters, the next issue they had to resolve was the problem of deciding on the step to be taken should that strategy fail. This is a crucial matter because it reflects directly on the question of how close to a military conflict, and even nuclear engagement, the superpowers were at the dénouement of the missile crisis. If JFK intended to react to a Soviet rejection of the Trollope ploy by carrying out an air strike or invasion of Cuba, then, given the likelihood of Soviet retaliation to that, the probability of a superpower war was high. If, however, Kennedy meant to follow up a Soviet decision to dismiss the Trollope initiative by implementing a diplomatic or other non-military strategy, then the chances of a Soviet-American engagement were correspondingly reduced. This was a question which preoccupied Kennedy throughout the 27 October ExComm meetings because he felt certain Khrushchev would in fact refuse to settle the crisis on the basis of his 26 October letter, as the United States now insisted, and would once again raise the issue of the Jupiters in Turkey. "The point of the matter," the president explained to his ExComm colleagues, "is Khrushchev's going to come back and refer to his thing this morning on Turkey. And then we're going to be screwing around for *another* forty-eight hours."[81]

Overall, Kennedy's performance during those crucial ExComm sessions on 27 October, particularly his thinking on the policy to be implemented if the Trollope ploy failed, was as impressive as it had been disturbing during the first two ExComm meetings on 16 October. Whereas McNamara had dominated the discussion on the opening day of the missile crisis, it was JFK who marshalled the deliberations on 27 October; and he did so with skill, asking pertinent questions, clarifying complex problems, and often bringing his colleagues back to the central issues. Whereas several administration officials made more circumspect and moderate policy proposals than those preferred by Kennedy on 16 October, the president, in contrast, strove on 27 October to temper the excessive zeal of some of his ExComm advisers.

There was a feeling, shared by many American officials on 27 October, that the time to attack Cuba had almost been reached. The JCS, Taylor reported to ExComm officials, recommended that "the big strike...be executed no later than Monday morning the 29th unless there is irrefutable evidence in the meantime that offensive weapons are being dismantled and rendered inoperable." An invasion of Cuba, Taylor added, should be carried out later. "That was a surprise," declared Robert Kennedy sardonically as Taylor finished. But outside of ExComm others agreed with the JCS. Acheson, for example, continued to make the case for an air strike limited to the missile sites. The news that a surface-to-air missile had shot down a U-2 plane over Cuba around noon and that the pilot, Major Rudolf Anderson, had been killed, increased the sentiment in favour of military action incrementally. "They've fired the first shot," was the reaction of one adviser. Notes taken by Lyndon Johnson express the sense that many ExComm officials had about the likelihood and imminence of an American assault on Cuba: "regarding the peace in the Caribbean – By strike no later than Mon a.m. Invasion."[82]

Linked to the interest policy-makers had in using force against Cuba was the general military build-up that took place in the United States during the second week of the missile crisis. That build-up involved readying a large number of fighter aircraft to carry out a strike against the missile sites and, secondly, transporting troops from various parts of the United States to Florida's southern coast in preparation for an invasion of Cuba. A private British report based on the observations of the Acting Consul in Miami conveyed the flavour of the situation well by comparing the atmosphere in Florida to "southern England before "D" Day." Military aircraft, it was observed, were leaving Miami's civilian airport at a rate of no less than one every minute on the morning of 26 October. The policy-making process in Washington took place against this background of a heightened readiness for war.[83]

What was striking about the move towards military action was that it occurred without the assurance that the Soviets had no warheads in Cuba. A 23 October CIA memorandum, for example, reported that, "While we are unable to confirm the presence of nuclear warheads, photo coverage continues to reveal the construction at several sites of buildings which we suspect are for nuclear storage." Hence, the CIA could not confirm the absence of warheads in Cuba. There was the possibility, therefore, that the Soviets might be able to respond to an American assault on Cuba with a nuclear attack using warheads and missiles from the island. Yet American officials were undeterred. Many of them ignored the critical question of whether warheads were present, and continued to believe that military action against Cuba was necessary.[84]

Warheads, it is now clear, were on the island at that time. Twenty of the forty intended for Cuba had already reached the island. Also forty-two of the forty-eight medium-range ballistic missiles, although none of the thirty-two intermediate-range missiles, had been installed before the initiation of the blockade. Moreover, General Anatoly I. Gribkov, stationed in Cuba during October 1962, revealed at a January 1992 Havana conference that the Soviets had managed to deploy a number of short-range, tactical missile launchers equipped with warheads. Those missiles could not reach the United States, intended instead for use against any invasion force that Kennedy dispatched. This missile arsenal was buttressed by 42 000 Soviet troops and around 270 000 Cuban soldiers and militia. Obviously, any American invasion would have met with redoubtable resistance from a combined Soviet-Cuban force of over 300 000 men armed with both conventional and nuclear weaponry.[85]

Kennedy himself was acutely aware of the feeling in his administration that the time for military action against Cuba was approaching. At several points in the ExComm meetings on 27 October he spoke of the likelihood that the United States would have to attack Cuba in the next few days. In discussing the NATO countries, he noted that, "They don't have any notion that we're about to *do* something." A few

minutes later in the discussion he explained what he meant
by that: "They don't realize that in two or three days we
may have a military strike which could bring perhaps the
seizure of Berlin or a strike on Turkey." Following McNamara's
advice, Kennedy agreed to intensify the pressure on the Soviets
and to help prepare for an invasion of Cuba by calling up
twenty-four air reserve squadrons.[86]

As the ExComm deliberations continued, however, it became clear that Kennedy viewed military action against Cuba
as a last resort. "I'm not convinced yet of the invasion," he
told his advisers. Rather, he was interested in trying two
other approaches before considering that alternative. The
first was the arrangement of a trade involving the Jupiters
in Turkey. In exploring that option, Kennedy had to ignore
the exhortations of many advisers who strongly opposed the
removal of the Jupiters. Nitze advised the president "to say
that we're prepared only to discuss *Cuba* at this time. After
the Cuban thing is settled we can thereafter be prepared to
discuss anything." Rusk argued that the question of missiles
in Turkey "is a separate problem [from the Cuban issue]
and ought to be discussed between NATO and [the] Warsaw
Pact." Bundy felt that Khrushchev's proposal on the Jupiters
was unacceptable because it would give the impression that
"we were trying to sell our allies for our interests. That would
be the view in all of NATO."[87]

Undeterred by the scepticism of his advisers, Kennedy
proceeded to examine in depth the possibility of a *quid pro
quo* involving the Jupiters. In a conversation during the
morning with Ambassador Ormsby Gore, he stated that "from
many points of view the removal of missiles from Turkey
and Cuba to the accompaniment of guarantees of the integrity of the two countries had considerable merit." He made
the same point more forcefully inside the ExComm group.
The gist of his argument was that if the Trollope ploy failed,
the United States should be ready to arrange the withdrawal
of the Jupiters from Turkey. Kennedy made this case partly
on the grounds that such a trade was equitable and partly
because his administration had been considering the removal
of those antiquated missiles for some time anyway, with the
implication being that a trade would be useful in that it
would facilitate the fulfilment of a long-held policy objec-

tive. "In the first place," JFK explained, "we last year tried to get the [Jupiter] missiles out of there because they're not militarily useful, number 1. Number 2, it's going to – to any man at the United Nations or any other rational man it will look like a very fair trade."[88]

Kennedy also claimed that forfeiting the Jupiters was acceptable because it was better than starting a war by attacking Cuba. Showing a genuine and appropriate concern over the consequences of a military engagement in the Caribbean, the president said that he was:

> thinking about what – what we're going to have to do in a day or so, which is ... sorties ..., and possibly an invasion, all because we wouldn't take missiles out of Turkey, and we all know how quickly everybody's courage goes when the blood starts to flow, and that's what's going to happen in NATO, when they – we start these things, and they [the Soviets] grab Berlin, and everybody's going to say, "Well that was a pretty good proposition." Let's not kid ourselves. . . . Today it sounds great to reject it [the Jupiter trade], but it's not going to, after we do something.

Kennedy reiterated the point later on: "We can't very well invade Cuba with all its toil, and long as it's going to be, when we could have gotten them out by making a deal on the same missiles in Turkey. If that's part of the record I don't see how we'll have a very good war." For JFK, then, trading the Jupiters was preferable to military conflict over Cuba.[89]

The difficulty about Khrushchev's proposal on the Jupiters, as Kennedy saw it, was that the Soviet leader had made it in public. "He's put this out in a way that's caused maximum tension and embarrassment," groused the president. "It's not as if it was a private proposal, which would give us an opportunity to negotiate with the Turks." Openly accepting the Jupiter trade as offered in Khrushchev's 26 October public message was problematic because it would convey the undesirable impression to the American public, NATO, and the international community in general that the United States was acceding under pressure to Soviet demands. For that reason, JFK developed an alternative strategy for removing the Jupiters. Assuming the Trollope ploy failed, the United States would attempt to coax Turkey and the other NATO allies into proposing the Jupiter trade themselves by explaining the imminence of an American attack on Cuba and how that might provoke Soviet reprisals in Berlin and Turkey, and by promising to replace the Jupiter deterrent in Turkey with Polaris submarines in the Mediterranean.[90]

Kennedy provided the clearest description of this approach when crafting a telegram to Raymond Hare, his ambassador to Turkey, late in the evening on 27 October:

> We're trying to get it back on the original proposition of last night [i.e. Khrushchev's 26 October letter], and – because we don't want to get into this [Jupiter] trade. If we're unsuccessful, then we – it's *possible* that we may have to get back on the Jupiter thing. If we *do*, then we would of course want it to come from the Turks themselves and NATO, rather than just the United States. We're hopeful, however, that that won't come. If it does,...we're prepared to do the Polaris.[91]

Swapping the Jupiters in Turkey publicly for the missiles in Cuba was only one of two strategies that Kennedy would almost certainly have employed before approving military action against Cuba. The second was the extension of the blockade to POL in order to intensify the pressure on Khrushchev and perhaps increase the chances that he would seek a quick settlement to the crisis. In an exchange with Bundy, Kennedy made clear that he would "rather go the total blockade route, which is a lesser step then the military action," if Turkey and NATO were unwilling to approve the withdrawal of the Jupiters. When Rusk talked later about the need to heighten the pressure on the Soviets, Kennedy noted that in the, "First place we've got the POL." Whereas JFK was relatively isolated in his support for a public trade of the Jupiters if required, his interest in adding POL to the list of items prohibited by the blockade was shared more generally by his ExComm colleagues. Bundy revealed that "the enlargement of the blockade" had "been on my mind a good deal." Nitze felt that one viable alternative was "to make a blockade, total." Robert Kennedy asked the question: "Tomorrow morning add POL?" It is highly probable, therefore, that the president would have ordered an extension of the blockade to POL before contemplating the use of force against Cuba.[92]

A less impressive aspect of Kennedy's handling of the crisis on 27 October was his continued reluctance to concede what Khrushchev had demanded in both his 26 and 27 October letters: a promise not to invade Cuba. "There are disadvantages" in Khrushchev's 26 October proposals, he told his advisers, because they involved "a guarantee of Cuba." McGeorge Bundy recalls that, "The president initially resisted a direct assurance against invasion, for he knew that influential forces favored such an invasion. The editors of *Time* among others had been pressing for it even before the crisis." Ultimately, Kennedy did decide to promise the Soviet leader that he would not attack Cuba, but the use of force against the Caribbean island was an option he would rather not have abandoned.[93]

The hallmarks of Kennedy's handling of the crisis on 27 October, none the less, were caution and temperance. Desperate to avoid military conflict over Cuba, he focused on a public trade of the Jupiters and an extension of the blockade as measures to be implemented before the possible use of force against Cuba. In addition, he decided to inform the Soviets privately of his intention to take the missiles out of Turkey in the near future. In an Oval Office meeting with his closest advisers, Kennedy asked his brother to offer this assurance to Dobrynin that evening.[94]

According to Robert Kennedy, he adopted a "carrot and stick" approach to his talk with Dobrynin at the Justice Department. The stick was the suggestion that unless Khrushchev promptly accepted the terms just offered by JFK, American military action would be carried out against Cuba. The carrot was the promise that the missiles in both Turkey and Italy would be removed "within a short time after this crisis was over," although that concession could not be part of the public deal. Dobrynin recalled that RFK was "very nervous throughout our meeting. In any case, it was the first time I had seen him in such a state. He did not even try to argue with me over this or that point, as he usually did, but repeated again and again that time pressed." Dobrynin has also maintained that Robert Kennedy did not present him with an ultimatum and that he suggested the Jupiters could be part of a formal settlement. Dobrynin apparently did acquire the latter impression, as Rusk has revealed that the Soviet ambassador "brought back to Bobby Kennedy a memo of conversation recording their exchange on the Turkish Jupiters, implying that we had made an official arrangement." Dobrynin was soon disabused of the notion. The letter was returned to him as if it had not even been opened.[95]

Although JFK's comments in ExComm and his decision to dispatch Bobby Kennedy to Dobrynin showed that he was anxious on 27 October to avoid a military conflict, it would be inaccurate to describe the missile crisis as anything other than highly dangerous. Despite Kennedy's (and Khrushchev's) best efforts, the confrontation could still have resulted in war. For instance, ExComm officials were unaware of the fact that during the crisis an American test ICBM was launched, and, moreover, it was situated near to ICBMS that had actually been alerted. Soviet intelligence might have inferred from this that an American ICBM attack was underway. Also an attempt to recall a CIA team, which had been infiltrated into Cuba during the crisis as part of Operation Mongoose, failed. The group carried out its mission, destroying a Cuban industrial facility on 8 November. It was not possible for Kennedy to micromanage the missile crisis, therefore, and this meant that events might still have spun out of control, despite his caution at key moments during the confrontation.[96]

As Saturday, 27 October, turned into Sunday, 28 October, the tension mounted. Many American officials continued to feel that military action against Cuba was virtually unavoidable. That sense was no doubt increased in the early morning of 28 October by a report from the CIA indicating that work on the missile sites in Cuba was "continuing its rapid pace. All 24 MRBM [medium range ballistic missiles] now appear to have reached full operational readiness." The memorandum added that three Soviet ships, in addition to the dry cargo vessels and tankers being tracked by American intelligence, were en route for Cuba.[97]

For Khrushchev, this was undoubtedly a soul-searching time. A number of recent developments had caused him acute anxiety. The downing of the American U-2 plane over Cuba, for instance, had occurred at the behest of local Soviet commanders without his authorisation. A Khrushchev aide recalls that the Soviet leader was "seriously worried" by the incident. Certainly, it must have furnished him with a sense that the crisis was spiralling out of his control. He also received a disturbing telegram from Castro on 27 October, written the previous night, predicting that within one to three days the United States would carry out an air strike or possibly an invasion of Cuba. If there was an American invasion aimed at occupying the island, advised Castro, the Soviet Union should "eliminate such danger forever through an act of clear legitimate defense, however harsh and terrible the solution would be, for there is no other." In other words, if Kennedy invaded Cuba, the Soviets should carry out a nuclear strike on the United States. Oleg Troyanovsky, who called Khrushchev to convey the contents of Castro's telegram, recalls that he:

> interrupted me several times and asked me to repeat the most important passages. It seems to me that he was not so much worried by the recommendation to deliver a missile strike at the USA if it invaded Cuba since Fidel himself regarded such an invasion less probable. Khrushchev was disturbed by the statement of the Cuban leader that the latter believed that aggression in the next 24 to 72 hours was practically imminent, most likely an air raid "on particular targets."

Capping the news about the U-2 incident and Castro's letter, ominous intelligence information reached Khrushchev on 27 October, indicating that an American attack on Cuba was imminent.[98]

On the morning of 28 October Khrushchev convened a meeting of the Central Committee in the government mansion in Novo-Ogaryovo in order to decide upon the next step to be taken. All the senior officials, including Gromyko, Mikoyan, and Malinovsky, were in attendance. New developments, in addition to the sequence of troubling news he had received the day before, encouraged Khrushchev to seek an immediate settlement to the crisis during his deliberations at Novo-Ogaryovo. The first was the receipt of an encoded telegram from Dobrynin, transmitting a record of his previous evening's talk with Robert Kennedy. Gromyko's assistant Vladimir Suslov passed on the telegram by phone to Troyanovsky, who read it out twice to the meeting then in progress between Khrushchev and his advisers. Robert Kennedy's assertion that Khrushchev needed to accept his brother's 27 October offer if he wished to avoid an American attack on Cuba sobered Soviet officials. "The content of the telegramme made the atmosphere in the [meeting] hall even more tense," recalled Troyanovsky. "It was said that Kennedy's proposal had to be accepted because in the final count it gave Cuba what we were striving for: a guarantee of non-invasion."[99]

The intercession of General Semyon Ivanov also influenced the thinking of Khrushchev and his advisers. After taking a telephone call, Ivanov told his colleagues of a report that Kennedy was set to make another address to the American people at 5:00 p.m. Moscow time. Although Ivanov's information was erroneous, Soviet policy-makers assumed it was not and that JFK would use the speech to announce that military action was to be carried out against Cuba. Disturbed by the array of disturbing developments during the past twenty-four hours – the U-2 episode, Castro's letter, intelligence indicating that an American attack was close at hand, Robert Kennedy's ultimatum, and the news of another Kennedy speech – Khrushchev now decided to end the crisis by accepting the terms of settlement proposed by JFK in his 27 October message.[100]

After composing his response to Kennedy's letter, Khrushchev instructed an offical to carry it by hand to Radio Moscow so that it could be broadcast immediately. In the message, he told Kennedy that he had just issued "a new order to dismantle the arms which you described as offensive, and to crate and return them to the Soviet Union." He said that he regarded "with respect and trust the statement you made in your message of 27 October 1962 that there would be no attack, no invasion of Cuba," by the United States or any other nations in the Western Hemisphere. That commitment, he explained, would ensure the fulfilment of the original objective behind the missile deployment: the defence of Cuba. Khrushchev did not mention the Jupiters in Turkey.[101]

The Soviet premier also wrote to Castro on 28 October. In deciding to withdraw the missiles from Cuba, Khrushchev had not consulted the Cuban leader. Castro, who heard about the settlement over the radio, felt humiliated – and angry. "Son of a bitch! Bastard! Asshole," were only the initial expletives in a whole series that he directed at Khrushchev on learning the news. Khrushchev obviously needed to justify his decision to the Cuban dictator, and this he did by arguing that the deployment of missiles had accomplished the goal of ensuring Cuban security. The settlement embodied in the Kennedy-Khrushchev messages, explained the Soviet leader, "allows for the question to be settled in your favor, to defend Cuba from an invasion and prevent war from breaking out." Alluding to Castro's support in his recent letter for a nuclear strike on the United States following an invasion of Cuba, Khrushchev warned that "we mustn't allow ourselves to be carried away by provocations," and exhorted Castro "to show patience." Pentagon officials, he argued, were trying to undermine the proposed settlement by finding a pretext to attack Cuba, and so it was important for Castro to resist supplying them with one.[102]

Khrushchev's message to Kennedy was received in Washington around 9:00 a.m. A few members of the military were dismayed by news of the settlement. Admiral George W. Anderson declared that, "We've been sold out." A belligerent General LeMay argued that the United States should bomb Cuba on Monday, 29 October, anyway. The president, according to his brother, was disappointed and disturbed by those reactions. Others doubted whether Khrushchev's 28 October message signified an end to the confrontation. Acheson, for example, kept reminding Rusk how the Korean Armistice talks had dragged on interminably. Even as late as 31 October, the former secretary of state felt, as he indicated in a letter to a friend, that the crisis was "not at, or apparently near a solution yet." [103]

But most American officials were relieved. At the ExComm meeting that morning Rusk congratulated all of his colleagues for helping to secure this "highly advantageous resolution" to the crisis. Bundy interjected that "everyone knew who were hawks and who were doves, but that today was the doves' day." Kennedy, on the advice of McNamara and Rusk, ordered all air reconnaissance scheduled that day to be postponed. He also emphasised the importance of arranging for UN surveillance of Cuba to replace that which had been provided hitherto by the U-2 flights. In subsequent negotiations, the president added, the United States should try to secure the removal of the IL-28 bombers from Cuba as well as the surface-to-surface missiles. He indicated, though, that the consummation of the settlement on Cuba should not be made dependent on Soviet withdrawal of the IL-28s. As for the public posture of his aides, Kennedy advised circumspection. Khrushchev's 28 October offer should be embraced, but, "We should point out that we were under no illusion that the problem of Soviet weapons in Cuba is solved."[104]

The president also approved a message to Khrushchev welcoming Radio Moscow's broadcast. It was, Kennedy acknowledged, "an important contribution to peace." In reiterating and clarifying the terms of settlement to the crisis, he added that, "I consider my letter to you of October twenty-seventh and your reply of today as firm undertakings on the part of both our governments which should be promptly carried out." Kennedy concluded by expressing the hope that a successful resolution of the crisis over Cuba would lead to tangible progress in negotiations on disarmament and a nuclear test ban. Apart from his letter to Khrushchev, the president also endorsed the Soviet leader's radio broadcast in a short public statement.[105]

As far as American relations with its NATO allies were concerned, the resolution to the missile crisis came not a moment too soon. On Sunday morning the United States convened a NATO Council session to inform America's allies of the probability that Kennedy would have to use force against Cuba. This was apparently part of JFK's strategy of trying to scare NATO into recommending the removal of the Jupiters. The meeting erupted as representatives of all fourteen countries protested. The discussion became so heated that Charles Bohlen felt compelled to arrange a meeting with de Gaulle to explain the American case. As Bohlen was preparing for the flight down to the French leader's country house at Colombey-les-Deux-Eglises, news arrived of Khrushchev's radio broadcast.[106]

The resolution of the crisis was further cemented in the continuing dialogue between Robert Kennedy and Ambassador Dobrynin. Having received news of Khrushchev's 28 October message from Rusk while at the Washington Armory horse show with his daughters, the attorney general went quickly to the White House. There he received a call from Dobrynin who requested another meeting. At 11:00 a.m. the two crisis-weary officials met in Robert Kennedy's office. In sharp contrast to the previous evening's meeting, the discussion was cordial. Dobrynin assured Kennedy that Khrushchev would withdraw the missiles from Cuba and said that the Soviet leader had asked him to convey his best wishes to the president and the attorney general.[107]

After his meeting with Dobrynin, a relieved Robert Kennedy returned to the White House. With what must have been a considerable sense of jubilation, the president and the attorney general reflected at length on the momentous recent events. "This is the night I should go to the theater," mused John Kennedy in obvious reference to his predecessor of a century before. "If you go," his brother responded, "I want to go with you."[108]

Conclusion

From the end of October to December 1962, the last ves-
tiges of the Cuban missile crisis dissolved. One thorny issue,
created by Castro's refusal to permit UN officials on Cuban
soil, was the provision of adequate inspection for the monitoring of the withdrawal of the missiles. That dilemma was
resolved when Moscow agreed to discard the tarpaulins covering the weapons on the ships returning to the Soviet Union,
thereby making it a simple matter for American U-2 planes
to photograph the missiles on the departing vessels. The
question of which Soviet weapons were to be regarded as
offensive was another problem. Reversing the position he
had taken in the ExComm meeting on 28 October, Kennedy
began to argue that the IL-28 bombers were offensive weapons
and so had to be removed. When Khrushchev acceded to
that demand and forced Castro to go along with it as well,
JFK announced on 20 November that he would end the
naval blockade. The Soviets withdrew all their IL-28s by 6
December. In this way, the settlement to the crisis over Cuba,
forged by Kennedy and Khrushchev at the end of October,
was implemented.[1]

John and Robert Kennedy, Nikita Khrushchev, Adlai Stevenson,
Kenneth Keating, and Dean Acheson had all played a role
in making the Cuban missile crisis – or at least exacerbating
it. It was Khrushchev who made the critical decision to install nuclear weapons in Cuba, but JFK's campaign to overthrow Castro (including, probably, Robert Kennedy's
implementation of Operation Mongoose), helped to convince
the Soviet leader that missiles were needed in Cuba to
discourage an American attack. The president's policy of
expanding America's nuclear arsenal and his decision to stress
his country's strategic superiority in public also brought
Khrushchev to the conclusion that he should emplace missiles on the Caribbean island. Keating, along with other Republicans, had in large measure caused Kennedy to promise
the American public that he would take vigorous action to

resist any Soviet missile deployment in Cuba, a pledge that made JFK feel compelled to confront Khrushchev in mid-October when he discovered that nuclear weapons were on the island. Even Stevenson had increased Cuban isolation and Castro's dependence on Khrushchev by laying the groundwork for the subsequent ejection of Cuba from the OAS during his trip to Latin America in the summer of 1961. Acheson, by insisting in the ExComm meetings that Kennedy order an air strike on the missile sites, made the crisis more dangerous than it would otherwise have been.

After the missile crisis, these six men travelled along divergent but in general equally hapless paths. A group of Kremlin rivals which included Leonid Brezhnev ousted Khrushchev from power in 1964, the same year that Keating lost his seat in the Senate to Robert Kennedy after a bitterly fought campaign. Assassins' bullets struck down John and Bobby Kennedy in 1963 and 1968. A heart attack on a London street in the summer of 1965 also cut short the life of Adlai Stevenson. Dean Acheson fared the best. Used by Presidents Johnson and Nixon as an *ad hoc* adviser, his reputation, tarnished in the early 1950s by the Korean War and McCarthy's attacks, continued its rehabilitation.[2]

External and internal factors coalesced to bring about the Cuban missile crisis – and to determine the way it played out. External considerations were certainly important. Among the probable considerations prompting Khrushchev to put nuclear weapons in Cuba was the belief that this would help close the strategic gap with the United States, undercut the Chinese criticism that he was failing to support revolutionary clients, and provide him with a bargaining chip he could use to extract concessions from the West in Berlin. Kennedy's pre-missile crisis policies towards Cuba were propelled in part by the standard assumptions that generally underpinned American policy during the Cold War: monolithism, dominoes, and the lessons of the 1930s. Kennedy tried to overthrow Castro because he regarded him as Khrushchev's puppet and so felt his position as Cuban leader represented an unacceptable extension of Soviet power. He suspected that the Cuban Revolution, unless quashed quickly, might prove to be the first of a long sequence of leftist revolutions through-

out Latin America. He believed that the failure of appeasement in the 1930s showed the necessity of an American commitment to counter the expansion of communist influence
anywhere and especially in America's own backyard, as with
Cuba.

The internal factors that were equally important in bringing about the missile crisis have usually received less attention from historians. Kennedy's relationship with the liberals
in his administration, especially Stevenson, shaped his policies towards Cuba in important ways. If JFK had been more
receptive to their arguments before the Bay of Pigs, he would
have rejected the plan. If he had embraced their views after it, he would not have organised such a concerted campaign to overthrow Castro during the second half of 1961
and 1962. A Cuban policy grounded in the ideas of these
liberals would have mitigated Khrushchev's fear of an imminent American attack on the island, and hence reduced
the likelihood that he would have deployed missiles in order to protect Cuba. Furthermore, a decision by Kennedy
to implement Stevenson's proposals during the first week
of the October confrontation, offering Khrushchev a negotiated settlement at the same time that the blockade was
announced, could have brought about a prompter and thus
safer resolution to the crisis.

Kennedy's relationship with Republican opponents, particularly Senator Keating, also influenced his Cuban policies. Determined to refute their charges that he had responded
weakly to the dangerous Soviet military build-up that was
taking place in Cuba during the fall of 1962, Kennedy explained to the American public that the build-up was not a
threat to the United States because it did not include offensive weapons. In this way, JFK acknowledged that the deployment of surface-to-surface nuclear missiles would represent
an unacceptable challenge to American security, one requiring
a swift and decisive response from his administration; and
this in large measure was why he felt bound during the first
week of the crisis to remove the missiles from Cuba with
either a military strike, his initial preference, or a blockade,
the alternative he came to prefer, rather than by means of
the diplomatic strategy developed by Stevenson. The public
commitments Keating and other Republicans had elicited

in September 1962 also ensured that Kennedy would not react to the news in mid-October of missiles in Cuba by simply tolerating the deployment and explaining that decision to the American public (which he could possibly have done by saying the Soviets already had the ability to strike the American mainland with its ICBMs and by noting that the United States already had in Turkey what the Soviets had just acquired – nuclear weapons on the border of its adversary). Those September public pledges helped sustain JFK's determination to remove the missiles from Cuba during the second week of the crisis as well. His citation of them on numerous occasions indicated that they were always an important reference point for him.

Kennedy's campaign for the presidency in 1960 may have contributed to the coming of the missile crisis. To bolster his chances of reaching the White House, JFK pointed to the Eisenhower administration's failure to prevent Castro's rise to power, and promised to make amends by overthrowing the Cuban leader if elected. Kennedy, therefore, probably authorised the Bay of Pigs operation in part to make good on his election promise. Khrushchev's fear after the Bay of Pigs that Kennedy would try once again to remove Castro, but on the next occasion use American force directly to ensure success, was one of the key factors behind his decision to install missiles in Cuba. Hence, it can be argued that there was a nexus between the 1960 campaign and the missile crisis, with the former helping to bring about the Bay of Pigs operation, which in turn helped convince Khrushchev of the need for missiles to protect Cuba, which obviously brought about the confrontation in October 1962.

Kennedy's conception of the relationship between public opinion and the foreign policy-making process also helped define his approach towards Castro. One of the lessons he drew from Britain's appeasement of Hitler in the late 1930s was that the public can exert an unhealthy influence over the pursuit of the national interest. In that case, the pressure applied by various interest groups had prevented British leaders from increasing military spending, a step made necessary by the threat of German aggression. In seeking to oust Castro, Kennedy was thus attracted to secret operations which could be used without triggering a public debate over the merits of that approach and objective. This explains why so many of JFK's Cuban policies, such as Mongoose, military contingency planning, and the assassination attempts he probably approved, were covert.

Domestic concerns were among the cluster of considerations that lay behind Khrushchev's decision to deploy missiles in Cuba. The Soviet leader probably felt that nuclear weapons in the Caribbean were helpful in part because they would allow him to make the argument to the rest of the Soviet leadership that this improvement to their strategic position meant that it was now safe to resume his suspended programme of cutting troop numbers in order to release resources for the civilian economy. Missiles in Cuba would also allow Khrushchev to use again the strategy of brinksmanship which the Kennedy administration's public assertion of American nuclear superiority had undermined in the fall of 1961. Fundamentally, brinksmanship was a device for accomplishing foreign policy objectives through rhetoric rather than the application of actual resources. In other words, it was part of Khrushchev's overall goal of concentrating more on domestic than defence needs.

Kennedy and Khrushchev were jointly responsible for the missile crisis. Khrushchev's decision to install medium and intermediate-range missiles in Cuba was an unnecessary risk. He could have enhanced Cuban security (and thereby undercut the Chinese charge that Moscow's support for leftist revolutions was inadequate) by deploying only troops and conventional weaponry on the island (and perhaps short-range, tactical nuclear weapons as well). Faced with the prospect of a direct clash with Soviet forces, Kennedy, in all likelihood, would have jettisoned any plan to attack Cuba. By accelerating the Soviet ICBM programme and by highlighting that policy in public, Khrushchev would have been able to placate the Soviet military, indulge his penchant for brinksmanship with credibility, repair the strategic nuclear balance that lay so conspicuously in America's favour, and to accomplish all that without moving the superpowers and Cuba to the brink of nuclear disaster.

Kennedy, however, was equally culpable. The sequence of events is important here. While it was obviously Khrushchev who made the decision to put missiles in Cuba, he did so only *after* Kennedy had ordered a CIA-organised invasion of the island, attempted to bring the Cuban economy to a standstill with a tight embargo on trade, arranged the diplomatic isolation of Cuba by working for its removal from the OAS, approved large-scale military manoeuvres in the Caribbean, and, although it is not clear whether Khrushchev knew of these, encouraged Operation Mongoose and contingency planning for an attack on Cuba, and probably approved various assassination attempts on Castro. That Kennedy showed no indication of even suspecting that these policies might appear threatening to Cuba's chief ally, the Soviet Union, was testimony to a remarkable myopia on his part. He likewise failed to perceive how the general increase in defence spending he carried out, his October 1961 decision to inform the public of America's nuclear superiority over the Soviets, and his tendency to emphasise this thereafter might have troubled Khrushchev. In the 1960 presidential campaign, JFK had predicted that the Cold War would reach its summit during the early 1960s. His policies towards Cuba and the Soviet Union helped make that a self-fulfilling prophecy.

Kennedy, moreover, may have missed opportunities to ameliorate relations with Moscow in early 1961, and with Havana both at that time and in August 1961 in the wake of the Che Guevara–Goodwin meeting. The offers made by Khrushchev and Castro could have been disingenuous, and even if they were not, they may have turned out to be problematic for JFK. For example, even though Khrushchev was interested in a Soviet–American rapprochement in early 1961, he may not have been willing to accept the status quo in Berlin as part of a *modus vivendi*, and this was plainly an essential requirement for the United States. None the less, Kennedy should have made a greater effort to explore these overtures. The Soviet and Cuban leaders were motivated to seek an improvement in relations with the United States out of self-interest, the former so that he could justify his defence cuts, and the latter to lessen the chances of a United States invasion and to help Cuba's ailing economy by, for example, encouraging Kennedy to restore Cuban–American trade to its pre-1959 levels. Precisely because Khrushchev and Castro were motivated by selfish rather than altruistic considerations, their attempts to open a dialogue with JFK were probably made in good faith. That their overtures were essentially at the private, diplomatic level also suggests that they were not public relations gimmicks. Despite all that, JFK did not respond to the offers from Moscow and Havana. Clearly, any improvement in the triangular Soviet–Cuban–American relationship that might have emerged from a decision by Kennedy to take advantage of these opportunities would have reduced the chances of Khrushchev offering and Castro accepting the deployment of missiles in Cuba.

Although Kennedy and Khrushchev shared the responsibility for causing the missile crisis, they also deserve the credit for defusing it. They managed to avoid a military clash on the seas. Khrushchev, with the letter he sent to JFK on 26 October, proved himself willing to be the first leader to offer the other concessions, and that message provided the basis for the final settlement. But Kennedy, ably assisted by his advisers, was able to dispel the confusion created by Khrushchev's two different offers on 26 and 27 October and to devise a shrewd and effective response to them.

Too often, portrayals of Kennedy's Cuban policies, as with assessments of his presidency in general, have been prone to oversimplification and exaggeration. JFK's record on Cuba was neither brilliant in the way that his supporters have insisted nor disastrous as his detractors have claimed: it was mixed. Kennedy's approach towards Castro before the missile crisis was utterly misguided. He tinkered with but never altered the assumptions on which American Cold War policies had been based. He exaggerated the threat posed by Castro to the United States. He implemented policies towards Cuba that were excessively hostile. He failed to take advantage of opportunities to improve relations with Havana and Moscow. He failed to listen to advisers who proposed creative alternatives to the policies he was carrying out.

During the first week of the missile crisis, Kennedy's performance was a mixture of the impressive and the disconcerting. If it had not been for the restraining hand of his advisers, especially Robert Kennedy, he may well have ordered a military strike on Cuba. Kennedy, in addition, should have paid far greater heed to Stevenson, whose policy proposals were on balance the most sensible and potentially efficacious of those devised by American officials during the

early days of the crisis. On the other hand, the basic decision made by JFK during the first week – that a naval blockade should be implemented instead of the military attack
recommended by the likes of Acheson – was sound. An air
strike or invasion, given the likelihood that they would provoke the sort of forceful Soviet response that would make
war virtually inevitable, were unacceptably dangerous alternatives.

During the second week of the crisis, Kennedy's overall
performance was superb. He was perhaps excessively concerned with the presentation of the American case to the
public, press, and international community; and, to be sure,
his reluctance to promise not to invade Cuba, as Khrushchev
requested, was the most disappointing feature of his thinking during the last days of the confrontation. None the less,
as the crisis progressed, he became more flexible and conciliatory, more earnest in his efforts to avoid war. He resisted the temptation to react forcibly to seemingly intolerable
Soviet provocations, like the shooting down of the U-2. At
the height of the crisis on 27 October he turned to the
removal of the Jupiters and the extension of the blockade
to POL as ways of avoiding the military options that some
of his advisers wished to implement if Khrushchev rejected
the Trollope ploy. In the end, Kennedy proved willing to
make the concessions – the withdrawal of the Jupiters and
the non-invasion pledge – needed to resolve the crisis. It is
impossible to prove what JFK would have done had
Khrushchev dismissed the Trollope initiative, demanded that
the deal on the Jupiters be a public arrangement, and ignored any decision by JFK to add POL to the quarantine.
At the end of that hypothetical lies a frightening area of
uncertainty. Still, the weight of evidence, particularly
Kennedy's comments during the 27 October ExComm meetings (though not the Cordier ploy), suggests that he would
have accepted a public trade of the Jupiters before resort-
ing to military action.

As with JFK, an evaluation of Khrushchev needs to be bal-
anced. His decision in the spring of 1962 to install nuclear
weapons in Cuba was probably not needed to fulfill his various
foreign, domestic, and defence policy objectives. His belief
that American intelligence would fail to detect the missiles

in Cuba before the completion of the deployment was mistaken. Most importantly, Khrushchev should have realised that the Kennedy administration would not tolerate missiles in Cuba, that a confrontation over the issue was thus inevitable, and hence the decision to put nuclear weapons on the island was simply too dangerous a risk to take. Like JFK, however, Khrushchev's performance was far more impressive during the crisis itself. His decision to respect and not challenge the blockade on 24 October, the settlement he offered Kennedy two days later, and his willingness on 28 October to embrace the Trollope initiative were all crucial contributions to the resolution of the crisis.

Why were Kennedy and Khrushchev so much more effective in extricating themselves from the missile crisis than in preventing it? JFK's inability to challenge the assumptions behind American foreign policy during the Cold War and to think about the long-term consequences of his actions explain in part his anti-Castro policies and his unwillingness to respond positively to Khrushchev's initiatives. Khrushchev, with his de-Stalinisation drive, the military cutbacks he attempted, and his development of the concept of peaceful coexistence, showed signs of being capable of revising the premises behind the foreign policy he inherited. But his risk-taking proclivities and impulsiveness – in other words, his general lack of caution – meant that he was capable of committing an error as egregious as installing nuclear missiles in Cuba.

Despite these shortcomings, Kennedy and Khrushchev were quick on their feet, and that mental agility helped them on 27 and 28 Ocober to stay probably two or three steps away from the point at which a military confrontation might have taken place. The other attribute that enabled them to reach a settlement was the genuine fear of nuclear war that they shared. This enlarged their willingness to offer concessions to end the crisis. Khrushchev, despite his use of brinksmanship, had expressed concern about the possibility of a nuclear exchange throughout his years as Soviet leader. For Kennedy, the crisis itself had a dramatic and educative effect on his thinking, creating in the midst of the confrontation the deepseated fear of nuclear war that he did not previously appear to possess.

If it had not been for Kennedy's consistently hostile policies towards Cuba and the Soviet Union and for Khrushchev's miscalculations in the spring of 1962, there would have been no missile crisis. If, however, leaders with less ability than Kennedy and Khrushchev had been at the helm in October 1962, the outcome of that confrontation might not have been a peaceful settlement. For Kennedy and Khrushchev, then, the Cuban missile crisis represented both the summit and nadir of their foreign policies.

Notes and References

Introduction

1. John F. Kennedy, radio and television report to the American people on the Soviet arms build-up in Cuba, 22 October 1962, *Public Papers of the Presidents of the United States: John F. Kennedy, 1962* (Washington, DC: United States Government Printing Office, 1963), 806–8.
2. John Bartlow Martin, *Adlai Stevenson and the World: The Life of Adlai E. Stevenson* (Garden City, NY: Doubleday, 1977), 725; Arthur M. Schlesinger, Jr, *A Thousand Days: John F. Kennedy in the White House* (London: Mayflower-Dell reprint, 1967), 629; Kenneth B. Keating, "My Advance View of the Cuban Crisis," *Look* 28 (3 November 1964): 103; Richard P. Nathan, interview with author, 2 October 1992; notes from conversations with Jean Monnet, Charles Bohlen, *et al.*, Papers of Richard Estabrook, document number 1860, National Security Archive (NSA), Washington, DC; Finletter telegram to Rusk, 23 October 1962, document no. 953, NSA; Oleg Troyanovski, "The Caribbean Crisis: A View from the Kremlin," *International Affairs* 4–5 (April–May 1992): 150–1; Theodore C. Sorensen, telephone interview with author, 4 May 1995.
3. See, for example, Philip Brenner, "Thirteen Months: Cuba's Perspective on the Missile Crisis," in James A. Nathan, ed., *The Cuban Missile Crisis Revisited* (New York: St Martin's Press, 1992); James G. Blight, Bruce J. Allyn, and David A. Welch, *Cuba on the Brink: Castro, the Missile Crisis, and the Soviet Collapse* (New York: Pantheon, 1993).

1 Approaching Camelot: John F. Kennedy and the Tools of a New Frontiersman

1. Oral history of G. Mennen Williams, 1, John F. Kennedy Library (JFKL), Boston, Massachusetts.
2. Oral history of Dean Acheson, 6, JFKL; Walter Isaacson and Evan Thomas, *The Wise Men: Six Friends and the World They Made* (New York: Simon and Schuster, 1986), 585.
3. Oral history of U. Alexis Johnson, 28, oral history of George A. Smathers, interview I, tape 2, 6, oral history of Maxwell D. Taylor, 24, all in JFKL.
4. Herbert S. Parmet, *Jack: The Struggles of John F. Kennedy* (New York: Dial, 1980), 60–78; oral history of Arthur Krock, 5, JFKL.
5. U.S. Department of State, *Foreign Relations of the United States, 1940* (Washington, DC: United States Government Printing Office, 1958), 35, 37. For a specific example of Joe Kennedy's contribution to the actual writing of his son's book, see Joseph P. Kennedy to John F. Kennedy, 20 May 1940, President's Office Files (POF), box 129, JFKL.

6. John F. Kennedy, *Why England Slept*, 2nd ed. (New York: W. Funk, 1961), 215–31.

7. Ibid., 66; oral history of Mark Dalton, 26–7, JFKL.

8. *Congressional Record*, 80th Congress, 1st session, appendix, 1422–3; James MacGregor Burns, *John Kennedy: A Political Profile* (New York: Avon reprint, 1961), 88; *Congressional Record*, 82nd Cong., 2nd sess., 3871.

9. *Congressional Record*, 82nd Cong., 1st sess., 10179, 10185–6, and 81st Cong., 2nd sess., 10645.

10. Ibid., 81st Cong., 1st sess., 532–3.

11. Ibid., 81st Cong., 1st sess., appendix, 993.

12. Ibid., 82nd Cong., 1st sess., 10179, 10185–6.

13. *New York Times*, 16 July 1960, 8; *Congressional Record*, 83rd Cong., 2nd sess., 2904.

14. *Congressional Record*, 85th Cong., 1st sess., 10780–8, 15450–3; John F. Kennedy, "The War in Indochina," *Vital Speeches of the Day* 20 (1 May 1954): 418–24; John F. Kennedy, *The Strategy of Peace*, ed. Allan Nevins (New York: Harper, 1960), 19–30.

15. Kennedy, "Report on his Trip to the Middle and Far East," 14 November 1951, Pre-Presidential Papers, box 95, JFKL; Parmet, *Jack*, 336–9; Kenneth P. O'Donnell and David F. Powers with Joe McCarthy, *"Johnny, We Hardly Knew Ye": Memories of John Fitzgerald Kennedy* (Boston: Little, Brown, 1972), 127–8. For an analysis of Kennedy's attempts to woo liberals during the 1950s, see Parmet, *Jack*, 465–78.

16. David Halberstam, *The Best and the Brightest* (New York: Penguin reprint, 1983), 19–20.

17. For a lucid description of Nixon's 1946 and 1950 campaigns, see Stephen E. Ambrose, *Nixon: The Education of a Politician, 1913–1962* (New York: Simon and Schuster, 1987), 117–40, 197–223.

18. Kennedy, *Strategy of Peace*, 33–45.

19. Richard N. Goodwin, *Remembering America: A Voice from the Sixties* (Boston: Little, Brown, 1988), 124.

20. Oral history of Smathers, 2–3, JFKL.

21. *New York Times*, 7 October 1960, 20, and 8 October 1960, 10.

22. Ibid., 21 October 1960, 18. Fulgencio Batista was the Cuban dictator whom Castro ousted in 1959.

23. Ibid., 22 October 1960, 8.

24. Allen W. Dulles to Eisenhower, 3 August 1960, box 88, Dulles memorandum for the record, 21 September 1960, box 89, *Baltimore Sun* clipping, "Seaton Supports Nixon on Cuba," 27 March 1962, box 105, all in the Papers of Allen W. Dulles, Seely Mudd Library, Princeton University, Princeton, New Jersey.

25. Richard M. Nixon, *Six Crises* (New York: Simon and Schuster reprint, 1990), 353–5.

26. United Press International Bulletin, text of Salinger's statement, 20 March 1962, Dulles Papers, box 101; Dulles to McCone, 20 March 1962, Dulles Papers, box 105.

27. McGeorge Bundy to JFK, "Nixon's comments on Your Briefing on Cuba before the Election," 14 March 1962, National Security Files

(NSF), box 36, JFKL.

28. Oral history of Robert F. Kennedy, volume 1, 40e, JFKL; JFK to Eisenhower, 18 July 1960, Dulles Papers, box 105; Dulles memorandum for record, 21 September 1960, Dulles Papers, box 89; *Washington Post* and *Times Herald* clipping, "Nixon Cites Ike to Back Cuba Charge," 22 March 1962, Dulles Papers, box 101. Apart from Dulles' briefings, Kennedy could have learned of the training of Cuban exiles for an invasion of Cuba from press accounts during the summer and autumn of 1960. See Stanley J. Grogan to Dulles, 22 March 1962, Dulles Papers, box 104.

29. Goodwin, *Remembering America*, 125; *New York Times*, 21 October 1960, 18; Herbert S. Parmet, *JFK: The Presidency of John F. Kennedy* (New York: Dial, 1983), 48–9.

30. Trumbull Higgins, *The Perfect Failure: Kennedy, Eisenhower, and the CIA at the Bay of Pigs* (New York: Norton, 1989), 67; Harris Wofford, *Of Kennedys and Kings: Making Sense of the Sixties* (New York: Farrar, Straus, Giroux, 1980), 344; oral history of Acheson, 5, JFKL.

31. Oral history of Alexis Johnson, 20, JFKL; George McGovern, "A Senator's View," in Kenneth W. Thompson, ed., *The Kennedy Presidency: Seventeen Intimate Perspectives of John F. Kennedy* (Lanham, MD: University Press of America, 1985), 47.

32. Oral history of Taylor, 2nd transcript, 3, JFKL; oral history of Walt W. Rostow, 154, JFKL; oral history of Smathers, interview III, tape 2, 4–6, JFKL. Reston and Alsop were veteran journalists, and Graham was the editor of the *Washington Post*.

33. Joseph P. Berry, Jr., *John F. Kennedy and the Media: The First Television President* (Lanham, MD: University Press of America, 1987), 62; David Halberstam, "Introduction," in *The Kennedy Presidential Press Conferences* (New York: E.M. Coleman Enterprises, 1978), iii; oral history of Dean Rusk, volume JJJ JJJ, "Reflections on John F. Kennedy," tape 2, 17–18, Dean Rusk Oral History Collection, University of Georgia, Athens, Georgia.

34. Acheson to Truman, 14 July 1961, Papers of Dean G. Acheson, box 166, Harry S. Truman Library, Independence, Missouri.

35. William E. Leuchtenburg, *In the Shadow of FDR: From Harry Truman to Ronald Reagan*, rev. ed. (Ithaca: Cornell University Press, 1985), 64, 74.

36. Parmet, *Jack*, 172–5, 212, 245–6, 307–11.

37. Theodore C. Sorensen, *Kennedy* (New York: Harper, 1965), 45–6.

38. Leuchtenburg, *In the Shadow of FDR*, 64, 75, 77; oral history of Smathers, interview III, tape 1, 16, JFKL.

39. Leuchtenburg, *In the Shadow of FDR*, 63, 66; W.W. Rostow, *The Diffusion of Power: An Essay in Recent History* (New York: Macmillan, 1972), 129.

40. Oral history of Robert S. McNamara, 9, JFKL; oral history of Adam Yarmolinsky, 23, JFKL. For background on the New Frontiersmen, see Halberstam, *Best and the Brightest*.

41. Benjamin C. Bradlee, *Conversations with Kennedy* (New York: Norton, 1975), 122. For reflections on and evidence of Kennedy's voracious sexual appetite, macho ethos, and competitiveness, see Garry Wills,

The Kennedy Imprisonment: A Meditation on Power (Boston: Little, Brown, 1982), 28–34; oral history of Henry Luce, 7, JFKL; *Time,* 2 December 1957, 19.

42. Michael R. Beschloss, *The Crisis Years: Kennedy and Khrushchev, 1960–1963* (New York: Edward Burlingame, 1991), 98–9; Thomas C. Reeves, *A Question of Character: A Life of John F. Kennedy* (New York: Free Press, 1991), 137–8; Bradlee, *Conversations,* 27; Dean Rusk, as told to Richard Rusk, *As I Saw It,* ed. Daniel S. Papp (New York: Norton, 1990), 294–5.

43. Kennedy, *Why England Slept,* 215–31.

44. Theodore C. Sorensen, *The Kennedy Legacy* (London: Weidenfeld and Nicolson reprint, 1970), 185–6; David C. Martin, "The CIA's 'Loaded Gun': The Life and Times of 'America's James Bond,' William King Harvey," *Washington Post,* 10 October 1976, C1; Wofford, *Of Kennedys and Kings,* 362.

45. Stewart Alsop, *The Center: The Anatomy of Power in Washington* (London: Hodder and Stoughton, 1968), 245.

46. Rusk, *As I Saw It,* 293; Wofford, *Of Kennedys and Kings,* 360–1.

47. Oral history of Rusk, Volume KKK KKK, "Reflections on John F. Kennedy," tape 2, Rusk Oral History Collection.

48. Oral history of Alexis Johnson, 11, JFKL.

2 Kennedy's Cuban Policies: Misconceptions and Missed Opportunities

1. Wilton B. Pearsons, memorandum re. discussion between DDE, JFK, *et al.,* 19 January 1961, Post-Presidential Papers, box 2, Dwight D. Eisenhower Library, Abilene, Kansas; Norman Brook to William Elliot, 14 December 1960, Prime Minister's Records (PREM) 11/3608, Public Record Office (PRO), Kew, Richmond, England.

2. John F. Kennedy, "For the Freedom of Man: We Must All Work Together," *Vital Speeches of the Day* 27 (1 February 1961): 226–7.

3. Ibid.: 227.

4. Oral history of W. Averell Harriman, 37, JFKL; P.H. Scott, minutes, "Cuban/United States Relations: Decision of United States Government to sever relations with Cuba," 5 January 1961, Foreign Office Records (FO) 371/156175, PRO; N. Khrushchev and L. Brezhnev, message to the president, 20 January 1961, *Public Papers of the Presidents of the United States: John F. Kennedy, 1961* (Washington, DC: United States Government Printing Office, 1962), 3n.

5. Higgins, *Perfect Failure,* 70–1, 79–80; Marchant to Foreign Office, 3 January 1961, FO 371/156175, PRO; telegram from Havana to Foreign Office, 21 January 1961, FO 371/156176, PRO; Marchant to Foreign Office, 5 February 1961, FO 371/156176, PRO; I.J.M. Sutherland to R.H.G. Edmonds, FO 371/156177, PRO.

6. Oral history of Harriman, 37, JFKL.

7. Walter Johnson, ed., *The Papers of Adlai E. Stevenson* (Boston: Little, Brown, 1977), VII, 615–17.

8. JFK, annual message to the Congress on the State of the Union, 30

January 1961, *Public Papers of the Presidents, 1961*, 22–3.

9. Ibid., 23–4.

10. United Press International, text of a government statement, 20 March 1962, Dulles Papers, box 101; Higgins, *Perfect Failure*, 67.

11. Bundy, memorandum of discussion on Cuba, 28 January 1961, NSF, box 35A, JFKL.

12. Bundy to JFK, 6 February 1961, NSF, box 35A, JFKL; memorandum of meeting with the president on Cuba, 8 February 1961, NSF, box 35A, JFKL; Higgins, *Perfect Failure*, 88; National Security Action Memorandum No. 31, 11 March 1961, NSF, box 329, JFKL.

13. Higgins, *Perfect Failure*, 92–6; Bundy to JFK, "Meeting on Cuba, 4:00 PM," 15 March 1961, NSF, box 35A, JFKL.

14. JFK, address at a White House reception for members of Congress and for the diplomatic corps of the Latin American Republics, 13 March 1961, *Public Papers of the Presidents, 1961*, 170–5; Goodwin, *Remembering America*, 150, 160–1.

15. Oral history of Smathers, interview 1, 5, JFKL; JFK to Bundy, National Security Action Memorandum No. 19, 15 February 1961, NSF, box 328, JFKL; Rusk to JFK, 24 February 1961, POF, box 115, JFKL; Rusk press conference, 9 March 1961, *Press Conferences of the Secretaries of State*, series III, reel no. 14, January 1958–December 1965.

16. Nikita S. Khrushchev, "Khrushchev Reviews 81–Party Moscow Conference," *Current Digest of the Soviet Press* 13 (22 February 1961): 8, 9, 11.

17. Maxwell D. Taylor, *Swords and Plowshares* (New York: Norton, 1972), 200; oral history of Walter Lippmann, 9, JFKL; Arthur M. Schlesinger, Jr., "A Biographer's Perspective," in Thompson, ed., *The Kennedy Presidency*, 29; oral history of Rostow, 124, JFKL; Chester Bowles, *Promises to Keep: My Years in Public Life, 1941–1969* (New York: Harper & Row, 1971), 344–5.

18. Schlesinger, "A Biographer's Perspective," 29.

19. CIA report, "The Sino-Soviet Dispute and Its Significance," 1 April 1961, NSF, box 176, JFKL; oral history of Robert Kennedy, vol. 2, JFKL.

20. State Department pamphlet, "Cuba," 3 April 1961, in Council on Foreign Relations, *Documents on American Foreign Relations, 1961* (New York: Harper, 1962), 446–8; president's news conference, 12 April 1961, *Public Papers of the Presidents, 1961*, 259. One example of an internal memorandum which referred to the "Sino-Soviet Bloc" was National Security Council Action Memorandum No. 2422, NSF, box 313, JFKL.

21. Schlesinger to JFK, "Joseph Newman on Cuba," 31 March 1961, Papers of Arthur M. Schlesinger, Jr, box WH-5, JFKL; Foreign Office to Washington, 28 April 1961, FO 371/156181, PRO; Foreign Office brief on Cuba for Bermuda meeting between JFK and Harold Macmillan, December 1961, FO 371/156185, PRO. The CIA came to the private conclusion that only one-quarter of Cubans opposed Castro. See Higgins, *Perfect Failure*, 91.

22. President's news conference, 8 February 1961, *Public Papers of the*

Presidents, 1961, 74. For another application of the domino theory to Cuba, see State Department pamphlet, "Cuba," 448–51.

23. Oral history of Dean Rusk, vol. 2, 317, JFKL.
24. Robert F. Kennedy, *Thirteen Days: A Memoir of the Cuban Missile Crisis* (New York: Norton, 1969), 90; oral history of McNamara, 17, JFKL.
25. J. William Fulbright to Kennedy, "Cuba Policy," 29 March 1961, Papers of J. William Fulbright, series 48:14, box 38, University of Arkansas Library, Fayetteville, Arkansas; Higgins, *Perfect Failure,* 110–11.
26. Schlesinger, *A Thousand Days,* 214–17; Schlesinger to Rusk, 7 April 1961, Schlesinger Papers, box WH-5; oral history of Robert Kennedy, vol. 1, 44–5, JFKL; Bowles, *Promises to Keep,* 327–8; Rusk, *As I Saw It,* 209–10; Paul H. Nitze with Ann M. Smith and Steven L. Rearden, *From Hiroshima to Glasnost: At the Center of Decision* (New York: Grove Weidenfeld, 1989), 184; oral history of Harlan Cleveland, 21–3, JKFL; Martin, *Adlai Stevenson and the World,* 624; oral history of Acheson, 13–14, JFKL; Peter Wyden, *Bay of Pigs: The Untold Story* (New York: Simon and Schuster, 1979), 316; Thomas G. Paterson, "Fixation with Cuba: The Bay of Pigs, Missile Crisis, and Covert War Against Fidel Castro," in Paterson, ed., *Kennedy's Quest for Victory: American Foreign Policy, 1961–1963* (New York: Oxford University Press, 1989), 135.
27. Sorensen, however, did learn of the plan by accident. See Wyden, *Bay of Pigs,* 165.
28. Schlesinger to JFK, 10 April 1961, Schlesinger Papers, box WH-5; Wyden, *Bay of Pigs,* 315, 316; Higgins, *Perfect Failure,* 90, 97, 105.
29. Lucien S. Vandenbroucke, "Anatomy of a Failure: The Decision to Land at the Bay of Pigs," *Political Science Quarterly* 99 (Fall 1984): 484–5.
30. Higgins, *Perfect Failure,* 126–40.
31. Ibid., 141–9.
32. Clark Clifford with Richard Holbrooke, *Counsel to the President: A Memoir* (New York: Random House, 1991), 349; Wofford, *Of Kennedys and Kings,* 351–2, 354; oral history of Rusk, volume 000 000, "The Kennedy Years," Rusk Oral History Collection; C. David Heymann, *A Woman Named Jackie* (New York: Lyle Stuart, 1989), 276; Richard J. Whalen, *The Founding Father: The Story of Joseph P. Kennedy* (New York: New American Library, 1964), 474; oral history of McNamara, 19, JFKL.
33. "U.S.S.R. Government Statement in Connection with Armed Invasion of Cuba," and "Message from N.S. Khrushchev, Chairman of the U.S.S.R. Council of Ministers, to U.S. President J. Kennedy," *Current Digest of the Soviet Press* 13 (17 May 1961): 3–5.
34. JFK, message to Chairman Khrushchev concerning the meaning of events in Cuba, 18 April 1961, *Public Papers of the Presidents, 1961,* 286.
35. JFK, address before the American Society of Newspaper Editors, 20 April 1961, ibid., 304–5; Goodwin, *Remembering America,* 180–1.
36. F. Roberts to Foreign Office, 20 April 1961, FO 371/156180, PRO; "U.S.S.R. Government Statement," 4.
37. Rostow, *Diffusion of Power,* 210; Goodwin, *Remembering America,* 187;

Bowles, *Promises to Keep*, 329–31.

38. Eisenhower, notes on luncheon meeting with JFK at Camp David, 22 April 1961, Post-Presidential Papers, box 2, Eisenhower Library; Richard M. Nixon, *RN: The Memoirs of Richard Nixon* (London: Sidgwick & Jackson, 1978), 234.

39. Barry M. Goldwater with Jack Casserly, *Goldwater* (St. Martin's: New York, 1988), 170–3. Goldwater recalls his talk with JFK as taking place on 15 April. This seems rather early, though. It was not clear by this point that the Bay of Pigs would fail. Perhaps the JFK-Goldwater meeting took place a little later and Goldwater misremembered.

40. Bowles, *Promises to Keep*, 331; Nixon, *RN*, 234–5; oral history of Robert Kennedy, 48, JFKL.

41. Goodwin, *Remembering America*, 188.

42. Bowles to Kennedy, 20 April 1961, Papers of Chester Bowles, box 297, Sterling Library, Yale University, New Haven, Connecticut.

43. Wofford, *Of Kennedys and Kings*, 341; Schlesinger, *A Thousand Days*, 358–64.

44. Stevenson to Kennedy, "Some lessons from Cuba," 23 April 1961, Papers of Adlai E. Stevenson, box 830, Mudd Library, Princeton University, Princeton, New Jersey.

45. Ibid.

46. Ibid.

47. JFK, address before the American Society of Newspaper Editors, 306.

48. National Security Action Memorandum No. 2422, "U.S. Policy Toward Cuba," 5 May 1961, NSF, box 313, JFKL.

49. Ibid.; Sorensen, *The Kennedy Legacy*, 182.

50. NSC Action Memorandum No. 2422; Eisenhower, notes on luncheon meeting with JFK at Camp David.

51. Rusk to all US diplomatic posts in other American republics, 5 May 1961, NSF, box 250, JFKL; memorandum of conversation between JFK, Stevenson, Rusk, and Cleveland, 24 May 1961, NSF, box 250, JFKL; JFK, press statement, 27 May 1961 [released to press on 29 May 1961], Stevenson Papers, box 832.

52. Stevenson to White House, 14 June 1961, NSF, box 250, JFKL; Stevenson to Rusk, 17 June 1961, NSF, box 250, JFKL; Stevenson, report to the president on South American Mission, 27 June 1961, in Walter Johnson, ed., *The Papers of Adlai E. Stevenson* (Boston: Little, Brown, 1979), VIII, 81–2.

53. U.S. Senate Select Committee to Study Governmental Operations with Respect to Intelligence Activities, interim report, S.Rept. 94–465, 94th Congress, 1st session, *Alleged Assassination Plots Involving Foreign Leaders*, 73–82. Historian Michael Beschloss suggests that Kennedy may have authorised the Bay of Pigs, despite the odds against its success (1500 exiles against a Cuban army and militia totalling well over 200 000), because he knew about the assassination attempt, hoped that it would be successfully carried out, and thought that this would give the Bay of Pigs operation a chance to succeed. See Beschloss, *Crisis Years*, 137–9.

54. *Alleged Assassination Plots*, 123–4; oral history of Smathers, interview

1, tape 2, 6–7, JFKL; Victor Marchetti and John D. Marks, *The CIA and the Cult of Intelligence* (London: Jonathan Cape, 1974), 306n.

55. Various FBI memoranda in Athan Theoharis, ed., *From the Secret Files of J. Edgar Hoover* (Chicago: Ivan R. Dee, 1991), 32–33, 36–37, 40; Kitty Kelley, "The Dark Side of Camelot," *People,* 29 February 1988, 109–11.

56. Kelley, "The Dark Side of Camelot," 111; Goodwin, *Remembering America,* 189; Lansdale to Harriman, 26 February 1977, Papers of Edward G. Lansdale, box 3, Hoover Institution, Stanford, CA. My thanks to Jonathan Nashel for alerting me to the Lansdale document. Giancana's brother and godson have recently contended that JFK was in fact transmitting secret FBI memoranda to Giancana, not material about the assassination attempts on Castro. This correspondence, they maintain, was intended to give Giancana a sense of the FBI's activities so that he "would always be one step ahead of the game." It was assumed the President was doing this in return for the help he had received from organised crime during the 1960 Presidential season. See Sam and Chuck Giancana, *Double Cross* (New York: Warner, 1992), 411–12.

57. JFK, address before the American Society of Newspaper Editors, 305–06.

58. *Alleged Assassination Plots,* 135–6; Goodwin, *Remembering America,* 187–8.

59. Newspaper clipping, "James Bond Qualities for the U.S. Guerrilla Fighter," *The Times* (London), 27 April 1961, POF, box 115, JFKL.

60. Memorandum of conversation between JFK and Khrushchev, 3:00 p.m., 3 June 1961, POF, box 126, JFKL.

61. Memorandum of conversation between JFK and Khrushchev, 10:15 a.m., 4 June 1961, and 3:15 p.m., June 4, 1961, POF, box 126, JFKL.

62. Memorandum of conversation between JFK and Khrushchev, 10:15 a.m., 4 June 1961, POF, box 126, JFKL; oral history of Rusk, 165, JFKL; Charles E. Bohlen, *Witness to History, 1929–1969* (New York: Norton, 1973), 483; memorandum of conversation between JFK and the Congressional leadership, 7 June 1961, NSF, box 317, JFKL; oral history of Robert Kennedy, 630, JFKL.

63. Goodwin to JFK, 22 August 1961, Papers of Theodore C. Sorensen, box 48, JFKL; Goodwin, *Remembering America,* 195–202.

64. Goodwin, *Remembering America,* 202.

65. Ibid., 203; Goodwin to JFK, 22 August 1961, POF, box 115, JFKL.

66. Castro and Dorticos, joint statement in telegram from Marchant to Foreign Office, 28 April 1961, FO 371/156182, PRO; Paterson, "Fixation with Cuba," 139; Szulc to Schlesinger, 23 June 1961, and Schlesinger to JFK, 26 June 1961, Schlesinger Papers, box WH-5.

67. Szulc to Schlesinger, 23 June 1961; G.G. Brown to R.H.G. Edmonds, 25 August 1961, FO 371/156185, PRO.

68. Goodwin, *Remembering America,* 152; *Alleged Assassination Plots,* 141; Bowles, *Promises to Keep,* 368–9.

69. *Alleged Assassination Plots,* 139–40; oral history of Alexis Johnson, 30, JFKL.

70. Lansdale to JFK *et al.*, "The Cuba Project," 18 January 1962, document no. 141, NSA; *Alleged Assassination Plots*, 142–3, 145.
71. *Alleged Assassination Plots*, 140–1, 146; John Prados, *Presidents' Secret Wars: CIA and Pentagon Covert Operations since World War II*, rev. ed. (New York: Morrow, 1986), 230; James G. Hershberg, "Before the 'Missiles of October'": Did Kennedy Plan a Military Strike against Cuba?" *Diplomatic History* 14 (Spring 1990): 175–6.
72. *Alleged Assassination Plots*, 140; Hershberg, "Before "'The Missiles of October,'" 176.
73. National Security Council meeting, 18 January 1962, NSF, box 313, JFKL.
74. Jean R. Moenk, "USCONARC Participation in the Cuban Crisis 1962 (U)," October 1963, 1, 3, document no. 3164, NSA; Robert L. Dennison, "CINCLANT Historical Account of Cuban Crisis – 1963 (U)," 29 April 1963, 17–21, document no. 3087, NSA.
75. Hershberg, "Before "'The Missiles of October,'" 174, 177–8.
76. Rostow, *Diffusion of Power*, 215, 218; Resolution of the O.A.S. Council, 4 December 1961, in Council on Foreign Relations, *Documents on American Foreign Relations, 1961*, 460–1, incl. 461n; Foreign Office brief on Cuba for Bermuda meeting between JFK and Macmillan, December 1961, FO 371/156185, PRO; National Security Council meeting, 18 January 1962, NSF, box 313, JFKL.
77. Various resolutions in Council on Foreign Relations, *Documents on American Foreign Relations, 1962* (New York: Harper, 1963), 336–48; Dean Rusk, press statement, 31 January 1962, Stevenson Papers, box 846; president's news conference, 31 January 1962, *Public Papers of the Presidents, 1962*, 90.
78. Rostow, *Diffusion of Power*, 219; newspaper clipping of a John Crosby article, "Shiny Words and Dollars," Stevenson Papers, box 846; Lansdale memorandum, "The Cuba Project," 18 January 1962, document no. 141, NSA.
79. Lansdale memorandum, "The Cuba Project"; JFK, proclamation on an Embargo of All Trade with Cuba, 3 February 1962, POF, box 114a, JFKL; White House statement concerning the embargo on trade with Cuba, 3 February 1962, *Public Papers of the Presidents, 1962*, 106.
80. "Big Maneuver Opens," *New York Times*, 10 April 1962; "President Sees Atlantic Fleet Hunt and Destroy 'Enemy' Submarine," *New York Times*, 15 April 1962; Chronology of the National Security Archive, 44.

3 Nikita Khrushchev and the Decision to Deploy

1. See, for instance, the Soviet reminiscences in James G. Blight and David A. Welch, *On the Brink: Americans and Soviets Reexamine the Cuban Missile Crisis* (New York: Noonday, 1990).
2. Dean G. Acheson, *Present at the Creation: My Years in the State Department* (New York: Norton, 1969); James F. Byrnes, *Speaking Frankly* (New York: Harper, 1947), and *All in One Lifetime* (New York: Harper, 1958); Harry S. Truman, *Memoirs*, I and II (Garden City, NY:

Doubleday, 1955–56); Sorensen, *Kennedy*; Schlesinger, *A Thousand Days*; Pierre Salinger, *With Kennedy* (Garden City, NY: Doubleday, 1966); Bowles, *Promises to Keep*.

3. Blight and Welch, *On the Brink*, 229, 238; Bruce J. Allyn, James G. Blight, and David A. Welch, eds, *Back to the Brink: Proceedings of the Moscow Conference on the Cuban Missile Crisis, January 27–28, 1989* (Lanham, MD: University Press of America, 1992), 7; essays by Raymond L. Garthoff, Barton J. Bernstein, and Thomas G. Paterson in *Diplomatic History* 14 (Spring 1990): 225, 232, 249–56.

4. Beschloss, *Crisis Years*, 329–30, 370–2; Blight and Welch, *On the Brink*, 242–3.

5. Blight and Welch, *On the Brink*, 252; Nikita S. Khrushchev, *Khrushchev Remembers*, ed. and trans. Strobe Talbott (Boston: Little, Brown, 1970), 431.

6. Edward Crankshaw, *Khrushchev* (London: Collins, 1966), 11–13; Fedor Burlatsky, *Khrushchev and the First Russian Spring*, trans. Daphne Sillen (London: Weidenfeld and Nicolson, 1991), 161; memorandum of conversation, 30 October 1959, POF, box 126, JFKL; Beschloss, *Crisis Years*, 16.

7. Crankshaw, *Khrushchev*, 11; memorandum of conversation, 30 October 1959, POF, box 126, JFKL; Macmillan to Eisenhower, 29 July 1959, PREM 11/2867, PRO.

8. Khrushchev, *Khrushchev Remembers* (1970), 32.

9. State Department Background Paper, "Khrushchev: The Man, His Manner, His Outlook, and His View of the United States," 25 May 1961, POF, box 126, JFKL; Khrushchev, *Khrushchev Remembers* (1970), 342.

10. Sergei Khrushchev, *Khrushchev on Khrushchev: An Inside Account of the Man and His Era*, ed. and trans. William Taubman (Boston: Little, Brown, 1990), 21–2; Raymond L. Garthoff, *Soviet Strategy in the Nuclear Age*, rev. ed. (New York: Praeger, 1962), 150–1; Michael P. Gehlen, *The Politics of Coexistence: Soviet Methods and Motives* (Bloomington: Indiana University Press, 1967), 67–108; Khrushchev, *Khrushchev Remembers* (1970), 469–70.

11. Stephen S. Kaplan *et al.*, *Diplomacy of Power: Soviet Armed Forces as a Political Instrument* (Washington, DC: Brookings Institution, 1981), 163–4; Nikita S. Khrushchev, *Khrushchev Remembers: The Last Testament*, ed. and trans. Strobe Talbott (Boston: Little, Brown, 1974), 24–34.

12. George F. Minde II and Michael Hennessey, "Reform of the Soviet Military under Khrushchev and the Role of America's Strategic Modernization," in Robert O. Crummey, ed., *Reform in Russia and the U.S.S.R.: Past and Prospects* (Urbana and Chicago: University of Illinois Press, 1989), 182.

13. Robert C. Tucker, *Political Culture and Leadership in Soviet Russia: From Lenin to Gorbachev* (New York: Norton, 1987), 121–5; Khrushchev, *Khrushchev Remembers* (1974), 12, 219–20; Garthoff, *Soviet Strategy*, 57; William T. Lee, *The Estimation of Soviet Defense Expenditures, 1955–1975: An Unconventional Approach* (New York: Praeger, 1977), 98.

14. Vasilii D. Sokolovskii, ed., *Soviet Military Strategy*, trans. and intro. Herbert S. Dinerstein, Leon Goure, and Thomas W. Wolfe (Englewood Cliffs, NJ: Prentice-Hall, 1963), 14–15.

15. Khrushchev, "Arms Budget Raised One-Third, Khrushchev Discloses," *Current Digest of the Soviet Press* 13 (2 August 1961): 3–6; Norman Gelb, *The Berlin Wall* (London: Michael Joseph, 1986), 71; Sokolovskii, ed., *Soviet Military Strategy*, 19–20.

16. Khrushchev, *Khrushchev Remembers* (1974), 397; typescript of conversation between Khrushchev and Stevenson, 5 August 1958, in Johnson, ed., *Papers of Adlai E. Stevenson*, VII, 268, 270–1. The emphasis in the quotation is in the original memorandum.

17. Khrushchev, *Khrushchev Remembers* (1974), 400.

18. Stevenson memorandum, 25 January 1960, Stevenson Papers, box 791.

19. Ibid.; Stevenson to Menshikov, 22 January 1960, Stevenson Papers, box 791.

20. Stevenson memorandum, 25 January 1960.

21. Khrushchev, *Khrushchev Remembers* (1970), 458; Beschloss, *Crisis Years*, 15; memorandum of conversation, 15 September 1959, POF, box 126, JFKL.

22. Khrushchev, *Khrushchev Remembers* (1974), 490–1, 491n.

23. Khrushchev, "For Friendship Among All Peoples, For Peace throughout the World," *Current Digest of the Soviet Press* 13 (1 February 1961): 24.

24. Oral history of Harriman, 37, JFKL.

25. "Message from N.S. Khrushchev, Chairman of the U.S.S.R. Council of Ministers, to U.S. President J. Kennedy," *Current Digest of the Soviet Press* 13 (17 May 1961): 4–5, 7–9; Minde and Hennessey, "Reform of the Soviet Military," 195–6.

26. Khrushchev, "Arms Budget Raised," 3–6; Garthoff, *Soviet Strategy*, 57.

27. Tucker, *Political Culture and Leadership*, 124.

28. Gehlen, *Politics of Coexistence*, 126–7. See, also, Harry Hanak, "Introduction," in Hanak, ed., *Soviet Foreign Policy since the Death of Stalin* (London: Routledge and K. Paul, 1972), 11.

29. Khrushchev, *Khrushchev Remembers* (1970), 405; memorandum of conversation between Khrushchev and Harriman, 23 June 1959, POF, box 126, JFKL; Gelb, *Berlin Wall*, 120. See, also, John Prados, *The Soviet Estimate: U.S. Intelligence Analysis and Russian Military Strength* (New York: Dial, 1982), 77–8; Allyn *et al.*, eds., *Back to the Brink*, 64.

30. Joseph L. Nogee and Robert H. Donaldson, *Soviet Foreign Policy since World War II* (New York: Pergamon, 1981), 110–11.

31. Beschloss, *Crisis Years*, 329–32; Hanak, "Introduction," 11.

32. Gelb, *Berlin Wall*, 51–64.

33. Khrushchev, "On Peaceful Coexistence," *Foreign Affairs* 38 (October 1959): 11; Khrushchev to Macmillan, 13 December 1961, PREM 11/3539, PRO.

34. Bryant Wedge, "Khrushchev at a Distance – A Study of Public Personality," *Trans-Action* 5 (October 1968): 27; Walter Lippmann, "Today and Tomorrow," *Washington Post*, 19 April 1961, in POF, box 126, JFKL.

35. Memorandum of conversation between Khrushchev and Harriman,

23 June 1959; F. Roberts to Foreign Office, 3 July 1961, PREM 11/ 3603, PRO; Stephen E. Ambrose, *Rise to Globalism: American Foreign Policy, 1938–1976*, rev. ed. (New York: Penguin, 1976), 259; Hope M. Harrison, "Ulbricht and the Concrete "Rose": New Archival Evidence on the Dynamics of Soviet-East German Relations and the Berlin Crisis," Cold War International History Project, Woodrow Wilson Center (1993), 56.

36. Stephen E. Ambrose, *Eisenhower: The President* (London: George Allen & Unwin, 1984), 502–4, 516–21, 525–6.
37. Harrison, "Ulbricht," 54–56; Gelb, *Berlin Wall*, 105–7, 134–6, 142–8.
38. Richard Lowenthal, "After Cuba, Berlin?" *Encounter* 19 (December 1962): 49; Burlatsky, *Khrushchev and the First Russian Spring*, 174.
39. Adam B. Ulam, *Expansion and Coexistence: The History of Soviet Foreign Policy, 1917–1967* (New York: Praeger, 1968), v; Burlatsky, *Khrushchev and the First Russian Spring*, 156.
40. Nogee and Donaldson, *Soviet Foreign Policy*, 208–13; Lowell Dittmer, *Sino-Soviet Normalization and Its International Implications, 1945–1990* (Seattle: University of Washington Press, 1992), 5–7, 23, 29–32.
41. Nogee and Donaldson, *Soviet Foreign Policy*, 214; Dittmer, *Sino-Soviet Normalization*, 17–22.
42. Jacques Lévesque, *The USSR and the Cuban Revolution*, trans. Deanna Drendel Leboeuf (New York: Praeger, 1978), 9–13.
43. Hugh Thomas, *Cuba or the Pursuit of Freedom* (London: Eyre & Spottiswoode, 1971), 1263–6, 1279, 1289–91.
44. Lévesque, *USSR and the Cuban Revolution*, 18.
45. Ibid., 16, 24, 36; Khrushchev, "Khrushchev Reviews 81-Party Moscow Conference," 11.
46. Memorandum of conversation between Karl L. Rankin and Edvard Kardelj, 19 April 1961, Papers of Karl L. Rankin, box 40, Mudd Library, Princeton University, Princeton, New Jersey.
47. Explorations of how the Sino-Soviet split influenced Khrushchev's decision to install missiles in Cuba include Robert D. Crane, "The Sino-Soviet Dispute on War and the Cuban Crisis," *Orbis* 8 (Fall 1964): 537–49; Lévesque, *The USSR and the Cuban Revolution*, 38–9.
48. William Taubman is one of the few scholars to suggest that Khrushchev may have put missiles in Cuba for reasons other than just wishing to repair the strategic gap and to protect Cuba. See Allyn *et al.*, eds., *Back to the Brink*, 121–2.
49. Burlatsky, *Khrushchev and the First Russian Spring*, 171.
50. See Mikoyan's comments in Blight and Welch, *On the Brink*, 238.
51. Ibid., 238–9.
52. Allyn *et al.*, eds, *Back to the Brink*, 150; Blight and Welch, *On the Brink*, 239.
53. Blight and Welch, *On the Brink*, 332; Allyn *et al.*, eds., *Back to the Brink*, 29, 50–1, 54–5, 151; Tad Szulc, *Fidel: A Critical Portrait* (New York: William Morrow, 1986), 578–9, 582; Blight, Allyn, and Welch, *Cuba on the Brink*, 198.
54. Roy A. Medvedev, *Khrushchev*, trans. Brian Pearce (Oxford: Blackwell, 1982), 184; Raymond L. Garthoff, "Cuban Missile Crisis: The Soviet

Story," *Foreign Policy* 72 (Fall 1988): 66.

55. Allyn *et al.*, eds., *Back to the Brink*, 51–2, 71, 123; 'Draft Agreement between Cuba and the USSR on Military Cooperation and Mutual Defense', August 1962, in Laurence Chang and Peter Kornbluh, eds, *The Cuban Missile Crisis, 1962: A Documents Reader* (New York: New Press, 1992), 54–6.

56. Bernd Greiner, "The Soviet View: An Interview with Sergo Mikoyan," *Diplomatic History* 14 (Spring 1990): 213–14.

57. Garthoff, "Cuban Missile Crisis," 67; Raymond L. Garthoff, *Reflections on the Cuban Missile Crisis*, rev. ed. (Washington, DC: Brookings Institution, 1989), 18; Martin Tolchin, "U.S. Underestimated Soviet Force in Cuba during '62 Missile Crisis,'" *New York Times*, 15 January 1992; Anatoli I. Gribkov and William Y. Smith, *Operation ANADYR: U.S. and Soviet Generals Recount the Cuban Missile Crisis* (Chicago: Edition Q, 1994), 28.

58. Garthoff, *Reflections*, 20; Gribkov and Smith, *Operation ANADYR*, 26–27. There is some confusion over the precise number of medium and intermediate-range missiles that were to be deployed. See the previous Gribkov citation for somewhat different figures.

59. Arthur M. Schlesinger, Jr., "Four Days with Fidel: A Havana Diary," *New York Review of Books*, 26 March 1992, 23; Malinovsky to Pliyev, quoted in *Cold War International History Project Bulletin* 2 (Fall 1992): 40; Mark Kramer, "Tactical Nuclear Weapons, Soviet Command Authority, and the Cuban Missile Crisis," and James G. Blight, Bruce J. Allyn, and David A. Welch, "Kramer vs. Kramer: Or, How Can You Have Revisionism in the Absence of Orthodoxy?" *Cold War International History Project Bulletin* 3 (Fall 1993): 40–50; Gribkov and Smith, *Operation ANADYR*, 4–6, 27–28, 46, 62–63.

60. Garthoff, "Cuban Missile Crisis," 68.

61. Greiner, "The Soviet View," 214–15; Graham T. Allison, *Essence of Decision: Explaining the Cuban Missile Crisis* (New York: HarperCollins, 1971), 107–8.

4 The Fall Offensive of Senator Keating

1. Bobbie Kilberg, interview with author, 25 June 1992; Richard P. Nathan, telephone interview with author, 2 October 1992. For a succinct account of the 1964 Senate race in New York, see Arthur M. Schlesinger, Jr, *Robert Kennedy and His Times* (New York: Ballantine, 1979), 718–29. Keating's role in the events leading up to the missile crisis has been largely ignored by historians. The only scholarship devoted specifically to him is Thomas G. Paterson, "The Historian as Detective: Senator Kenneth Keating, the Missiles in October, and His Mysterious Sources," *Diplomatic History* 11 (Winter 1987): 67–70.

2. *Biographical Directory of the United States Congress, 1774–1989* (Washington, DC: United States Government Printing Office, 1989), 1290; John E. Findling, *Dictionary of American Diplomatic History* (Westport, CT: Greenwood, 1980), 256–7; Nelson Lichtenstein, ed., *Political Profiles: The Kennedy Years* (New York: Facts on File, 1976), 261; *Wall*

Street Journal, 19 April 1963, 10; Schlesinger, *Robert Kennedy and His Times,* 724; Jacob K. Javits with Rafael Steinberg, *Javits: The Autobiography of a Public Man* (Boston: Houghton Mifflin, 1981), 357; Kilberg interview; Robert R. McMillan, interview with author, 12 June 1992.

3. Patricia Shakow, telephone interview with author, 16 June 1992; Abbott A. Leban, telephone interview with author, 8 June 1992; oral history of Kenneth B. Keating, Eisenhower administration project, oral history project, Columbia University, New York.

4. Nathan interview; Shakow interview; Kilberg interview; McMillan interview; Milton Eisenberg, telephone interview with author, 28 September 1992; Eleanor Merrill, telephone interview with author, 28 October 1992.

5. Keating interview, Columbia Oral History Project; Shakow interview; Kilberg interview; Mary Pitcairn Keating, interview with author, 15 May 1992.

6. Keating, "My Advance View," 96, 99.

7. Keating memorandum, "Senator Keating's Record on Cuba," 12 October 1964, Papers of Kenneth B. Keating, series II, box 489, Rush Rhees Library, Rochester, New York; Keating, "My Advance View," 99.

8. Keating to Robert Fay, 18 August 1959, Keating Papers, series II, box 10.

9. *Congressional Record,* 87th Cong., 1st sess., 2708, 4733.

10. Ibid., 87th Cong., 1st sess., 6076.

11. Press release, "Keating Suggests Naval Blockade and Trade Embargo of Cuba," 30 April 1961, Keating Papers, series II, box 478.

12. *Congressional Record,* 87th Cong., 1st sess., 12581.

13. Ibid., 87th Cong., 2nd sess., 18360.

14. Ibid., 18361.

15. Mary Pitcairn Keating interview.

16. Marianda C. Arensberg to Keating, 10 August 1961, series II, box 1026, Fernando Garcia-Chacon, 23 April 1962, series II, box 1026, letter, unauthored and undated, beginning "Yours of Sep. 24 and 29," series II, box 828, Keating to Rusk, 18 October 1962, series II, box 828, Rusk to Keating, 29 October 1962, series II, box 828, Keating to Rusk, 29 October 1962, all in Keating Papers.

   Investigative reporter Warren Hinckle and ex-FBI agent William W. Turner believe that Keating received some of his information on the Soviet build-up from the Cuban Student Directorate's underground intelligence network in Cuba. See Hinckle and Turner, *Deadly Secrets: The CIA-Mafia War Against Castro and the Assassination of J.F.K.* (New York: Thunder's Mouth, 1992), 148.

17. Leban interview; McMillan interview.

18. McMillan interview.

19. Note (including a newspaper clipping) from McMillan to Keating, 23 October 1972, Keating Papers, series VII, box 48; McMillan interview; Robert R. McMillan, "A Look Back at Cuban Missile Crisis," *Newsday,* 14 October 1983, 72.

20. McMillan interview; McMillan, "A Look Back at the Cuban Missile

Crisis," 72; McMillan to Keating, "Visit to South America," 21 December 1961, Keating Papers, series VII, box 48; Harry S. Dent, telephone interview with author, 15 September 1992. As of December 1961, Khrushchev had not even authorised the construction of missile sites in Cuba. He apparently did not even consider doing so until spring 1962. Hence, O'Donnell's claims about missile sites in Cuba were mistaken. He had probably confused the increase in conventional Soviet equipment in Cuba like the MiGs with a missile deployment.

21. Dent interview; *Congressional Record*, 87th Cong., 2nd sess., 205; McMillan interview; McMillan, "A Look Back at Cuban Missile Crisis," 72.

22. McMillan interview; McMillan, "A Look Back at Cuban Missile Crisis," 72.

23. Dent interview. Dent recalls that J.Edgar Hoover also passed on secret information and advice to Thurmond, encouraging him to continue his assault on McNamara's Defense Department.

24. Keating interview, Columbia Oral History Project; oral history of Cleveland, 31–2, JFKL; Chronology of the NSA, 51; *Congressional Record*, 87th Cong., 2nd sess., 22957.

25. Merrill interview; Shakow interviews, June and December 1992; Vera Glaser, telephone interview with author, 28 October 1992.

26. For a summary of McCone's dissent on Cuba in the late summer and fall of 1962, see McCone memorandum, "Soviet MRBMs in Cuba," 31 October 1962, in Mary S. McAuliffe, ed., *CIA Documents on the Cuban Missile Crisis 1962* (Central Intelligence Agency: Washington, DC, October 1992), 13–17; ibid., v.

27. McCone, "Soviet. MRBMs," in ibid., 13.

28. Cline memorandum, "Notification of NSC Officials of Intelligence on Missile Bases in Cuba," 27 October 1962, in ibid., 149.

29. *U.S. News and World Report*, 19 November 1962, 86; oral history of Rusk, 312, JFKL; oral history of Roswell L. Gilpatric, 49–50, JFKL.

30. Mary Pitcairn Keating interview.

31. Oral history of Gilpatric, 49, JFKL; *Washington Post* clipping, "Data on Cuba was Official, Keating Says," Keating Papers, series II, box 950; Paterson, "The Historian as Detective," 70; Sorensen, *Kennedy*, 698.

32. Roger Hilsman, *To Move A Nation: The Politics of Foreign Policy in the Administration of John F. Kennedy* (Garden City, NY: Doubleday, 1967), 556. For some of the mail received by Keating from the public on Cuba in 1961 and 1962, see Keating Papers, series II, boxes 827, 828, 947.

33. Glaser to Keating, 7 September 1962, Keating Papers, series II, box 1028; Glaser interview.

34. Keating to the editor of the *Jamestown Post-Journal*, 26 February 1963, Papers of Nelson A. Rockefeller, reel no. 159, Name File, Gubernatorial Office Records, Rockefeller Archive Center, North Tarrytown, New York; McMillan interview.

35. Mary Pitcairn Keating and Nathan interviews.

36. Shakow (June 1992), Eisenberg, and Leban interviews.

37. *Congressional Record*, 87th Cong., 2nd sess., 18728, 20055.
38. Keating, "My Advance View," 99.
39. Glaser to Keating, 31 October 1962, Keating Papers, series II, box 828; *Wall Street Journal*, 19 April 1963, 10.
40. *Congressional Record*, 87th Cong., 2nd sess., 18438, 22957; Thomas L. Hughes to Bundy, 2 January 1963, document no. 2821, NSA.
41. Press release, "Keating Asserts U.S. Errs in Terming Cuban Buildup 'Defensive,'" 20 September 1962, Keating Papers, series II, box 480; press release of transcript, "'Ask Ken Keating:' A Television and Radio Program," 30 September 1962, Keating Papers, series II, box 480; U.S. Senate, Hearing Before the Committees on Foreign Relations and Armed Services, *Situation on Cuba*, 87th Cong., 2nd sess. (17 September 1962), 8–9; press release, "Keating Urges End to Aid Shipments in Vessels Supplying Castro," 24 September 1962, Keating Papers, series II, box 480.
42. Press release of transcript, "'Ask Ken Keating:' A Television and Radio Program," 16 September 1962, Keating Papers, series II, box 480; Senate Hearing, *Situation on Cuba*, 9, 11–12, 18; Shakow interview; press release, "Keating Urges End to Aid Shipments in Vessels Supplying Castro," 24 September 1962, Keating Papers, series II, box 480. The emphasis in the quotation is my own.
43. Republican Congressional Committee, "The Cuban Issue: A Chronology," May 1963, Papers of John Sherman Cooper, box 551, University of Kentucky Library, Lexington, Kentucky.
44. Montague Kern, Patricia W. Levering, Ralph B. Levering, *The Kennedy Crises: The Press, the Presidency, and Foreign Policy* (Chapel Hill: University of North Carolina Press, 1983), 108; NSA Chronology, 50–1.
45. Kern, Levering, and Levering, *Kennedy Crises*, 108–13.
46. American Opinion Summary, Public Opinion Studies Staff, Bureau of Public Affairs, State Department, 5, 6, 18, 27 September 1962, and 11 October 1962, documents 351, 362, 420, 465, 577, NSA; O'Donnell and Powers, *"Johnny, We Hardly Knew Ye"*, 308.
47. Dino A. Brugioni, *Eyeball to Eyeball: The Inside Story of the Cuban Missile Crisis*, ed. Robert F. McCort (New York: Random House, 1991), 168; Nicholas deB. Katzenbach, interview with author, 17 June 1992; Lichtenstein, ed., *Political Profiles: The Kennedy Years*, 261; Bradlee, *Conversations*, 74–5, 121.
48. JFK, transcript of interview with William Lawrence recorded for the program "Politics – '62," 14 October 1962, *Public Papers of the Presidents, 1962*, 777.
49. Oral history of Samuel B. Frankel, 450, document no. 3258, NSA; Brugioni, *Eyeball to Eyeball*, 112–13.
50. Victor Lasky, *It Didn't Start with Watergate* (New York: Dial, 1977), 81; Leban interview.
51. Memorandum, "Cuba Chronology – 1962," Keating Papers, series II, box 950; press release, "A Horse Trade on Berlin?," 10 September 1962, Keating Papers, series II, box 480; Katzenbach interview; Eisenberg interview.
52. Glaser interview; Merrill interview; Brugioni, *Eyeball to Eyeball*, 170–1.

53. Katzenbach interview; oral history of Hanson Baldwin, 687, document no. 3270, NSA; transcript of a news conference at the White House, 3 September 1962, document no. 336, NSA. The emphasis in the quotation is from the transcript.
54. Hilsman, *To Move A Nation*, 556; JFK, remarks in Harrisburg at a Democratic State Finance Committee Dinner, remarks by telephone to a dinner meeting of the Ohio State Democratic Convention in Columbus, transcript of interview with William Lawrence, 20 and 21 September and 14 October 1962, *Public Papers of the Presidents, 1962*, 696, 700, 779–80.
55. Lou Harris to JFK, "The New Shape of this Campaign," 4 October 1962, POF, box 105, JFKL.
56. National Security Action Memorandum No. 181, 23 August 1962, NSF, box 338, JFKL.
57. Transcript, news conference, 4 September 1962, NSF, box 36, JFKL; Kennedy, *Thirteen Days*, 2–5.
58. *U.S. News and World Report*, 19 November 1962, 86; Lasky, *J.F.K.*, 553; memorandum, "Cuba Chronology – 1962," Series II, box 950, Keating Papers; Alexander L. George, "The Cuban Missile Crisis, 1962," in George, David K. Hall, William E. Simons, *The Limits of Coercive Diplomacy: Laos, Cuba, Vietnam* (Boston: Little, Brown, 1971), 91.
59. President's news conference, 13 September 1962, *Public Papers of the Presidents, 1962*, 675; Sorensen memorandum for press conference marked "Final Version," 13 September 1962, Sorensen Papers, box 48; "Tass Statement on Aid to Cuba and United States 'Provocations,'" *Current Digest of the Soviet Press* 14 (10 October 1962): 13–15, 25; Bundy, "Memorandum on Cuba for the press conference," 13 September 1962, Sorensen Papers, box 48.
60. McCone memorandum on Mongoose meeting, 4 October 1962, document no. 520, NSA.
61. Dennison, "CINCLANT Historical Account of Cuban Crisis."
62. Ibid.
63. McNamara to JFK, "Presidential Interest in SA-2 Missile System and Contingency Planning for Cuba," 4 October 1962, document no. 515, Carl Kaysen to McNamara and the Joint Chiefs of Staff, 3 October 1962, document no. 512, C.V. Clifton to McNamara, 5 October 1962, document no. 531, all in NSA.
64. Oral history of William P. Mack, 390, document no. 3285, NSA.
65. Hershberg, "Before 'The Missiles of October,'" 183.
66. Beschloss, *Crisis Years*, 2–4.

5 Belligerent Beginnings: JFK on the Opening Day

1. Oral history of Rusk, 395, JFKL; Sorensen, *Kennedy*, 717; oral history of Robert Kennedy, 206, JFKL.
2. NSA Chronology, 54; Frank A. Sieverts, internal Kennedy administration history, "The Cuban Crisis, 1962," 22 August 1963, 34, document no. 3154, NSA; Elie Abel, *The Missile Crisis* (Philadelphia: Lippincott, 1966), 43–44.

3. Entry for 16 October 1962, President's Appointment Book, JFKL; Kennedy, *Thirteen Days*, 1; Sorensen, *Kennedy Legacy*, 168; Abel, *Missile Crisis*, 45.

4. Oral history of Charles E. Bohlen, 23, document no. 2304, NSA.

5. ExComm is a frequently used abbreviation for the Executive Committee of the National Security Council. Technically, Kennedy did not establish this group until 22 October. See National Security Action Memorandum 196, 22 October 1962, NSF, box 315, JFKL. The group, however, which convened to discuss the Cuban situation in the days between 16 and 21 October was essentially the same as that which met from 22 October onwards.

6. NSA Chronology, 54.

7. Oral history of Rusk, 395, JFKL; oral history of McNamara, 27, JFKL; oral history of Gilpatric, 50, JFKL.

8. Taylor, *Swords and Plowshares*, 265.

9. Kohler to Rusk, 16 October 1962, document no. 628, NSA; Sorensen draft of a message to Khrushchev, 18 October 1962, Sorensen Papers, box 48; Sorensen, *Kennedy*, 691.

10. Heymann, *A Woman Named Jackie*, 296–319, 541–545; Reeves, *A Question of Character*, 295–297. Kennedy's faith in Jacobsen was such that he even named a ship after him (the *S.S. Maximus*) and also tried to persuade him to live in the White House. In 1975 the New York State Board of Regents deemed Jacobsen's treatments to be dangerous and unethical, and thus rescinded his medical license.

11. "Off-the-Record Meeting on Cuba," 11:50 a.m.–12:57 p.m., 16 October 1962, Transcript (hereafter cited as ExComm Transcript, First Meeting), 20–21, Presidential Recordings, JFKL. In the first two ExComm meetings, Maxwell Taylor, Lyndon Johnson, and Douglas Dillon were the other "hawks" who recommended a military response to the Soviet missiles in Cuba.

    The transcripts for the 16 October ExComm meetings include such mannerisms of speech as "uh" and "er." These have been excluded from the quotations in this chapter.

12. Ibid., 27. In the original transcript, JFK actually says "we're getting ready to, to roll." I have deleted from this and all following quotations the repetition of words that are recorded in the transcripts. The emphasis in the quotation and all subsequent ones in this chapter are from the original transcripts.

13. "Off-the-Record Meeting on Cuba," 6:30 p.m.–7:55 p.m., 16 October 1962, Transcript (hereafter cited as ExComm Transcript, Second Meeting), 18–19, Presidential Recordings, JFKL.

14. Ibid., 23.

15. ExComm Transcript, First Meeting, 17–18, 29.

16. Johnson, ed., *Papers of Adlai E. Stevenson*, VIII, 299; Clayton Fritchey to Stevenson, 13 April 1965, Stevenson Papers, box 846; entry for 16 October 1962, President's Appointment Book, JFKL.

17. ExComm Transcript, First Meeting, 12, 21, 27; ExComm Transcript, Second Meeting, 9, 18–19, 46–47, 49.

18. ExComm Transcript, Second Meeting, 26.

19. ExComm Transcript, First Meeting, 13; ExComm Transcript, Second Meeting, 13, 14, 25, 35.
20. ExComm Transcript, Second Meeting, 12–13, 25.
21. Ibid., 11–12.
22. Ibid., 23.
23. Ibid., 11, 15, 36.
24. O'Donnell and Powers, *"Johnny, We Hardly Knew Ye"*, 309–310. See the excellent Thomas G. Paterson and William J. Brophy, "October Missiles and November Elections: The Cuban Missile Crisis and American Politics, 1962," *Journal of American History* 73 (June 1986): 87–119. They argue convincingly that the congressional elections were not important to the administration's handling of the Cuban issue either before or during the missile crisis.
25. ExComm Transcript, First Meeting, 21–22.
26. ExComm Transcript, Second Meeting, 29.
27. Robert L. Dennison, "CINCLANT Historical Account of Cuban Crisis," 2–3; Dennison, Report of the Commander in Chief U.S. Atlantic Fleet Upon Being Relieved, 30 April 1963, 31, document no. 3088, NSA.
28. ExComm Transcript, First Meeting, 11–12.
29. Ibid., 22, 29.
30. ExComm Transcript, Second Meeting, 9–10.
31. Ibid., 12, 45–46.
32. Ibid., 22.
33. Ibid., 44–49.
34. Sieverts, "The Cuban Crisis, 1962," 37.
35. Oral history of Robert Kennedy, 20–21, 83, JFKL.
36. ExComm Transcript, First Meeting, 8–9, 14–15, JFKL.
37. Ibid., 9–10.
38. ExComm Transcript, Second Meeting, 5–6; undated and unsigned draft of a message to "Mr. F.C.," Sorensen Papers, box 49.
39. ExComm Transcript, Second Meeting, 47–49.
40. Katzenbach interview.
41. Beschloss, *Crisis Years*, 5; Brugioni, *Eyeball to Eyeball*, 223; *Alleged Assassination Plots*, 146.
42. Handwritten note from Robert Kennedy to JFK, 16 October 1962, document no. 620, NSA; ExComm Transcript, First Meeting, 21, 31.
43. ExComm Transcript, Second Meeting, 25, 27. Marc Trachtenberg makes this cogent analysis of RFK's Tojo comment in "White House Tapes and Minutes of the Cuban Missile Crisis: Introduction to Documents," *International Security* 10 (Summer 1985): 167.
44. George McTurnan Kahin, *Intervention: How America Became Involved in Vietnam* (New York: Knopf, 1986).

6 The Battle for Blockade: Bobby Kennedy versus Dean Acheson

1. McGeorge Bundy, *Danger and Survival: Choices About the Bomb in the First Fifty Years* (New York: Random House, 1988), 399; oral history of Gilpatric, 81–2, JFKL; Bradlee, *Conversations*, 224–5. For a lucid

portrayal of Acheson in his post-secretary of state years, see Douglas Brinkley, *Dean Acheson: The Cold War Years, 1953–1971* (New Haven: Yale University Press, 1992).

2. Bowles, *Promises to Keep*, 448.
3. Oral history of Gilpatric, 50, 55, JFKL.
4. Leonard C. Meeker, minutes of 11:00 a.m. ExComm meeting, 19 October 1962, document no. 699, NSA.
5. Kennedy, *Thirteen Days*, 1.
6. Excerpt of a letter from Acheson to a friend, 31 October 1962, Acheson Papers, box 85; oral history of Acheson, 22, JFKL; Acheson, "Dean Acheson's Version of Robert Kennedy's Version of the Cuban Missile Affair: Homage to Plain Dumb Luck," *Esquire* 71 (February 1969): 76; Abel, *Missile Crisis*, 45.
7. Acheson, notes for meeting, 17 October 1962, Acheson Papers, box 85.
8. Ibid. Acheson probably furnished either John Kennedy or Rusk with this memorandum. See oral history of Acheson, 24, JFKL.
9. Acheson, "Dean Acheson's Version," 46.
10. Entry for 17 October 1962, President's Appointment Book, JFKL; Acheson, "Dean Acheson's Version," 76; Kennedy, *Thirteen Days*, 15–17; George W. Ball, *The Past Has Another Pattern: Memoirs* (New York: Norton, 1982), 290–1.
11. Ball, *Past Has Another Pattern*, 291; oral history of Elie Abel, 23–4, document no. 3252, NSA; Kennedy, *Thirteen Days*, 15–17; Acheson, "Dean Acheson's Version," 76.
12. Ball, *Past Has Another Pattern*, 291; Acheson, "Dean Acheson's Version," 76.
13. Excerpt of a letter from Acheson to a friend, 31 October 1962, Acheson Papers, box 85; Acheson, "Dean Acheson's Version," 76; oral history of Acheson, 23, JFKL.
14. Acheson, "Dean Acheson's Version," 76–7; Acheson to Patrick Devlin, undated, in David S. McLellan and David C. Acheson, eds, *Among Friends: Personal Letters of Dean Acheson* (New York: Dodd, Mead, 1980), 245.
15. Acheson, notes for meeting, 17 October 1962, document no. 653, NSA; Acheson to Devlin, undated, 245.
16. Oral history of Acheson, 23, JFKL; Acheson, "Dean Acheson's Version," 76.
17. Oral history of George C. McGhee, 11–12, document no. 3211, NSA.
18. Isaacson and Thomas, *Wise Men*, 128–9; Abel, *Missile Crisis*, 72; Blight and Welch, *On the Brink*, 143; Nitze, *From Hiroshima to Glasnost*, 224.
19. Acheson to Truman, 14 April 1960, in McLellan and Acheson, eds, *Among Friends*, 181.
20. Acheson, *Power and Diplomacy* (Cambridge, MA: Harvard University Press, 1958), 123–4; oral history of Acheson, 2, JFKL; Acheson to Truman, 31 August 1959, in McLellan and Acheson, eds., *Among Friends*, 170–1.
21. Brinkley, *Dean Acheson*, 126–7; Isaacson and Thomas, *Wise Men*, 612; Katzenbach interview; Harold Caccia to Frederick Hoyer Millar, 7

July 1961, PREM 11/3616, PRO.

22. Entry for 18 October 1962, President's Appointment Book, JFKL; Acheson, "Dean Acheson's Version," 76–7; Abel, *Missile Crisis*, 67–8; oral history of Acheson, 24, JFKL.

23. Entry for 18 October 1962, President's Appointment Book, JFKL; Sorensen, *Kennedy*, 690.

24. Andrei A. Gromyko, *Memoirs*, trans. Harold Shukman (New York: Doubleday, 1989), 176–7; Sorensen, *Kennedy*, 689–91.

25. Rusk, *As I Saw It*, 243.

26. Memorandum, "Chronology of the Cuban Crisis, October 15–28, 1962," 2 November 1962, document no. 1867, NSA; entry for 19 October 1962, President's Appointment Book, JFKL; Meeker, minutes of 11:00 a.m. ExComm Meeting, 19 October 1962.

27. Meeker, minutes of 11:00 a.m. ExComm Meeting, 19 October 1962.

28. Ibid.

29. Ibid.

30. Oral history of Acheson, 24, JFKL; Acheson, "Dean Acheson's Version," 77; Bundy, *Danger and Survival*, 400–1; O'Donnell and Powers, *"Johnny, We Hardly Knew Ye"*, 322.

31. Oral history of Acheson, 24–5, JFKL.

32. Ibid., 25, JFKL; entry for 21 October 1962, David K.E. Bruce diaries, document no. 1623, NSA.

33. McNamara, notes of National Security Council meeting no. 506 with JFK, 21 October 1962, NSF, box 313, JFKL.

34. Schlesinger, *Robert Kennedy and His Times*, 22; oral history of Williams, 3, JFKL.

35. Katzenbach interview; oral history of Rostow, 95, JFKL.

36. Oral history of Taylor, 24, JFKL; oral history of Rostow, 95, JFKL; oral history of Rusk, vol. 2, 306, JFKL; oral history of John P. Roche, vol. I, 58, Lyndon Baines Johnson Library (LBJL), Austin, Texas; oral history of Alexis Johnson, 36–7, JFKL.

37. Oral history of Robert Kennedy, vol. 1, 76–7, and vol. 8, 610–12, JFKL; Bradlee, *Conversations*, 204–5. Bradlee incorrectly states that this incident occurred during the missile crisis.

38. *Alleged Assassination Plots*, 147.

39. For a full account of the role played by Acheson in the early Cold War period, see Isaacson and Thomas, *Wise Men*, 322–6, 338–40, 356–72, 387–9, 392–6, 405–8.

40. Ibid., 581; Acheson, *Power and Diplomacy*, 50–1. For more detail on Acheson's disdain for Dulles, see Brinkley, *Dean Acheson*, 10–37.

41. Isaacson and Thomas, *Wise Men*, 610.

42. Ibid., 610.

43. Oral history of Theodore C. Sorensen, 51–2, JFKL.

44. Isaacson and Thomas, *Wise Men*, 490–1.

45. David S. McLellan, *Dean Acheson: The State Department Years* (New York: Dodd, Mead & Co., 1976), 225–6; Isaacson and Thomas, *Wise Men*, 492–3; Alsop, *Center*, 102.

46. Isaacson and Thomas, *Wise Men*, 492, 494; Acheson, *Present at the Creation*, 402. For evidence of the disdain with which Acheson viewed

the Wisconsin senator, see Acheson memorandum, "Reasons for Censuring McCarthy," Acheson Papers, box 89.

47. Acheson, *A Democrat Looks at His Party* (New York: Harper, 1955), 114–88; Bohlen, *Witness to History,* 302.

48. Schlesinger, *Robert Kennedy and His Times,* 106–15; Ball, *Past Has Another Pattern,* 291.

49. Acheson to Manlio Brosio, 28 October 1959, in McLellan and Acheson, eds, *Among Friends,* 173; McLellan, *Dean Acheson,* 413–14; Johnson, ed., *Papers of Adlai E. Stevenson,* VIII, xv; Isaacson and Thomas, *Wise Men,* 563, 579–81, 583.

50. McCone memorandum, "Brief Discussion with the President," 17 October 1962, in McAuliffe, ed., *CIA Documents,* 165.

51. McCone memorandum, 19 October 1962, in ibid., 184; Bundy, *Danger and Survival,* 400; Meeker, minutes of 11:00 a.m. ExComm meeting, 19 October 1962; Nitze, *From Hiroshima to Glasnost,* 224.

52. Kennedy, *Thirteen Days,* 26–7; McNamara, notes of National Security Council meeting no. 506 with JFK.

53. McCone memorandum, "Conversation with General Eisenhower," 17 October 1962, McCone, "Memorandum of Discussion with the President Alone," 21 October 1962, both in McAuliffe, ed., *CIA Documents,* 167–8, 243.

54. Quoted in John A. Garraty and Mark C. Carnes, eds, *Dictionary of American Biography,* supplement eight, 1966–1970 (New York: Charles Scribner's Sons, 1988), 323; oral history of Robert Kennedy, vol. 1, 58, 65, JFKL.

55. Edwin O. Guthman and Jeffrey Shulman, eds, *Robert Kennedy in his Own Words: The Unpublished Recollections of the Kennedy Years* (New York: Bantam, 1988), 335; Kennedy, *Thirteen Days,* 1, 25–6.

56. Oral history of Edward A. McDermott, 44, document no. 3205, NSA.

57. Kennedy, *Thirteen Days,* 14; McCone memorandum, 19 October 1962, in McAuliffe, ed., 185.

58. Acheson, "Dean Acheson's Version," 76.

59. Oral history of Alexis Johnson, 37, JFKL.

60. McNamara notes, National Security Council meeting no. 506 with JFK.

7 Adlai Stevenson: Hamlet in New York

1. Wills, *Kennedy Imprisonment,* 177; Richard N. Goodwin, *The Sower's Seed: A Tribute to Adlai Stevenson* (New York: New American Library, 1965), 14.

2. Stewart Alsop and Charles Bartlett, "In Time of Crisis," *Saturday Evening Post,* 8 December 1962, 17–20.

3. Bowles, *Promises to Keep,* 430–1; Martin, *Adlai Stevenson and the World,* 743; "The Big Flap – Doves, Hawks, 'Dawks,' 'Hoves,'" *Newsweek* 17 December 1962, 18–19, in Stevenson Papers, box 846; Charles Bartlett, "Portrait of a Friend," in Thompson, ed., *The Kennedy Presidency,* 16–17.

4. JFK to Stevenson, 4 and 5 December 1962, excerpts from JFK's press conference, 12 December 1962, both in Stevenson Papers, box 850.

5. Stevenson to Myron M. Cowen, 7 December 1962, Stevenson Papers, box 846; transcript of an interview of Stevenson by Hugh Downs on the NBC–TV program, "Today," 5 December 1962, Stevenson Papers, box 846; Stevenson to JFK, 8 December 1962, Stevenson Papers, box 850; oral history of Cleveland, 29, JFKL.
6. Bartlett to JFK, 29 and 31 October 1962, POF, box 28, JFKL.
7. Entry for 11 November 1962, President's Appointment Book, JFKL; Bradlee, *Conversations*, 120–1.
8. Alsop, *Center*, 192; Johnson, ed., *Papers of Adlai E. Stevenson*, VIII, 351; oral history of Charles Bartlett, 135, JFKL.
9. Johnson, ed., *Papers of Adlai E. Stevenson*, VIII, 351–2.
10. Stewart Alsop, *Stay of Execution: A Sort of Memoir* (Philadelphia: Lippincott, 1973), 152–4, 202; Bundy to Stevenson, no date [but probably in December 1962], Stevenson Papers, box 909b; Fritchey, press statement, 21 January 1963, Stevenson Papers, box 860; John Bartlow Martin, *Adlai Stevenson of Illinois: The Life of Adlai E. Stevenson* (Garden City, NY: Anchor Press/Doubleday, 1977), 644–5; Johnson, ed., *Papers of Adlai E. Stevenson*, VII, 151, 369 (incl. 369n); newspaper article clipping, "Deep-Laid Political Power Play Lies Behind Charges Against Stevenson," in Acheson Papers, box 85.
11. Halberstam, *Best and the Brightest*, 188–9; Stevenson to Barbara Jackson, 12 January 1963, in Johnson, ed., *Papers of Adlai E. Stevenson*, VIII, 371.
12. Martin, *Adlai Stevenson and the World*, 735. For the favourable correspondence received by Stevenson in the aftermath of his 25 October showdown with Zorin, see Stevenson Papers, box 847.
13. W. LeRoy Garth to Stevenson, 13 December 1962, Stevenson Papers, box 847; oral history of Harlan Cleveland, 43, JFKL.
14. Reeves, *A Question of Character*, 413–21.
15. Fritchey to Stevenson, 13 April 1965, Stevenson Papers, box 846; Abel, *Missile Crisis*, 49; Johnson, ed., *Papers of Adlai E. Stevenson*, VIII, 299.
16. Stevenson memorandum, "Notes and Questions," 17 October 1962, Stevenson Papers, box 846.
17. Ibid.
18. Ibid.
19. Ibid.; Bundy, *Danger and Survival*, 412.
20. Stevenson memorandum, "Notes and Questions."
21. Stevenson to JFK, 17 October 1962, Sorensen Papers, box 49.
22. Ibid. The emphasis in the quotation is Stevenson's.
23. Ibid. The emphasis is Stevenson's own.
24. Johnson, ed., *Papers of Adlai E. Stevenson*, VIII, 299n; Sorensen, *Kennedy*, 695–6.
25. Fritchey to Stevenson, 13 April 1965.
26. Meeker, minutes of 11:00 a.m. ExComm meeting, 19 October 1962.
27. Stevenson memorandum, "Political Program to be Announced by the President," 20 October 1962, document no. 723, NSA.
28. Ibid. Stevenson also produced a "Memorandum Concerning Security Council Presentation" of a political settlement to the crisis over

Cuba. It was undated but probably written on 20 October.

29. Ball, *Past Has Another Pattern*, 294–5; Stevenson to Schlesinger, undated but around 31 January 1963, in Johnson, ed., *Papers of Adlai E. Stevenson*, VIII, 386.

30. Ball, *Past Has Another Pattern*, 294–5; Schlesinger, *Robert Kennedy and His Times*, 555–6.

31. O'Donnell and Powers, *"Johnny, We Hardly Knew Ye"*, 325–6; Martin, *Adlai Stevenson and the World*, 724.

32. O'Donnell and Powers, *"Johnny, We Hardly Knew Ye"*, 322–3; Abel, *Missile Crisis*, 96; Martin, *Adlai Stevenson and the World*, 724; oral history of Robert A. Lovett, 53–4, document no. 3221, NSA; Schlesinger, *Robert Kennedy and His Times*, 556. O'Donnell and Powers maintain that during their conversation on the Truman Balcony after the 20 October ExComm meeting, the president defended Stevenson after Robert Kennedy had criticised him. Given that John Kennedy responded to Stevenson's performance in the missile crisis by trying to humiliate him through the Alsop-Bartlett article, and given that he did in fact accept his brother's advice on sending McCloy to New York, it is doubtful whether the president did make such positive statements about Stevenson after the meeting on 20 October, as O'Donnell and Powers allege.

33. Abel, *Missile Crisis*, 96; Stevenson memorandum, 21 October 1962, in Johnson, ed., *Papers of Adlai E. Stevenson*, VIII, 304–6.

34. Stevenson memorandum, 21 October 1962; Meeker, minutes of 11:00 a.m. ExComm meeting, 19 October 1962.

35. Edward P. Doyle, ed., *As We Knew Adlai: The Stevenson Story by Twenty-Two Friends* (New York: Harper & Row, 1966), 162; oral history of Barbara Jackson Ward, 6, JFKL.

36. Krock memorandum, 26 May 1960, Papers of Arthur Krock, box 31, Mudd Library, Princeton University, Princeton, New Jersey; Ball, *Past Has Another Pattern*, 158; Guthman and Shulman, eds, *Robert Kennedy*, 38.

37. Parmet, *Jack*, 172–5, 212, 245–52, 310; Mary Pitcairn Keating interview. For other evidence of Kennedy's friendship with McCarthy, see oral history of Smathers, interview III, tape 2, 2, JFKL; oral history of Harriman, 2, JFKL.

38. Oral history of Williams, 7–10, JFKL; Bowles, *Promises to Keep*, 285–6; Schlesinger, *A Thousand Days*, 19, 26; Eleanor Roosevelt to Mary Lasker, 15 August 1960, POF, box 32, JFKL.

39. Bradlee, *Conversations*, 62–3.

40. Schlesinger, *Robert Kennedy and His Times*, 145–6; Guthman and Shulman, eds., *Robert Kennedy*, 204–5.

41. Curt Gentry, *J. Edgar Hoover: The Man and the Secrets* (New York: Norton, 1991), 402–3; Richard Gid Powers, *Secrecy and Power: The Life of J. Edgar Hoover* (New York: Free Press, 1987), 171–3; Theoharis, ed., *From the Secret Files of J. Edgar Hoover*, 282–91. See especially in Theoharis, informal memo from FBI Supervisor William Cleveland to FBI Assistant Director Courtney Evans, 31 October 1964, 291.

42. Quoted in Reeves, *A Question of Character*, 152; oral history of Smathers,

interview III, tape 2, 7, JFKL; Guthman and Shulman, eds, *Robert Kennedy*, 38; Heymann, *A Woman Named Jackie*, 473.

43. Guthman and Shulman, eds, *Robert Kennedy*, 39, 419.
44. Stevenson explained the need to withdraw from Guantánamo in order to bring about the "neutralization" of Cuba in his 21 October memorandum.
45. Nitze, *From Hiroshima to Glasnost*, 227.
46. Stuart Chase, "Two Worlds," *Bulletin of the Atomic Scientists* 19 (June 1963): 18–20.
47. Schlesinger, *Robert Kennedy and His Times*, 555–6.
48. In his posthumous memoir of the missile crisis, Robert Kennedy distorted Stevenson's views by saying he advocated a trade, while failing to mention his unequivocal support for the blockade. Various scholars have similarly misrepresented his position. Raymond Garthoff, James Blight, and David Welch have all discussed his predilection for a diplomatic trade without acknowledging that he also endorsed the blockade. See Kennedy, *Thirteen Days*, 27; Garthoff, *Reflections*, 52; Blight and Welch, *On the Brink*, 359n.

8 Dénouement

1. Minutes of the 507th meeting of the NSC, 22 October 1962, NSF, box 313, JFKL.
2. Ibid.
3. Allyn *et al.*, eds, *Back to the Brink*, 141.
4. Rusk, *As I Saw It*, 234–5; Fulbright to J.M. Yantis, 2 August 1963, Fulbright Papers, series 48:14, box 38; Russell notes, 23 October 1962, Papers of Richard B. Russell, series XV, sub series EE, Richard B. Russell Library, University of Georgia, Athens, Georgia; McCone memorandum, "Leadership meeting on October 22nd at 5:00 p.m.," 24 October 1962, in McAuliffe, ed., *CIA Documents*, 275–9.
5. Rusk, *As I Saw It*, 235; Bernd Greiner, "The Soviet View," 213–14; Blight and Welch, *On the Brink*, 240; Anatoly Dobrynin, "The Caribbean Crisis: An Eyewitness Account," *International Affairs* 8 (August 1992): 51–2.
6. Kennedy to Khrushchev, 22 October 1962, in Ronald R. Pope, ed., *Soviet Views on the Cuban Missile Crisis: Myth and Reality in Foreign Policy Analysis* (Washington, DC: University Press of America, 1982), 28–9. Kohler also delivered the text of Kennedy's speech. See NSA Chronology, 61.
7. JFK, radio and television report to the American people on the Soviet arms build-up in Cuba, 806–7.
8. Ibid., 807–9. Emphasis is in the original.
9. Troyanovski, "The Caribbean Crisis," 152.
10. Nathan interview.
11. "Cuba: From Protests to Removal of Soviet Missiles," *Current Digest of the Soviet Press* 14 (21 November 1962), 4; CIA report on Soviet Bloc Shipping to Cuba, 23 October 1962, NSF, box 315, JFKL; János Rádványi, *Hungary and the Superpowers: The 1956 Revolution and*

Realpolitik (Stanford, CA: Hoover Institution Press, 1972), 130.
12. Khrushchev to Kennedy, 23 October 1962, in Pope, ed., *Soviet Views*, 30; NSA Chronology, 64.
13. Kennedy to Khrushchev, 23 October 1962, in Pope, ed., *Soviet Views*, 31.
14. Executive Committee minutes, 10:00 a.m., 23 October 1962, NSF, box 315; Lyndon Baines Johnson (LBJ) notes on NSC meeting, 10:00 a.m., 23 October 1962, Vice Presidential Security Files (VPSF), box 8, LBJL.
15. Executive Committee minutes, 10:00 a.m., 23 October 1962, NSF, box 315, JFKL; LBJ notes on NSC meeting, 10:00 a.m., 23 October 1962.
16. Executive Committee minutes, 10:00 a.m., 23 October 1962, NSF, box 315, JFKL; Executive Committee Record of Action, 6:00 p.m., 23 October 1962, NSF, box 315, JFKL; JFK, proclamation 3504: interdiction of the delivery of offensive weapons to Cuba, 23 October 1962, *Public Papers of the Presidents, 1962*, 809–11; Executive Order by the president, 23 October 1962, NSF, box 47, JFKL; LBJ notes on NSC meeting, 10:00 a.m., 23 October 1962.
17. Executive Committee Minutes, 10:00 a.m., 23 October 1962, NSF, box 315, JFKL; oral history of Luce, 32–4, JFKL.
18. Ormsby Gore to Foreign Office, 24 October 1962, FO 371/162375, PRO.
19. Rusk, text of a speech at a Council of the OAS special meeting, 23 October 1962, from a *New York Times* clipping, 24 October 1962, NSF, box 37, JFKL; Rusk, *As I Saw It*, 236–237; NSA Chronology, 62–3.
20. Kennedy, *Thirteen Days*, 41, 43–4; Ormsby Gore to Foreign Office, 24 October 1962, PREM 11/3690, PRO.
21. Abel, *Missile Crisis*, 112; Lyon to Rusk, 22 October 1962, document no. 1024, NSA.
22. Lyon to Rusk, 22 October 1962; oral history of Acheson, 26–7, JFKL.
23. Oral history of Acheson, 27–8, JFKL.
24. Lyon to Rusk, 22 October 1962, document no. 1024, NSA; oral history of Acheson, 28, JFKL.
25. Oral history of Acheson, 28–9, JFKL; Acheson to Lady Pamela Berry, 3 December 1962, in McLellan and Acheson, eds, *Among Friends*, 239.
26. Conclusions of a Cabinet meeting, 23 October 1962, Cabinet Records 128/36 (PT.2), PRO.
27. Thomas K. Finletter to Rusk, 23 October 1962, document no. 953, NSA; oral history of Acheson, 29, JFKL.
28. Lyon to Rusk, 23 October 1962, document no. 1019, NSA; Dowling to Rusk, 24 October 1962, document no. 1224, NSA; Acheson to John Cowles, 2 November 1962, in McLellan and Acheson, eds, *Among Friends*, 237; Abel, *Missile Crisis*, 128.
29. Acheson, "Dean Acheson's Version," 44.
30. Kennedy, *Thirteen Days*, 45.
31. Ibid., 47–8.
32. Ibid., 49; quote in Alsop and Bartlett, "In Time of Crisis," 15; LBJ

notes on NSC meeting, undated, VPSF, box 8, LBJL.

33. Executive Committee Record of Action, 10:00 a.m., 24 October 1962, NSF, box 315, JFKL; Kennedy, *Thirteen Days*, 49–52, 54–5. Kennedy made the final decision not to intercept the *Bucharest* in the Ex-Comm meeting on the morning of 25 October. See Executive Committee Record of Action, 10:00 a.m., 25 October 1962, NSF, box 315, JFKL.

34. Executive Committee Record of Action, 10:00 a.m., 24 October 1962, NSF, box 315, JFKL; McCone memorandum, "Notes on Leadership Meeting on October 24th, 1962, at 5:00 p.m.," 25 October 1962, in McAuliffe, ed., *CIA Documents*, 298.

35. Hilsman to Rusk, 26 October 1962, NSF, box 36, JFKL.

36. Khrushchev to Kennedy, 24 October 1962, in Pope, ed., *Soviet Views*, 32–6.

37. *New York Times*, 24 October 1962, 20, and 25 October 1962, 22.

38. Summary Record of NSC Executive Committee meeting no. 5, 5:00 p.m., 25 October 1962, NSF, box 315, JFKL.

39. Executive Committee Record of Action, 10:00 a.m., 25 October 1962, Summary Record of NSC Executive Committee meeting no. 5, 5:00 p.m., 25 October 1962; unauthored memorandum, "Political Path," 25 October 1962; unauthored and undated memorandum, "Scenario for Airstrike against offensive missile bases and bombers in Cuba," all of these are in NSF, box 315, JFKL. See, also, Rostow memorandum, "The Possible Role of a Progressive Economic Blockade Against Cuba," 25 October 1962, NSF, box 36, JFKL; McCone memorandum, "Meeting of the NSC Executive Committee, 25 October, 5:00 P.M.," 26 October 1962, in McAuliffe, ed., *CIA Documents*, 309.

40. Rusk to various US embassies, 25 October 1962, NSF, box 41, JFKL; Summary Record of NSC Executive Committee meeting no. 5, 5:00 p.m., 25 October 1962, NSF, box 315, JFKL; Bundy, *Danger and Survival*, 410.

41. Kennedy to Khrushchev, 25 October 1962, in Pope, ed., *Soviet Views*, 36–7.

42. Blight and Welch, *On the Brink*, 83–4; Dean to Foreign Office, 25 October 1962, FO 371/162387, PRO.

43. Blight and Welch, *On the Brink*, 83–4; James G. Blight, *The Shattered Crystal Ball: Fear and Learning in the Cuban Missile Crisis* (Savage, MD: Rowman & Littlefield, 1990), 115.

44. Dean to Foreign Office, 25 October 1962.

45. Fritchey to Stevenson, 13 April 1965.

46. U Thant, *View from the UN* (Garden City, NY: Doubleday, 1978), 155, 157.

47. Oral history of Cleveland, 8, JFKL; Adlai E. Stevenson, "The Cuban Crisis: A Base for Communist Aggression," *Vital Speeches of the Day* 29 (15 November 1962): 70–4.

48. Stevenson, "The Cuban Crisis," 73–5.

49. Martin, *Adlai Stevenson and the World*, 729; Stevenson, statement to the press, 8:45 p.m., 23 October 1962, Stevenson Papers, box 846; Abel, *Missile Crisis*, 148–9.

50. Adlai E. Stevenson and Valerian A. Zorin, "Has the U.S.S.R. Missiles in Cuba? United Nations Debate," *Vital Speeches of the Day* 29 (15 November 1962): 77–9; Blight and Welch, *On the Brink*, 392n.
51. Stevenson and Zorin, "Has the U.S.S.R. Missiles in Cuba?": 80–2; Abel, *Missile Crisis*, 169–70.
52. Dean to Foreign Office, 24 October 1962, PREM 11/3690, PRO; U Thant to Kennedy and Khrushchev, 24 October 1962, Kennedy to U Thant, 25 October 1962, Khrushchev to U Thant, 25 October 1962, in Council on Foreign Relations, *Documents on American Foreign Relations, 1962*, 386–9; Martin, *Adlai Stevenson and the World*, 731.
53. U Thant to Khrushchev, U Thant to Kennedy, Kennedy to U Thant, all on 25 October 1962, Khrushchev to U Thant, 26 October 1962, in Council on Foreign Relations, *Documents on American Foreign Relations, 1962*, 389–92.
54. NSC Executive Committee Record of Action, meeting no. 6, 10:00 a.m., 26 October 1962, NSF, box 316, JFKL; Kennedy, *Thirteen Days*, 59–60; NSA Chronology, 68.
55. NSC Executive Committee Record of Action, meeting no. 6; LBJ notes on NSC meeting, 10:00 a.m., 26 October 1962, VPSF, box 8, LBJL.
56. NSC Executive Committee Record of Action, meeting no. 6; LBJ notes on NSC meeting, 10:00 a.m., 26 October 1962.
57. NSC Executive Committee Record of Action, meeting no. 6; Fritchey to Stevenson, 13 April 1965.
58. Harriman to Ball, 26 October 1962, NSF, box 36, JFKL.
59. Walter Lafeber, ed., *Eastern Europe and the Soviet Union*, II (New York: Chelsea House Publishers, 1973), 699.
60. Ibid., 699–703.
61. Dobrynin, "The Caribbean Crisis," 54–5.
62. Kennedy, *Thirteen Days*, 68–9; Scali, notes of first meeting with Fomin, 26 October 1962, in Chang and Kornbluh, eds., *Cuban Missile Crisis, 1962*, 184; Rusk, *As I Saw It*, 238; Garthoff, "Cuban Missile Crisis," 73; Allyn et al., eds, *Back to the Brink*, 112–114, 117–118.
63. Kennedy, *Thirteen Days*, 68; Summary Record of NSC Executive Committee meeting no. 6, 10:00 a.m., 26 October 1962, NSF, box 316, JFKL.
64. Abel, *Missile Crisis*, 182.
65. Carter to McCone, "MONGOOSE Operations and General Lansdale's Problems," 25 October 1962, McCone memorandum, "Meeting of the NSC Executive Committee, 26 October, 1962 10:00 A.M.," 26 October 1962, McCone, "Memorandum of MONGOOSE meeting in the JCS Operations Room, October 26, 1962, at 2:30 p.m.," 29 October 1962, all in McAuliffe, ed., *CIA Documents*, 311–312, 317, 319–321.
66. CIA memorandum, "The Crisis: USSR/Cuba," 6:00 a.m, 27 October 1962, NSF, box 316, JFKL; Taylor, *Swords and Plowshares*, 275–6; Summary Record of NSC Executive Committee meeting no. 7, 10:00 a.m., 27 October 1962, NSF, box 316, JFKL; Kennedy, *Thirteen Days*, 71, 75.
67. For the full text of this message, see Council on Foreign Relations, *Documents on American Foreign Relations, 1962*, 392–5.

68. Allyn *et al.*, eds, *Back to the Brink*, 110, 130; Garthoff, "Cuban Missile Crisis," 80.
69. Garthoff, "Cuban Missile Crisis," 74.
70. Kennedy, *Thirteen Days*, 79–80; Allyn *et al.*, eds., *Back to the Brink*, 93.
71. Cuban Missile Crisis Meetings, 27 October 1962, Transcript (hereafter cited as 27 October Transcript), 2, 3, 8, Presidential Recordings, JFKL.
72. Ibid., 3, 4.
73. Rusk, *As I Saw It*, 240; oral history of Cleveland, 34, JFKL; oral history of Francis T.P. Plimpton, 15, JFKL.
74. Forrestal to JFK, 27 October 1962, NSF, box 36, JFKL; 27 October Transcript, 5–6, 28–9.
75. 27 October Transcript, 6, 9.
76. Ibid., 29, 31–2.
77. Oral history of Gilpatric, 59, JFKL; oral history of Cleveland, 34, JFKL.
78. Oral history of Alexis Johnson, 48, JFKL; Summary Record of NSC Executive Committee meeting no. 8, 4:00 p.m., 27 October 1962, NSF, box 316, JFKL; 27 October Transcript, 22.
79. 27 October Transcript, 28–39; Summary Record of the NSC Executive Committee meeting no. 8, 4:00 p.m., 27 October 1962; JFK, message to Chairman Khrushchev calling for removal of Soviet missiles from Cuba, 27 October 1962, *Public Papers of the Presidents, 1962*, 813–14; Sorensen, *Kennedy*, 714.
80. JFK, message to Chairman Khrushchev calling for removal of Soviet missiles from Cuba, 813–14.
81. 27 October Transcript, 29.
82. Ibid., 38–9, 45–56; Acheson, "Dean Acheson's Version," 44; undated LBJ notes on NSC meeting [apparently written on 27 October], VPSF, box 8, LBJL.
83. Allyn *et al.*, eds., *Back to the Brink*, 95; I.J.M. Sutherland to R.I.T. Cromartie, 26 October 1962, FO 371/162391, PRO.
84. CIA memorandum, Readiness Status of Soviet Missiles in Cuba, 23 October 1962, NSF, box 315, JFKL.
85. Garthoff, *Reflections*, 39–40. Schlesinger, "Four Days with Fidel," 22–3; Tolchin, "U.S. Underestimated Soviet Force in Cuba"; J. Anthony Lukas, "Fidel Castro's Theater of Now," *New York Times*, 20 January 1992; Gribkov and Smith, *Operation ANADYR*, 27–28, 46. Other warheads, such as those for cruise missiles, may also have been on the island. See the previous Gribkov citation.
86. 27 October Transcript, 23, 24, 70–1.
87. Ibid., 2, 4–5, 41.
88. Ormsby Gore to Foreign Office, 27 October 1962, PREM 11/3691, PRO; 27 October Transcript, 2–3.
89. 27 October Transcript, 27, 67.
90. Ibid., 5.
91. Ibid., 81.
92. Ibid., 26, 27, 28, 48, 73.
93. Ibid., 4; Bundy, *Danger and Survival*, 431.

94. Allyn *et al.*, eds, *Back to the Brink*, 92.
95. Kennedy, *Thirteen Days*, 85–7; Dobrynin, "The Caribbean Crisis," 58; Rusk, *As I Saw It*, 240; Allyn *et al.*, eds, *Back to the Brink*, 86, 92–3. Dobrynin did not also meet with Robert Kennedy on 26 October, as he claimed in 1989. See Allyn *et al.*, eds, *Back to the Brink*, 80–1; Kramer, "Tactical Nuclear Weapons," 40; Dobrynin, "The Caribbean Crisis."
96. Laurence Chang, "The View from Washington and the View from Nowhere: Cuban Missile Crisis Historiography and the Epistemology of Decision Making," in James A. Nathan, ed., *The Cuban Missile Crisis Revisited* (New York: St Martin's, 1992), 147–8.
97. CIA memorandum, "The Crisis: USSR/Cuba," 6:00 a.m., 28 October 1962, NSF, box 316, JFKL.
98. Allyn *et al.*, eds, *Back to the Brink*, 30–31, 89–90; Troyanovski, "The Caribbean Crisis," 153; Castro to Khrushchev, 26 October 1962, in Chang and Kornbluh, eds, *Cuban Missile Crisis, 1962*, 81, 189; Dobrynin, "The Caribbean Crisis," 58.
99. Troyanovski, "The Caribbean Crisis," 153–4.
100. Ibid., 154.
101. Ibid., 155; Khrushchev to Kennedy, 28 October 1962, in Council on Foreign Relations, *Documents on American Foreign Relations, 1962*, 398–9.
102. Carlos Franqui, *Family Portrait with Fidel*, trans. Alfred MacAdam (London: Jonathan Cape, 1983), 194; Khrushchev to Castro, 28 October 1962, in Chang and Kornbluh, eds, *Cuban Missile Crisis, 1962*, 239.
103. Oral history of Robert Kennedy, 609–10, JFKL; Kennedy, *Thirteen Days*, 97; NSA Chronology, 74; excerpt of a letter from Acheson to a friend, 31 October 1962.
104. Summary Record of NSC Executive Committee meeting no. 10, 11:10 a.m., 28 October 1962, NSF, box 316, JFKL. Bundy's use of "hawks" and "doves" suggests that he may have been the official who furnished Alsop and Bartlett with these terms for their article.
105. JFK, message in reply to a broadcast by Chairman Khrushchev on the Cuban crisis, statement by the president following the Soviet decision to withdraw missiles from Cuba, both 28 October 1962, *Public Papers of the Presidents, 1962*, 814–15.
106. Richard H. Estabrook, notes from conversations with Monnet, Bohlen, Durbrow, *et al.*, 2 November 1962, document no. 180, NSA.
107. Kennedy, *Thirteen Days*, 87–8.
108. Ibid., 88.

Conclusion

1. For a good description of the aftermath to the crisis, see Garthoff, *Reflections*, 97–129.
2. Beschloss, *Crisis Years*, 698–700; Schlesinger, *Robert Kennedy and His Times*, 718–29; Martin, *Adlai Stevenson and the World*, 862–3; Brinkley, *Dean Acheson*, 204–302.

Selected Bibliography

ARCHIVES AND MANUSCRIPT COLLECTIONS

Acheson, Dean G. Papers. Harry S. Truman Library, Independence, Missouri.

Bowles, Chester. Papers. Sterling Library, Yale University, New Haven, Connecticut.

Cabinet Records. Public Record Office (PRO), Kew, Richmond, England.

Cooper, John Sherman. Papers. University of Kentucky Library, Lexington, Kentucky.

The Cuban Missile Crisis, 1962 collection. National Security Archive (NSA), Washington, DC.

Dulles, Allen W. Papers. Seely Mudd Library, Princeton University, Princeton, New Jersey.

Eisenhower, Dwight D. Post-Presidential Papers. Dwight D. Eisenhower Library, Abilene, Kansas.

Foreign Office Records. PRO.

Fulbright, J. William. Papers. University of Arkansas Library, Fayetteville, Arkansas.

Johnson, Lyndon B. Vice Presidential Security Files. Lyndon Baines Johnson Library (LBJL), Austin, Texas.

Keating, Kenneth B. Papers. Rush Rhees Library, University of Rochester, Rochester, New York.

Kennedy, John F. National Security Files. John F. Kennedy Library (JFKL), Boston, Massachusetts.

Kennedy, John F. Pre-Presidential Papers. JFKL.

Kennedy, John F. President's Office Files. JFKL.

Kennedy, John F. White House Central Files. JFKL.

Kennedy, Robert F. Papers. JFKL.

Krock, Arthur. Papers. Mudd Library, Princeton University.

Lansdale, Edward G. Papers. Hoover Institution on War, Revolution and Peace, Stanford, California.

Lippmann, Walter. Papers. Sterling Library, Yale University.

President's Appointment Book. JFKL.

Presidential Recordings: "Off-the-Record Meeting on Cuba." 11:50 a.m.–12:57 p.m., 16 October 1962. Transcript. JFKL.

Presidential Recordings: "Off-the-Record Meeting on Cuba." 6:30 p.m.–7:55 p.m., 16 October 1962. Transcript. JFKL.

Presidential Recordings. Cuban Missile Crisis Meetings. 27 October 1962. Transcript. JFKL.

Prime Minister's Records. PRO.

Ranklin, Karl L. Papers. Mudd Library, Princeton University.

Rockefeller, Nelson A. Papers. Rockefeller Archive Center, North Tarrytown, New York.

Russell, Richard B. Papers. Richard B. Russell Library, University of Georgia, Athens, Georgia.
Schlesinger, Arthur M., Jr. Papers. JFKL.
Sorensen, Theodore C. Papers. JFKL.
Stevenson, Adlai E. Papers. Mudd Library, Princeton University.
Truman, Harry S. Post Presidential File. Truman Library.

PUBLISHED DOCUMENTS

Chang, Laurence, and Kornbluh, Peter, eds *The Cuban Missile Crisis, 1962: A Documents Reader*. New York: New Press, 1992.
Congressional Record.
Council on Foreign Relations. *Documents on American Foreign Relations, 1961–1962*. New York: Harper, 1962–63.
Johnson, Walter, ed. *The Papers of Adlai E. Stevenson*. 8 vols. Boston: Little, Brown, 1972–79.
The Kennedy Presidential Press Conferences. New York: E.M. Coleman Enterprises, 1978.
Lafeber, Walter, ed. *Eastern Europe and the Soviet Union*. Vol. II. New York: Chelsea House, 1973.
McAuliffe, Mary S., ed. *CIA Documents on the Cuban Missile Crisis 1962*. Washington, DC: Central Intelligence Agency, 1992.
McLellan, David S., and Acheson, David C., eds *Among Friends: Personal Letters of Dean Acheson*. New York: Dodd, Mead, 1980.
Pope, Ronald R., ed. *Soviet Views on the Cuban Missile Crisis: Myth and Reality in Foreign Policy Analysis*. Washington, DC: University Press of America, 1982.
Theoharis, Athan, ed. *From the Secret Files of J. Edgar Hoover*. Chicago: Ivan R. Dee, 1991.
U.S. Department of State. *Foreign Relations of the United States, 1940*. Washington, DC: US Government Printing Office, 1958.
— *Press Conferences of the Secretaries of State*. Series III, reel no. 14. January 1958–December 1965.
U.S. National Archives and Records Service. *Public Papers of the Presidents of the United States: John F. Kennedy, 1961–1963*. Washington, DC: United States Government Printing Office, 1962–64.
U.S. Senate. Hearing Before the Committee on Foreign Relations and the Committee on Armed Services. *Situation on Cuba*. 87th Cong., 2nd sess. Washington, DC, 17 September 1962.
— Proposed Nomination of Adlai E. Stevenson as United States Representative to the United Nations. *United States Senate Foreign Relations Committee*. 87th Cong., 1st sess. Washington, DC, 18 January 1961.
U.S. Senate Select Committee to Study Governmental Operations with Respect to Intelligence Activities. *Alleged Assassination Plots Involving Foreign Leaders*. Interim report, S.Rept. 94–465, 94th Congress, 1st session.

INTERVIEWS

Abel, Elie. Oral history, NSA.
Acheson, Dean G. Oral history, JFKL.
Bartlett, Charles. Oral history, JFKL.
Bohlen, Charles E. Oral history, NSA.
Bowles, Chester. Oral history, JFKL.
Cleveland, Harlan. Oral history, JFKL.
Dalton, Mark. Oral history, JFKL.
Dent, Harry S. Interview with author, 15 September 1992.
Eisenberg, Milton. Interview with author, 28 September 1992.
Gilpatric, Roswell L. Oral history, JFKL.
Glaser, Vera. Interview with author, 28 October 1992.
Harriman, W. Averell. Oral history, JFKL.
Johnson, U. Alexis. Oral history, JFKL.
Katzenbach, Nicholas deB. Interview with author, 17 June 1992.
Keating, Kenneth B. Oral history, Eisenhower administration collection,
    Columbia University, New York.
Keating, Mary Pitcairn. Interview with author, 15 May 1992.
Kennedy, Robert F. Oral history, JFKL.
Khrushchev, Nikita S. Oral history, JFKL.
Kilberg, Bobbie. Interview with author, 25 June 1992.
Kohler, Foy D. Oral history, JFKL.
Krock, Arthur. Oral history, JFKL.
Leban, Abbott A. Interview with author, 8 June 1992.
Lippmann, Walter. Oral history, JFKL.
Lovett, Robert A. Oral history, NSA.
Luce, Henry. Oral history, JFKL.
McCone, John A. Oral history, JFKL.
McDermott, Edward A. Oral history, NSA.
McGhee, George C. Oral history, NSA.
McMillan, Robert R. Interview with author, 12 June 1992.
McNamara, Robert S. Oral history, JFKL.
Merrill, Eleanor. Interview with author, 28 October 1992.
Nathan, Richard P. Interview with author, 2 October 1992.
Plimpton, Francis T.P. Oral history, JFKL.
Roche, John P. Oral history, LBJL.
Rostow, Walt W. Oral history, JFKL.
Rusk, Dean. Oral history, JFKL.
Rusk, Dean. Tapes 000 000 on the Kennedy Years; JJJ JJJ on John F.
    Kennedy; KKK KKK on John F. Kennedy; Q on the Bay of Pigs; V on the
    Cuban missile crisis. Dean Rusk Oral History Project. University of Georgia.
Shakow, Patricia. Interviews with author, 16 June 1992, December 1992.
Smathers, George A. Oral history, JFKL.
Sorensen, Theodore C. Oral history, JFKL.
Taylor, Maxwell D. Oral history, JFKL.
Thompson, Llewellyn E. Oral history, JFKL.
U Thant. Oral history, JFKL.
Ward, Barbara Jackson. Oral history, JFKL.

Williams, G. Mennen. Oral history, JFKL.
Wofford, Harris. Oral history, JFKL.

BOOKS

Abel, Elie. *The Missile Crisis.* Philadelphia: Lippincott, 1966.
Acheson, Dean G. *A Citizen Looks at Congress.* New York: Harper, 1957.
— *A Democrat Looks at His Party.* New York: Harper, 1955.
— *Grapes from Thorns.* New York: Norton, 1972.
— *Morning and Noon.* Boston: Houghton Mifflin, 1965.
— *The Pattern of Responsibility.* Ed. McGeorge Bundy. Boston: Houghton Mifflin, 1952.
— *Power and Diplomacy.* Cambridge, MA: Harvard University, 1958.
— *Present at the Creation: My Years in the State Department.* New York: Norton, 1969.
— *Sketches from Lives of Men I have Known.* New York: Harper, 1961.
Allison, Graham T. *Essence of Decision: Explaining the Cuban Missile Crisis.* New York: HarperCollins, 1971.
Allyn, Bruce J., James G. Blight, and David A. Welch, eds *Back to the Brink: Proceedings of the Moscow Conference on the Cuban Missile Crisis, January 27–28, 1989.* Lanham, MD: University Press of America, 1992.
Alsop, Stewart. *The Center: The Anatomy of Power in Washington.* London: Hodder and Stoughton, 1968.
— *Stay of Execution: A Sort of Memoir.* Philadelphia: Lippincott, 1973.
Ambrose, Stephen E. *Eisenhower: The President.* London: George Allen & Unwin, 1984.
— *Nixon: The Education of a Politician, 1913–1962.* New York: Simon and Schuster, 1987.
— *Rise to Globalism: American Foreign Policy, 1928–1976.* Rev. ed. New York: Penguin, 1976.
Ball, George W. *The Past Has Another Pattern: Memoirs.* New York: Norton, 1982.
Berry, Joseph P., Jr. *John F. Kennedy and the Media: The First Television President.* Lanham, MD: University Press of America, 1987.
Beschloss, Michael R. *The Crisis Years: Kennedy and Khrushchev, 1960– 1963.* New York: Edward Burlingame, 1991.
Biographical Dictionary of the United States Congress, 1774–1989. Washington, DC: US Government Printing Office, 1989.
Blight, James G. *The Shattered Crystal Ball: Fear and Learning in the Cuban Missile Crisis.* Savage, MD: Rowman & Littlefield, 1990.
— Bruce J. Allyn, and David A. Welch. *Cuba on the Brink: Castro, the Missile Crisis, and the Soviet Collapse.* New York: Pantheon, 1993.
Blight, James G., and David A. Welch. *On the Brink: Americans and Soviets Reexamine the Cuban Missile Crisis.* New York: Noonday, 1990.
Bohlen, Charles E. *Witness to History, 1929–1969.* New York: Norton, 1973.
Bowles, Chester. *Promises to Keep: My Years in Public Life, 1941– 1969.* New York: Harper & Row, 1971.
Bradlee, Benjamin C. *Conversations with Kennedy.* New York: Norton, 1975.

Brinkley, Douglas. *Dean Acheson: The Cold War Years, 1953–1971.* New Haven: Yale University Press, 1992.

Brugioni, Dino A. *Eyeball to Eyeball: The Inside Story of the Cuban Missile Crisis.* Ed. Robert F. McCort. New York: Random House, 1991.

Brune, Lester H. *The Missile Crisis of October 1962: A Review of Issues and References.* Claremont, CA: Regina, 1985.

Bundy, McGeorge. *Danger and Survival: Choices About the Bomb in the First Fifty Years.* New York: Random House, 1988.

Burlatsky, Fedor. *Khrushchev and the First Russian Spring.* Trans. Daphne Sillen. London: Weidenfeld and Nicolson, 1991.

Burns, James MacGregor. *John Kennedy: A Political Profile.* New York: Avon reprint, 1961.

Chayes, Abram. *The Cuban Missile Crisis: International Crises and the Role of Law.* New York: Oxford University Press, 1974.

Clifford, Clark, with Richard Holbrooke. *Counsel to the President: A Memoir.* New York: Random House, 1991.

Clinch, Nancy Gager. *The Kennedy Neurosis.* New York: Grosset and Dunlap, 1973.

Cochran, Bert. *Adlai Stevenson: Patrician Among the Politicians.* New York: Funk and Wagnalls, 1969.

Cohen, Warren I. *Dean Rusk.* Totowa, NJ: Cooper Square, 1980.

Crankshaw, Edward. *Khrushchev.* London: Collins, 1966.

Crummey, Robert O., ed. *Reform in Russia and the U.S.S.R.: Past and Prospects.* Urbana and Chicago: University of Illinois Press, 1989.

Dallin, David J. *Soviet Foreign Policy after Stalin.* Philadelphia: Lippincott, 1961.

Davis, John H. *The Kennedys: Dynasty and Disaster, 1848–1983.* New York: McGraw-Hill, 1984.

Davis, Kenneth S. *The Politics of Honor: A Biography of Adlai E. Stevenson.* New York: Putnam, 1967.

Detzer, David. *The Brink: Cuban Missile Crisis, 1962.* New York: Crowell, 1979.

Dinerstein, Herbert S. *The Making of a Missile Crisis, October 1962.* Baltimore: Johns Hopkins University Press, 1976.

Dittmer, Lowell. *Sino-Soviet Normalization and Its International Implications, 1945–1990.* Seattle: University of Washington Press, 1992.

Divine, Robert A., ed. *The Cuban Missile Crisis.* Chicago: Quadrangle, 1971.

— *Foreign Policy and U.S. Presidential Elections, 1952–1960.* New York: New Viewpoints, 1974.

Doyle, Edward P., ed. *As We Knew Adlai: The Stevenson Story by Twenty-Two Friends.* New York: Harper & Row, 1966.

Exner, Judith, as told to Ovid Demaris. *My Story.* New York: Grove, 1977.

Fairlie, Henry. *The Kennedy Promise: The Politics of Expectation.* Garden City, NY: Doubleday, 1973.

Findling, John E. *Dictionary of American Diplomatic History.* Westport, CT: Greenwood, 1980.

FitzSimons, Louise. *The Kennedy Doctrine.* New York: Random House, 1972.

Franqui, Carlos. *Family Portrait with Fidel.* Trans. Alfred MacAdam. London: Jonathan Cape, 1983.

Galbraith, John Kenneth. *Ambassador's Journal: A Personal Account of the Kennedy Years.* Boston: Houghton Mifflin, 1969.

Garraty, John A., and Mark C. Carnes, eds *Dictionary of American Biography.* Supplement 8, 1966–1970. New York: Charles Scribner's Sons, 1988.

Garthoff, Raymond L. *Reflections on the Cuban Missile Crisis.* Rev. ed. Washington, DC: Brookings Institution, 1989.

— *Soviet Strategy in the Nuclear Age.* Rev. ed. New York: Praeger, 1962.

Gehlen, Michael P. *The Politics of Coexistence: Soviet Methods and Motives.* Bloomington: Indiana University Press, 1967.

Gelb, Norman. *The Berlin Wall.* London: Michael Joseph, 1986.

Gentry, Curt. *J. Edgar Hoover: The Man and the Secrets.* New York: Norton, 1991.

George, Alexander L., David K. Hall, and William E. Simons. *The Limits of Coercive Diplomacy: Laos, Cuba, Vietnam.* Boston: Little, Brown, 1971.

Giancana, Sam and Chuck. *Double Cross.* New York: Warner, 1992.

Giglio, James N. *The Presidency of John F. Kennedy.* Lawrence: University Press of Kansas, 1991.

Goldwater, Barry, with Jack Casserly. *Goldwater.* New York: St Martin's, 1988.

Goodwin, Richard N. *Remembering America: A Voice from the Sixties.* Boston: Little, Brown, 1988.

— *The Sower's Seed: A Tribute to Adlai Stevenson.* New York: New American Library, 1965.

Gribkov, Anatoli I., and William Y. Smith, *Operation ANADYR: U.S. and Soviet Generals Recount the Cuban Missile Crisis.* Chicago: Edition Q, 1994.

Gromyko, Andrei A. *Memoirs.* Trans. Harold Shukman. New York: Doubleday, 1989.

Guthman, Edwin O., and Jeffrey Shulman, eds *Robert Kennedy in his Own Words: The Unpublished Recollections of the Kennedy Years.* New York: Bantam, 1988.

Halberstam, David. *The Best and the Brightest.* New York: Penguin reprint, 1983.

Hanak, Harry, ed. *Soviet Foreign Policy since the Death of Stalin.* London: Routledge and K. Paul, 1972.

Harper, Paul, and Joann P. Krieg, eds *John F. Kennedy: The Promise Revisited.* New York: Greenwood, 1988.

Heymann, C. David *A Woman Named Jackie.* New York: Lyle Stuart, 1989.

Higgins, Trumbull. *The Perfect Failure: Kennedy, Eisenhower, and the CIA at the Bay of Pigs.* New York: Norton, 1989.

Hilsman, Roger. *To Move A Nation: The Politics of Foreign Policy in the Administration of John F. Kennedy.* Garden City, NY: Doubleday, 1967.

Hinckle, Warren, and William W. Turner. *Deadly Secrets: The CIA-Mafia War Against Castro and the Assassination of J.F.K.* New York: Thunder's Mouth, 1992.

Isaacson, Walter, and Evan Thomas. *The Wise Men: Six Friends and the World They Made.* New York: Simon and Schuster, 1986.

Javits, Jacob K., with Rafael Steinberg. *Javits: The Autobiography of a Public Man.* Boston: Houghton Mifflin, 1981.

Kahin, George McT. *Intervention: How America Became Involved in Vietnam.* New York: Knopf, 1986.

Kaplan, Stephen S. *et al. Diplomacy of Power: Soviet Armed Forces as a Political Instrument.* Washington, DC: Brookings Institution, 1981.

Kennedy, John F. *The Strategy of Peace.* Ed. Allan Nevins. New York: Harper, 1960.

— *Why England Slept.* 2nd ed. New York: W. Funk, 1961.

Kennedy, Robert F. *Thirteen Days: A Memoir of the Cuban Missile Crisis.* New York: Norton, 1969.

Kern, Montague, Patricia W. Levering, and Ralph B. Levering. *The Kennedy Crises: The Press, the Presidency, and Foreign Policy.* Chapel Hill: University of North Carolina Press, 1983.

Khrushchev, Nikita S. *Khrushchev Remembers.* Ed. and trans. Strobe Talbott. Boston: Little, Brown, 1970.

— *Khrushchev Remembers: The Glasnost Tapes.* Trans. and ed. Jerrold L. Schecter with Vyacheslav V. Luchkov. Boston: Little, Brown, 1990.

— *Khrushchev Remembers: The Last Testament.* Ed. and trans. Strobe Talbott. Boston, 1974.

— *Khrushchev Speaks: Selected Speeches, Articles, and Press Conferences, 1949–1961.* Ed. Thomas P. Whitney. Ann Arbor: University of Michigan Press, 1963.

Khrushchev, Sergei. *Khrushchev on Khrushchev: An Inside Account of the Man and His Era.* Ed. and trans. William Taubman. Boston: Little, Brown, 1990.

Kohler, Foy D. *Understanding the Russians: A Citizen's Primer.* New York: Harper & Row, 1970.

Krock, Arthur. *Memoirs: Sixty Years on the Firing Line.* New York: Funk and Wagnalls, 1968.

Lasky, Victor. *It Didn't Start with Watergate.* New York: Dial, 1977.

— *J.F.K.: The Man and the Myth.* New York: Macmillan, 1963.

Lebow, Richard Ned. *Nuclear Crisis Management: A Dangerous Illusion.* Ithaca: Cornell University Press, 1987.

Lee, William T. *The Estimation of Soviet Defense Expenditures, 1955–1975: An Unconventional Approach.* New York: Praeger, 1977.

LeMay, Curtis E., with Dale O. Smith. *America is in Danger.* New York: Funk and Wagnalls, 1968.

Leuchtenburg, William E. *In the Shadow of FDR: From Harry Truman to Ronald Reagan.* Rev. ed. Ithaca: Cornell University Press, 1985.

Lévesque, Jacques. *The USSR and the Cuban Revolution.* Trans. Deanna Drendel Leboeuf. New York: Praeger, 1978.

Lichtenstein, Nelson, ed. *Political Profiles: The Kennedy Years.* New York: Facts on File, 1976.

Lincoln, Evelyn. *Kennedy and Johnson.* New York: Holt, Rinehart & Winston, 1968.

Lord, Donald C. *John F. Kennedy: The Politics of Confrontation and Conciliation.* Woodbury, NY: Barron's, 1977.

Marchetti, Victor, and John D. Marks. *The CIA and the Cult of Intelligence.* London: Jonathan Cape, 1974.

Martin, John Bartlow. *Adlai Stevenson of Illinois: The Life of Adlai E. Stevenson.*

Garden City, NY: Anchor Press/Doubleday, 1977.

— *Adlai Stevenson and the World: The Life of Adlai E. Stevenson.* Garden City, NY: Doubleday, 1977.

McCauley, Martin, ed. *Khrushchev and Khrushchevism.* Basingstoke: Macmillan, 1987.

McKeever, Porter. *Adlai Stevenson: His Life and Legacy.* New York: Morrow, 1989.

McLellan, David S. *Dean Acheson: The State Department Years.* New York: Dodd, Mead, 1976.

— and David C. Acheson, eds *Among Friends: Personal Letters of Dean Acheson.* New York: Dodd, Mead, 1980.

McNamara, Robert S. *Blundering into Disaster: Surviving the First Century of the Nuclear Age.* New York: Pantheon, 1986.

Medland, William J. *The Cuban Missile Crisis of 1962: Needless or Necessary.* New York: Praeger, 1988.

Medvedev, Roy A. *Khrushchev.* Trans. Brian Pearce. Oxford: Blackwell, 1982.

Miroff, Bruce. *Pragmatic Illusions: The Presidential Politics of John F. Kennedy.* New York: McKay, 1976.

Morley, Morris H. *Imperial State and Revolution: The United States and Cuba, 1952–1986.* New York: Cambridge University Press, 1987.

Nathan, James A., ed. *The Cuban Missile Crisis Revisisted.* New York: St Martin's, 1992.

Nixon, Richard M. *RN: The Memoirs of Richard Nixon.* London: Sidgwick & Jackson, 1978.

— *Six Crises.* New York: Simon and Schuster reprint, 1990.

Nitze, Paul H., with Ann M. Smith and Steven L. Rearden. *From Hiroshima to Glasnost: At the Center of Decision.* New York: Grove Weidenfeld, 1989.

Nogee, Joseph L., and Robert H. Donaldson. *Soviet Foreign Policy since World War II.* New York: Pergamon, 1981.

O'Donnell, Kenneth P., and David F. Powers, with Joe McCarthy. *"Johnny, We Hardly Knew Ye": Memories of John Fitzgerald Kennedy.* Boston: Little, Brown, 1972.

Pachter, Henry M. *Collision Course: The Cuban Missile Crisis and Coexistence.* New York: Praeger, 1963.

Parmet, Herbert S. *Jack: The Struggles of John F. Kennedy.* New York: Dial, 1980.

— *JFK: The Presidency of John F. Kennedy.* Dial, 1983.

Paterson, Thomas G., ed. *Kennedy's Quest for Victory: American Foreign Policy, 1961–1963.* New York: Oxford University Press, 1989.

Powers, Richard Gid. *Secrecy and Power: The Life of J. Edgar Hoover.* New York: Free Press, 1987.

Prados, John. *Presidents' Secret Wars: CIA and Pentagaon Covert Operations since World War II.* Rev. ed. New York: Morrow, 1986.

— *The Soviet Estimate: U.S. Intelligence Analysis and Russian Military Strength.* New York: Dial, 1982.

Rádványi, János. *Hungary and the Superpowers: The 1956 Revolution and Realpolitik.* Pan Alto, CA: Hoover Institution Press, 1972.

Reeves, Richard. *President Kennedy: Profile of Power.* New York: Simon and Schuster, 1993.

Reeves, Thomas C. *A Question of Character: A Life of John F. Kennedy.* New York: Free Press, 1991.

Rostow, W.W. *The Diffusion of Power: An Essay in Recent History.* New York: Macmillan, 1972.

Rusk, Dean, as told to Richard Rusk. *As I Saw It.* Ed. Daniel S. Papp. New York: Norton, 1990.

Salinger, Pierre. *With Kennedy.* Garden City, NY: Doubleday, 1966.

Schlesinger, Arthur M., Jr. *Robert Kennedy and His Times.* New York: Ballantine, 1979.

— *A Thousand Days: John F. Kennedy in the White House.* London: Mayflower-Dell reprint, 1967.

Schoenbaum, Thomas J. *Waging Peace and War: Dean Rusk in the Truman, Kennedy, and Johnson Years.* New York: Simon and Schuster, 1988.

Sievers, Rodney M. *The Last Puritan?: Adlai Stevenson in American Politics.* Port Washington, NY: Associated Faculty Press, 1983.

Smith, Gaddis. *Dean Acheson.* New York: Cooper Square, 1972.

Smith, Wayne S. *The Closest of Enemies: A Personal and Diplomatic Account of U.S.–Cuban Relations Since 1957.* New York: Norton, 1987.

Sokolovskii, Vasilli D., ed. *Soviet Military Strategy.* Trans. and intro. Herbert S. Dinerstein, Leon Goure, and Thomas W. Wolfe. Englewood Cliffs, NJ: Prentice-Hall, 1963.

Sorensen, Theodore C. *Kennedy.* New York: Harper, 1965.

— *The Kennedy Legacy.* London: Weidenfeld and Nicolson reprint, 1970.

Szulc, Tad. *Fidel: A Critical Portrait.* New York: William Morrow, 1986.

Taylor, Maxwell D. *Swords and Plowshares.* New York: Norton, 1972.

Thomas, Hugh. *Cuba or the Pursuit of Freedom.* London: Eyre & Spottiswoode, 1971.

Thompson, Kenneth W., ed. *The Kennedy Presidency: Seventeen Intimate Perspectives of John F. Kennedy.* Lanham, MD: University Press of America, 1985.

Thompson, Robert Smith. *The Missiles of October: The Declassified Story of John F. Kennedy and the Cuban Missile Crisis.* New York: Simon and Schuster, 1992.

Tucker, Robert C. *Political Culture and Leadership in Soviet Russia: From Lenin to Gorbachev.* New York: Norton, 1987.

U Thant, *View from the UN.* Garden City, NY: Doubleday, 1978.

Ulam, Adam B. *Expansion and Coexistence: The History of Soviet Foreign Policy, 1917–1967.* New York: Praeger, 1968.

Walton, Richard J. *Cold War and Counterrevolution: The Foreign Policy of John F. Kennedy.* New York: Viking Press, 1972.

— *The Remnants of Power: The Tragic Last Years of Adlai Stevenson.* New York: Coward-McCann, 1968.

Whalen, Richard J. *The Founding Father: The Story of Joseph P. Kennedy.* New York: New American Library, 1964.

White, Theodore H. *The Making of the President, 1960.* New York: Atheneum, 1961.

Wicker, Tom. *JFK and LBJ: The Influence of Personality Upon Politics.* New York: Morrow, 1968.

— *Kennedy Without Tears: The Man Beneath the Myth.* New York: Morrow, 1964.

Wills, Garry. *The Kennedy Imprisonment: A Meditation on Power.* Boston: Little, Brown, 1982.

Wofford, Harris. *Of Kennedys and Kings: Making Sense of the Sixties.* New York: Farrar, Straus, Giroux, 1980.

Wyden, Peter. *Bay of Pigs: The Untold Story.* New York: Simon and Schuster, 1979.

ARTICLES, NEWSPAPERS, PERIODICALS

Acheson, Dean G. "Dean Acheson's Version of Robert Kennedy's Version of the Cuban Missile Affair: Homage to Plain Dumb Luck." *Esquire* 71 (February 1969): 44, 46, 76–7.

Alsop, Stewart. "Footnote for the Historians." *Saturday Evening Post,* 26 January 1963.

— and Charles Bartlett. "In Time of Crisis." *Saturday Evening Post,* 8 December 1962, 15–20.

Beck, Kent M. "Necessary Lies, Hidden Truths: Cuba in the 1960 Campaign." *Diplomatic History* 8 (Winter 1984): 37–59.

Bernstein, Barton J. "The Cuban Missile Crisis: Trading the Jupiters in Turkey?" *Political Science Quarterly* 95 (Spring 1980): 97–125.

— "The Week We Almost Went to War." *Bulletin of the Atomic Scientists* 32 (February 1976): 13–21.

Chase, Stuart. "Two Worlds." *Bulletin of the Atomic Scientists* 19 (June 1963): 18–20.

Cold War International History Project Bulletin.

Crane, Robert D. "The Cuban Crisis: A Strategic Analysis of American and Soviet Policy." *Orbis* 6 (Winter 1965): 528–63.

— "The Sino-Soviet Dispute on War and the Cuban Crisis." *Orbis* 8 (Fall 1964): 537–49.

Current Digest of the Soviet Press.

Dobrynin, Anatoly. "The Caribbean Crisis: An Eyewitness Account." *International Affairs* 8 (August 1992): 47–60.

Garthoff, Raymond L. "Cuban Missile Crisis: The Soviet Story." *Foreign Policy* 72 (Fall 1988): 61–80.

— Barton J. Bernstein, Marc Trachtenberg, and Thomas G. Paterson. "Commentaries on "An Interview with Sergo Mikoyan." *Diplomatic History* 14 (Spring 1990): 223–56.

Greiner, Bernd. "The Soviet View: An Interview with Sergo Mikoyan." *Diplomatic History* 14 (Spring 1990): 205–21.

Gromyko, Anatolii A. "The Caribbean Crisis." *Soviet Law and Government* 11 (Summer 1972): 3–53.

Hafner, Donald L. "Bureaucratic Politics and 'Those Frigging Missiles': JFK, Cuba and U.S. Missiles in Turkey." *Orbis* 21 (Summer 1977): 307–33.

Hagan, Roger. "Triumph or Tragedy?" *Dissent* 10 (Winter 1963): 13–26.

Harrison, Hope M. "Ulbricht and the Concrete 'Rose': New Archival

Evidence on the Dynamics of Soviet-East German Relations and the Berlin Crisis, 1958–1961." Working Paper No. 5. Cold War International History Project, Woodrow Wilson Center, 1993.

Hershberg, James G. "Before 'The Missiles of October': Did Kennedy Plan a Military Strike against Cuba" *Diplomatic History* 14 (Spring 1990): 163–98.

Horelick, Arnold L. "The Cuban Missile Crisis: An Analysis of Soviet Calculations and Behavior." *World Politics* 16 (April 1964): 363–89.

Keating, Kenneth. "My Advance View of the Cuban Crisis." *Look* 28 (3 November 1964): 96–106 passim.

Kelley, Kitty. "The Dark Side of Camelot." *People,* 29 February 1988.

Khrushchev, Nikita S. "On Peaceful Coexistence." *Foreign Affairs* 38 (October 1959): 1–18.

Lebow, Richard Ned. "Domestic Politics and the Cuban Missile Crisis: The Traditional and Revisionist Interpretations Reevaluated." *Diplomatic History* 14 (Fall 1990): 471–92.

Lowenthal, Richard. "After Cuba, Berlin?" *Encounter* 19 (December 1962): 48–55.

Mackintosh, J. Malcolm. "Soviet Motives in Cuba." *Survival* 5 (Jan.– Feb. 1963): 16–18.

McMillan, Robert R. "A Look Back at Cuban Missile Crisis." *Newsday,* 14 October 1983, 72.

Nash, Philip. "Nuisance of Decision: Jupiter Missiles and the Cuban Missile Crisis." *Journal of Strategic Studies* 14 (1991): 1–26.

Nathan, James A. "The Missile Crisis: His Finest Hour Now." *World Politics* 27 (January 1975): 256–81.

New York Times.

Paterson, Thomas G. "Bearing the Burden: A Critical Look at JFK's Foreign Policy." *Virginia Quarterly Review* 54 (Spring 1978): 193–212.

— "The Historian as Detective: Senator Kenneth Keating, the Missiles in Cuba, and His Mysterious Sources." *Diplomatic History* 11 (Winter 1987): 67–70.

— and William J. Brophy. "October Missiles and November Elections: The Cuban Missile Crisis and American Politics, 1962." *Journal of American History* 73 (June 1986): 87–119.

Schlesinger, Arthur M. "Four Days with Fidel: A Havana Diary." *New York Review of Books,* 26 March 1992, 22–9.

Steele, John L. "The Adlai Stevenson Affair." *Life,* 14 December 1962, 44–6.

Time.

Trachtenberg, Marc. "The Influence of Nuclear Weapons in the Cuban Missile Crisis." *International Security* 10 (Summer 1985): 137–63.

— "White House Tapes and Minutes of the Cuban Missile Crisis: Introduction to Documents." *International Security* 10 (Summer 1985): 164–70.

Troyanovski, Oleg. "The Caribbean Crisis: A View from the Kremlin." *International Affairs* 4–5 (April–May 1992): 147–57.

U.S. News and World Report, 19 November 1962, 86.

Vandenbroucke, Lucien S. "Anatomy of a Failure: The Decision to Land at the Bay of Pigs." *Political Science Quarterly* 99 (Fall 1984): 471–91.

Vital Speeches of the Day.

Wall Street Journal, 19 April 1963, 10.

Washington Post.

Wedge, Bryant. "Khrushchev at a Distance – A Study of Public Personality." *Trans-Action* 5 (October 1968): 24–8.

White, Mark J. "Belligerent Beginnings: John F. Kennedy on the Opening Day of the Cuban Missile Crisis." *Journal of Strategic Studies* 15 (March 1992): 30–49.

— "Dean Rusk's Revelation: New British Evidence on the Cordier Ploy." *Society for Historians of American Foreign Relations Newsletter* 25 (September 1994): 1–9.

— "Hamlet in New York: Adlai Stevenson during the First Week of the Cuban Missile Crisis." *Illinois Historical Journal* 86 (Summer 1993): 71–84.

Wohlstetter, Roberta. "Cuba and Pearl Harbor: Hindsight and Foresight." *Foreign Affairs* 43 (July 1965): 691–707.

Index